Also by Thomas Hine

Populuxe

Facing
Tomorrow

11/5/19

for Kathy,
    fellow explorer of the
future(s) and of design.
    All the best

    [signature]

Facing
Tomorrow

What the Future Has Been
What the Future Can Be

Thomas Hine

Alfred A. Knopf   New York   *1991*

This Is a Borzoi Book Published by Alfred A. Knopf, Inc.

Copyright © 1991 by Thomas Hine

All rights reserved under International and Pan-American Copyright Conventions. Published in the United States by Alfred A. Knopf, Inc., New York, and simultaneously in Canada by Random House of Canada Limited, Toronto. Distributed by Random House, Inc., New York.

Library of Congress Cataloging-in-Publication Data

Hine, Thomas [date]
Facing tomorrow : what the future has been, what the future can be / Thomas Hine. —1st ed.
p.   cm.
ISBN 0-394-57785-X
1. Twenty-first century—Forecasts.   I. Title.
CB161.H56   1991
303.49'09'05—dc20   90-53560 CIP

Manufactured in the United States of America
First Edition

This book is dedicated to the memory of Ellen Lillis Duggan,
Marianne Dolan Coleman and Ruth Hawthorne Fay,
three who helped me find my own future.

Contents

Preface

This book grew out of a feeling that, as a society, we do not know where we are going, and we're going there awfully fast. I was concerned that the future had become, at best, a nostalgia item, something we remember with affection and condescension but don't take seriously. That's a dangerous situation because a denial of the future starves people's sense of possibility even as it absolves their responsibilities to unborn generations. People have become increasingly reluctant to view themselves as participants in history, who can transform a cultural and material inheritance into a legacy for many more human generations—or into garbage.

I began work in late summer, 1988, and it seemed, as I proceeded, that history had perversely decided to speed up. China had what seemed like a revolution on live television, the post–World War II era ended its forty-five-year run, the Berlin Wall came down, Eastern Europe was freed, environmental consciousness returned amid daily evidence that global pollution was getting worse. People started worrying about the condition of their banks, and everybody bought a fax machine. With the threat of the breakup of the Soviet Union, the euphoria vanished and new, less focused tensions returned. While the manuscript was at the typesetters, Iraq was crushed by a technologically advanced military force that restored a long-lost glamour to weapons of mass destruction. Hardly any of these things were foreseen by the experts on the future whose work I thought would provide the basis for my research.

Meanwhile, concern about the future was surfacing in books, magazine articles and television programs. Some prognosticators offered a vision of technological progress as fast, information-packed and inexorable as a Tomahawk cruise missile. Others saw environmental holocaust, global economic booms, endless entertainment in computer-generated alternate realities, new levels of human consciousness or salvation by extraterrestrial beings. Still others spoke of frightening new weapons and geopolitical strategies intended largely to keep the world from changing. There are books that tell you that the future will be whatever you want it to be. But while many addressed consumers of the future, few looked ahead from the point of view of active participants.

As the world kept changing faster than I could write, I decided that whatever comes next is less important than the way people respond to it. *Facing Tomorrow* is one person's attempt to think through some of the consequences of what is happening now and of what seems likely in the immediate future. Like anyone else, I have interests, preoccupations and limitations that color my view. I don't presume, however, to speak for everyone or provide definitive answers. The goal, rather, is to engage many diverse people in the issues of the future. The Western cultural perspective from which the book is written reflects my background, of course, but it is also intrinsic to the subjects being discussed. Western ideas of scientific inquiry, technological progress and human development have a strong impact on nearly everyone on earth, and their practical benefits are not likely to be abandoned. Such powerful concepts deserve to be constantly examined and reconsidered. *Facing Tomorrow* is addressed to that hypothetical concerned citizen on whose good judgment our political system is supposed to depend. It is a generalist's attempt to make sense of issues that have become the province of dozens of different species of experts, some of whom don't admit the insights of the others into the universes they consider. It assumes, of course, that it is possible to make sense, that people can think for themselves and what individuals do can be important. Grasping all the possibilities probably can't be done, but it is, if nothing else, good intellectual exercise and, I believe, vital to our civic health.

One reason that thinking about the future has become so difficult is that we know that earlier predictions of limitless possibilities have had unforeseen consequences. We know that we've clogged up our lives with traffic jams, foul air and trashy oceans. We know that the dreams of an information-based global economy can turn people's careers into frail abstractions that can burst like bubbles through no fault of their own. We know that people can change the world through trivial acts, such as using hairsprays that destroy the ozone layer, and through routine necessities, like taking the car to work. And we know that the world is full of dangers we cannot hear, smell or feel. The future seems to present more problems than it used to, but the very knowledge that makes it difficult to face tomorrow makes it morally imperative that we do so.

I do believe that we can be optimistic about our future. But this affirmation is possible only if we adjust our view of the world and of how we judge our actions and our lives. We need mature aspirations that recognize both real physical limits and the enormous range of possibilities that can be realized within those limits. We need to look particularly at precisely what we mean when we use the phrase "our way of life," which is what Western troops in the Persian Gulf were said to be fighting for. Too often, we equate personal freedom with license to foul the earth or to trample on the liberties of others. There is a special meaning to our way of life, but it cannot be measured in GNP or BTUs. It is now evident that the accelerating use of resources and endless personal expansiveness that seemed fundamental to our old ideas of progress exact great costs. Sometimes these take the form of environmental degradation. Sometimes the price is loss of human life and national treasure in warfare. Before we commit ourselves to such expensive courses of action, it is important to ask whether the goals pursued are truly worthwhile. We must not merely redefine what can be done; we must also consider what we really want. People don't like to lower their expectations, but they might be pleased to change them.

The word that expresses most of the grounds I find for hope is "subtlety." It describes a direction in which technology seems poised to go, if we choose to make it do so. We are able to direct technology much more precisely than we did in the past, largely because of our improved ability to measure and direct its effects. The same profusion of knowledge that makes the future so difficult to contemplate also offers the means to correct mistakes and achieve social and technological goals with greater precision and less waste. It is possible to make materials that offer the optimum performance in a specified task or to replace a gene that improves an organism without creating a monster. Computers are particularly useful tools for subtlety because they can help us recognize important patterns that weren't evident before and can identify relationships among seemingly disparate phenomena. New modes of manufacture promise to render obsolete mass production and an economy that depends on the inducement of mass consumption. Theoretically at least, it should be possible to provide goods and services that give greater satisfaction at lower costs.

Although it appears possible that subtler technologies can ameliorate many of our most pressing environmental, economic and social problems, I am not predicting that they will. Subtlety requires clear goals and a populace that is attuned to the environmental, geopolitical and social implications of technological choice. Subtlety demands that people engage technology, criticize it and never stop paying attention to it. Our enhanced ability to understand the consequences of our acts will make no difference if nobody moves to correct errors.

All of us carry the seeds of the future in our minds and make it happen, mostly through routine choices we are scarcely aware we are making. Residents of developed countries do so more than most people, because we use a disproportionate share of the world's resources without thinking, as if we deserved to. Yet the solution is not to undevelop, but to develop in new, more harmonious directions that leave more resources for others and provide a more workable model to which they can aspire.

If we have begun over the last few years to get over our fear of the future, we have still not truly begun to face it. Rather, we have been stirred to a more active acquiescence in the same technologies of speed and power that animated the old-time futures that failed us. The trajectory of the Tomahawk is not the only path that can be followed to what President Bush has termed "a new world order." There are more possibilities than we can begin to count.

Thus, the focus of *Facing Tomorrow* is not on impending supergadgets, what stocks to buy, next year's lifestyles or impending global collapse. The focus is not on the house of tomorrow, but rather on the architecture of imagination, the structures of meaning within which people make their lives. The future offers more than we can foresee, but its nature will be determined largely by the way we think about it. What follows is not intended to provide the answers but to spur your involvement in what I have found an exhilarating effort: to conceive a future worth looking forward to.

Philadelphia, March 1991

Acknowledgments

F*acing Tomorrow* was sparked by a work of art, or strictly speaking, a proposal for a work of art, by Krzysztof Wodiczko, which sought to use contemporary communications technology to make the tower of Philadelphia City Hall a nightly indicator of the city's health. A discussion of this work disappeared from the manuscript, but its attempt to scrutinize old images and find new ways to make them meaningful suffuses the book.

Many people helped shape this book, sometimes without their knowing it, by sharing ideas, arguing with me and recommending readings. Among them were Thomas P. Hughes, Marshall W. Berman, Arthur Shestack, Ann Mintz, Medard Gabel, Gene Roberts, Penny Balkin Bach, Marie Colman Nelson, Joseph Coates, David Snyder, Lebbeus Woods, Douglas Michels, Conald Prowler, Craig Hodgetts, Emilio Ambasz, Edmund N. Bacon, Barbara Kaplan, John Santos, Stephan Salisbury, Ligia Ravé, Ray Eames and, years earlier, Buckminster Fuller. Julian Fisher offered comments and reassurance on the final draft, and James Chan commented on and contributed to it throughout the research and writing.

My agent Barney Karpfinger believed in the project and offered important suggestions. As editor, Martha Kaplan displayed a calm confidence in the face of apparent chaos, combined with a subtle hand that might provide a model not just for working with an author and a manuscript but for facing the future itself.

Facing
Tomorrow

1 /   The End
of the Future

For at least two decades, no compelling,
comprehensive vision of the future has captured the American imagination. Our culture is like a child raised without adults: We have no
idea what we will be when we grow up. We don't know what to tell
our own children, though we dimly suspect we are setting a bad example. We condescend to past visions of the future—the progressivist
utopias of the turn of the previous century, the streamlined dreams of
the 1930s, the jet age exuberance of the 1950s. But we have nothing
to take their place.

Instead, our popular culture is filled with tainted dreams, manipulated horrific fantasies planted in the minds of innocents, which
come true when Freddy Krueger, the sleep-invading slasher from the
endless *Nightmare on Elm Street* movie cycle, comes to eviscerate the
dreamer and most of her friends, relatives and neighbors. Today, we
know all about what was wrong with the visions of the past and are,
we tell ourselves, more realistic. But we are more limited, too. Besides, there's no evidence, outside of the movies, that a refusal to
dream prevents nightmares from coming true.

When the world does not seem to be going your way, it is

worth finding out which way the world is going. If progress seems self-defeating, it is time to come up with a new definition of progress. It's time for a new future, one that will enable us make sense of the present and judge how the actions we take each day will shape tomorrow. We need to understand our past ideas of the future, in part so that we can understand the ways in which we have gone wrong. But we can't slap a new coat of paint on our old tomorrows. We need to conceive of our future new and whole, from the ground up. We have to examine our fears, to see if they are real, and our desires, to understand what we really want and what we can hope to get. Today, people become angry at the future because it is not going to provide what was once expected. We need a clearer idea of what we can anticipate, what we can achieve, what we can create, so that we can once again feel the exaltation of moving toward something we want rather than the bitterness of settling for less.

Finding that guide, that sense of the future, is the goal of all that follows. It takes the form of an exploration rather than a thesis because it is based on the belief that progress does not follow a single vector and that the future is the last thing about which anyone can afford to be doctrinaire.

It does, however, begin with a postulate: The future is a matter of life and death. Death is in each of our individual futures, but the human future should be dedicated to the continuation and enhancement of life. Human progress does not consist in a few people having control of immense power, but in all people having access to greater opportunities to live satisfying lives. We can look in the mirror and see evidence of our own mortality. We look to the future for its promise of a kind of immortality. We look to the future to celebrate life.

Looking to the future is, almost by definition, an optimistic exercise. Even those who see dire threats shout warnings because they believe the dangers can be avoided. One who looks to the future today—in the context of technology, the world's resources and population, our political, economic and social institutions—can find an enormous amount to worry about. For most of the last two centuries we have defined progress in terms of the ever larger organization and release of energy stored in the earth. To stay with that definition invites disappointment. But if we accept that civilization is moving on to another phase of its development, and see that we have technology that if used wisely can help it do so, there is plenty of room for hope. We understand more about how the world works and about the complex interactions of living things, whose efficiency, adaptability and ingenuity still make all human invention seem crude by comparison. Yet our potential for organizing the man-made systems that sustain our lives with far greater subtlety is increasing. Existing and imminent technologies will give us enormous powers that can be used for good or ill. A good future will not come inevitably. We cannot afford to let the society coast on automatic pilot. The most pressing issues are not matters of engineering, but of human values.

Most adults have no trouble remembering a time when Americans viewed themselves as the people of the future, and the rest of the world agreed. That future was a grand playground, a universe of gadgetry, a clean new world from which every vestige of the old had been expunged. More recently, the past has served as our playground, as we have used our traditions decoratively, ironically or cynically, with the thoughtlessness of spoiled children who know that there will always be something to play with. We used to have contempt for our ancestors and envy our descendants. Now we look wistfully toward our ancestors and think of our descendants hardly at all. The future was once a radiant city; now it's a slum.

How did this happen to our forward-looking society? Was the future shot, along with John and Robert Kennedy and Martin Luther King, Jr.? Was it missing in action in Vietnam? Did it get burnt out in the 1960s when many of the ideas smart people had developed over previous decades had a brief, sometimes disastrous tryout? Was it left on the moon among some astronaut's golf balls? Did it run out of gas, along with the rest of America, in 1973, when OPEC curtailed oil supplies and the citizens of Levittown, Pennsylvania, rioted at the pumps? Was it accidentally deleted by Rose Mary Woods, President Nixon's fortuitously fumbling private secretary? Did it just fall apart, like a rusted-out muscle car? Or is it alive and well and living in Japan?

The real answer is that the technology- and consumption-driven future of personal expansiveness outlived its usefulness. Many pieces of that vision were realized, but they have proven less satisfying than was promised. Changes in the society, and particularly in the role of women, have forced the rejection of many long-held expectations. And that remembered future assumed that American economic and military dominance of the world would continue indefinitely, something that has proven neither sustainable nor desirable.

Yet much contemporary behavior is still guided by that worn-out vision, simply because we have nothing so convincing to take its place. Society has no way to judge its progress, because there is little agreement about what progress is and how it is to be attained.

The word "future," as it is used here, does not mean a static utopia or a set of products that can be ordered from a catalogue. It is more concerned with choosing a direction than with establishing a timetable of the destinations we can expect to reach. The dates when things might happen are important to professional forecasters, who rely on demographic data, scientific discoveries, economic cycles and other current data to extrapolate into the future. There is no shortage of such specialized and highly focused predictions, many of them contradictory. What is lacking is a sense of the future as a project, a work of collective imagination and aspiration.

All consideration of the future is about the present. At times people look to the future to provide deliverance from the horrors of their own time, while at others they look ahead from good times to still better ones. Some have argued that the future is an age-old conspiracy of politicians, religious leaders and bankers to induce people to accept misery now in the hope of future rewards that will never come. That may, at times, be true, but it can hardly be the whole story. We look to the future to give moral weight to present actions. Before succeeding generations can live with the consequences of what we do, we must ask whether we can live with ourselves.

There is reason to believe that we can make the future better; there are plenty of dangers that could make it far, far worse. The problems are, in many cases, global in scope and centuries in the making. Human power is at the heart of most of our dilemmas. It is what makes consideration of the future not an act of arrogance or self-indulgence, but of moral necessity.

Three questions about human power—how we should use the world, how we should relate to each other and how we should use our abilities to both change material phenomena and organize people—are the key elements of having a sense of the future. They are not really separable: The organization of people largely determines how they change the world. Powerful people direct technology, which thus unleashes power in the physical world and thus reshapes society. We have tended to measure progress in terms of the amplification or replacement of human energy by energy sources stored within the earth—released and directed through technology.

Everything is connected to everything else and one of our chief problems today is that we separate economic questions from physical, botanical and even cultural issues. Our problems have been parceled out to specialists, whose goal is to reduce fundamental issues of human life to technical problems, which can then be solved. But when, as citizens, we try to imagine what is going on in our society and in the world, the connections are lost. It seems as if things are out of control, running off in all directions. We don't even know how to think of bringing them together and setting a course.

To get a handle on the future we need to accept its complexity and revel in its interconnectedness. It has the romance of a vast, overgrown garden whose many vines and tendrils have woven themselves into an unbreakable fabric. Yet, as with the garden, some weeding is needed if it is to be as beautiful and productive as it could be. We will find that many good ideas, such as personal freedom, have become entangled with and almost inseparable from parasites that stunt their growth, such as the ideal of endless physical consumption. The aim is not to destroy everything and replace it with something that is reductive and lifeless. It is, rather, to make sure that we are not so caught up in the tangle that we lose our ability to act.

How did we change from a people who felt that our fate was to make the world better to one that doesn't care to seriously consider that question? We can begin with a visit to the 1939–40 New York World's Fair, and specifically to its most popular exhibit, the General Motors Futurama.

"I have seen the future" was what the buttons said that were given to visitors when they emerged from the pavilion, and in hindsight we can say that they had. They had ridden moving chairs past an enormous diorama which depicted a transformed American landscape. As you would expect in a General Motors presentation, automobiles played a central role. There were wide, limited-access highways that linked gleaming streamlined cities to suburban houses that were themselves models of modernity and comfort. It was a sprawling preview of a landscape of personal expansiveness. It is difficult to imagine its impact on visitors who had lived through a decade of economic depression. Today we might say it all looked too simple, but in an era of chronic housing shortages, with aging city neighborhoods in which many of the houses lacked indoor plumbing and in which most of the outdoor space was filled with clotheslines, such a future must have looked like heaven, and perhaps like a pipe dream as well.

The slogan on the buttons echoed Lincoln Steffens's famous declaration upon his return from the newborn Soviet Union. This was a capitalist vision of a workers' paradise, one whose vision of automobile dependency was very much in the interest of General Motors. But it was a fairly comprehensive physical vision of society, one that linked work life, home life, civic life and the things that would have to be built, and be bought, to make them possible. Such an automobile-dependent society was surely not, in the long run, as good for America as it was for General Motors. Still, its dream of harnessing the country's industrial might to provide comfort and convenience for its citizens was more palatable than some then current alternative visions—such as Stalin's dictatorship of the proletariat and Hitler's thousand-year Reich.

At the New York Fair of 1964–65, General Motors used the same slogan on its buttons, and the same name for its pavilion. By that time, much of the future predicted in its earlier pavilion had come true. What the new model showed was essentially an update of the 1939 vision. Six-lane highways seemed a revolutionary idea when most roads had only two, though sixteen-lane highways didn't seem much different, and probably not better, than six. There were a few other new features, such as underwater cities, though without any explanation of why people would want to live in them. Even though the postwar euphoria was over, the recycled Futurama still drew large crowds who wanted to see what the future would be like.

By 1983, when "The World in Motion," GM's pavilion for Epcot Center at Walt Disney World, opened, the social vision was gone. As before, visitors ride through the pavilion in moving chairs, but what they see are cute cavemen inventing the wheel and people trying to fly by flapping their wings. Throughout, recorded voices sing the insistent refrain: "It's fun to be free!" It does have a small section on the future at the end, but it is all flashes and mirrors, a state of glitzy indeterminacy that feels like a late-1970s discotheque. General Motors had judged that its fate was not tied to a vision of the future, even though Epcot was intended by Walt Disney to be an "experimental prototype community of tomorrow."

At Vancouver's Expo '86, GM's Canadian subsidiary retreated still further from a social vision with its pavilion called "The Spirit Lodge." Visitors sat together in a large metal shed, and on the other side of a glass wall, a morose Indian sat staring at a campfire, pondering his existential depression. He conjured up animal spirits that appeared as holographic images. These spirits, such as the fox and the eagle, all agreed on a single message: "Life and the freedom to move are as one." The Indian was not pondering what lay ahead. He was, instead, looking for a way to stop feeling quite so glum. Certainly the Indian didn't want to hear about highways, or about how large numbers of people might be able to affirm their lives through motion, without getting in each other's way. He was, after all, by himself. And the eagle didn't tell him about the way the world would work. If you're an eagle, you don't need highways. You do need a suitable habitat of a kind that has been disappearing as the automobile has made almost everywhere habitable by humans. The eagle didn't mention that either. This eagle was a car salesman. When visitors left they were given a button that showed the head of a Northwest Indian totem, although when you looked at it a certain way, it could resemble the front end of an automobile. So much for the future.

General Motors' evolving visions provide a neat summation of the evolution of public consciousness—and the shrinking of the future from something that is built communally to something that is felt alone. They lead from the vibrant social visions of the era of Franklin D. Roosevelt and Robert Moses to the less fresh, more relentless visions of the era of Lyndon B. Johnson and Robert Moses to the Reagan era's assurance that personal needs, not social needs, are paramount. The two Futuramas sought acceptance of social change. The Epcot pavilion does not purport to show its visitors what the future will be like; it only assures them it will be fun. At Vancouver, GM's exhibition designers were shrewd in identifying a general spiritual discomfort that was prompting people to look within, not ahead.

There is a big difference between looking forward to driving your car on a wonderful big highway and dreaming of driving it away from the demons that haunt your life. The first is an achievable goal, something that is part of the real world. The second is a dream, one that might have its origins in idealism or spirituality, though General Motors is suggesting a very material cure. This is in keeping with the shift of the culture from concrete, achievable goals to abstract ones. It is easy to misunderstand this as a transition from materialism to a greater idealism, but in practice abstract goals are the most effective spurs to consumption because they can never be achieved. If, as in 1939, your dream is to possess an automobile to get to work, an automatic washer to clean your clothes and, most distantly, a television set to see the World Series, the possibility exists that your desires can be fulfilled. But if you are convinced that you buy to participate in the great pageant of progress, as advertising asserted in the 1950s and 1960s, or that you buy in order to make yourself less lonely and more complete, as much recent advertising has suggested, the likelihood is that you will buy and buy and buy. If we look to material goods to help us conquer personal spiritual dissatisfactions, there will never be enough things in the world. The Futuramas implied a massive public works program, whereas Epcot and Vancouver seemed to imply that there is no reality outside of ourselves.

Much of what was predicted in the first Futurama has not only come true; it has become the only America most of its citizens have ever known. It is unwise to buy your future ready-made from General Motors, and that corporation's apparent decision not to sell us one should probably come as a relief.

Still, it is even more dangerous to see the future only as a projection of our own insecurities and desires. It is easy to forget that there are other people in the world—lots of them—with their own fears and dreams. We do not soar like the eagle. We build our own man-made ecosystem of roads, towns, pipelines, supertankers, all so that we can indulge in the illusion of flying free. It is easy to forget that all of our actions have material consequences; they use energy, materials, space, and they can lead to pollution, shortages or congestion. We ignore the needs of other people and the realities of the material world only at great peril; we will face the consequences sooner or later. The future of private dreams has become a world of broken promises, where the present seems to be working so badly we can't bear to think about the future. We need a sense of the future, not so that we can conjure magical visions, but so that we can live our lives today.

It was possible in 1939 to sell a vision of the future, because even though Americans had gone through some very bad times, there was a sense, at least, that they had gone through them together. One of the stated aims of the fair was to give people a vision worth working for, which soon turned into a vision worth fighting for.

It is easy to have a sense of the future when things are going well and people feel that their horizons are expanding. People tend to feel that they deserve all the good fortune they have, and they look forward to something even better on the horizon. For Americans, the first two decades after World War II were times of enormous optimism and confidence, feelings that were solidly based on an economy that, while somewhat recession-prone, easily dominated the world along with military power. During that time, the United States remade its entire physical and economic landscape.

It's more difficult to think about the future when you are in the situation Americans are in now. The country, while still very powerful and very rich, is no longer under the illusion that nothing can go wrong. Our companies are losing out on world markets. Garbage is drifting up on beaches. Homeless people live on city streets. Basic infrastructure, such as bridges and water systems, is failing throughout the country. And the postwar confrontation with Communism, which defined the country's position in the world for forty-five years, has disappeared as Leninism has lost its authority, even in the Soviet Union, making way for the re-emergence of contending nationalist forces. The world situation has become far more challenging and confusing than it was, but it is also possibly more hopeful and liberating. It is a time when we can maturely choose what we're about, but such maturity is frightening. The old certainties are reassuring, but they have one problem: Many of them are no longer certain. It is necessary to really examine our values and decide which ones are essential and which have been distorted and produce results that are the opposite of those we desire.

Americans still seem to believe that there is something called progress. They just don't feel that it touches and improves their own lives as it used to. There is little sense of a better tomorrow taking shape. Such a sense is far more important, overall, than those aspects of standard of living that can be measured. By nearly any material standard, American life is substantially "richer" than it was in 1955, a year that set new records for consumption and gave rise to even more expansive projections. The country now burns about twice the amount of energy per person that it did in that near-euphoric year. And each of us occupies more than twice the amount of developed space—for our homes, workplaces, shopping centers, parking lots, roads, sewage treatment plants, landfills and everything else we need to sustain our lifestyle—than we did in what seemed a more expansive era. There are now more registered automobiles than licensed drivers, which indicates that some consumption barrier has been broken. There are also more televisions and dozens of television channels to choose from. Appliances that were once merely imagined are now commonplace. We get peaches in midwinter from South America, and foods we'd never even heard of then are now on supermarket shelves from all over the world. Our cars are more comfortable and a great deal more reliable. There are lasers in our phonographs, whose fidelity and clarity are close to perfect. We expect air conditioning almost everywhere. Back then, diapers were made of cloth and they had to be laundered; now they are disposable (so society as a whole— not just Mom—has to figure out what to do with them).

What many people have viewed as a time of decline has, in consumption at least, been one of tremendous growth. Indeed, compared with our current profligacy, 1955 seems an almost frugal time. If we could once again live at such consumption levels, some of the environmental problems that now seem overwhelming could be solved. It is true that many current problems were created, in large measure, by the visions and aspirations to be found in the world of 1955. But the material attainment of those goals has not brought greater happiness, merely nostalgia for a time when things seemed to be getting better.

Such expansiveness has been made possible, of course, by the shift from one-income to two-income households, staggering personal debt, increased teenage employment, all in the context of an economy that seems increasingly precarious. Such expansion has been accompanied by family instability and single-parent households increasing even more rapidly in the middle class than among the poor, lowered educational attainment and widespread drug abuse and narcotics-related crime. Higher unemployment levels have become increasingly acceptable politically, and the stock market drops when joblessness is reduced. People living on the street provide a constant reminder that it is possible to fall through the safety net, and their presence suggests that there may not actually be enough to go around. Moreover, the homeless have become such a fixture in the society that one federal court has allowed them to register to vote at the address of their steam vents.

This is an expansiveness that is no longer working. It frightens us and makes us cruel. What were once thought to be core values of the society, such as reward for hard work, respect for education, loyalty to your employers and to employees, have been jettisoned. Our quantitative standard of living may still be riding high, but our qualitative standard has plummeted. All was sacrificed in the name of crude material proliferation. The promotion of growth is a worthy social goal, but as with all living things, there is a point where the sheer physical expansion ends and other, less disruptive enlargement takes its place.

In trying to derive a useful sense of the future, it is important to recognize some of the things it is not. It is not a grand utopian ideal that can be quickly realized then left to technicians for maintenance. It is neither a forecast of what will happen three months from now nor a vision of what might happen in three hundred years. What we do today has an impact on both, but taking too short a view limits our vision, while a very long view tends to make our role in shaping the future seem insignificant. A sense of the future is not simple extrapolation of current trends. It expects major social and technological changes, but it does not rely on miracles or cataclysms. It is not a form of intellectual insider trading, a strategy for catching and profiting from the wave of history. The future is not something that you can buy, nor is it animated by any single invention or technology. Although the future is, in some sense, an aggregate of many individuals' expectations and aspirations, it is not something you can expect to encounter in a personal reverie, or through a technique that encourages you to imagine yourself apart from society and the rest of the physical world. The future does not come in tiny compartments, one for Americans and one for Thais, or one for accountants and another for pharmacists. Different people will experience the future differently, but nobody will do so wholly without reference to other people and the physical universe of which they are a part.

Our sense of the future will undoubtedly have an impact on public policy, but it cannot simply be a compilation of operational ideas. Indeed, one of the reasons that the future now seems so elusive is that we look at it in terms of classifications that may no longer be appropriate. For some, the key fact of the world's future is that the populations of rich countries are becoming older while the poor are ever younger. For others it is a matter of increasing ability to simulate human intelligence through microcircuitry, or accelerating worldwide soil erosion, or instantaneous global access to information. The future is not just one of those things, but all of them at once and a lot more besides. Few of us can expect to become experts in any or all of these matters, and besides, specific expertise has an ever shorter period of usefulness. Thus any attempt to derive a future that can become part of our public discourse and serve as a measure of our progress or waywardness must be based on general principles. It will inevitably be less about content—how we will organize our schools, clean our floors, feed our families—than about the way in which we consider it. Before we can think constructively about the future, we have to think about how we think about it.

A useful sense of the future should be both comprehensive and practical. That means that it should be broad enough to embrace disparate concerns and give an idea of how they will relate to one another. It cannot assume that human beings will suddenly be a different kind of creature, or that any fundamental physical laws will be suspended (though we might be able to make a few of them work to our advantage). A useful future provides a foundation for hope, but this foundation should rest squarely on the earth and not float somewhere in midair. A useful sense of the future must be firmly rooted in the physical and show respect—even awe—for the material environment that has brought us into being and provides the only source of sustenance we will ever know.

Yet when we make such an effort to derive a reality-based sense of our situation, we run smack up against the disconsolations of science. At least since Copernicus, science has been revealing human beings as ever more peripheral phenomena in the universe. Humans are passengers on a mote in the universe; individual lives span a time little more significant than the one-day maturity of the mayfly. People are chance events, temporary aggregations of matter and energy, effective carriers of an almost willful chemical called DNA. Because the nervous system settles for an approximation of reality, most of what is important happens on a scale either far larger or far smaller than anything we can perceive. And when we talk about the future, we are dealing with time, a phenomenon that our nervous systems allow us to experience in only a simplistic and distorted way.

Yet at the same time that science has displaced humanity from its once presumed central role in creation, it has given people ever more godlike powers to change the realm of existence in which we do live and to extend our dominion over other species and to remake the chemical nature of the earth itself. We're the ones with blast furnaces, with atomic bombs and genetic engineering. Everything we do affects the other creatures of the planet, the environment that gives them life and the world in which our descendants, those receptacles of odd pieces of our DNA, will live.

Thus we are left with a paradox. Centuries ago, when our precursors in the Western tradition believed that they occupied a central place in creation, there was a strong ethical basis for concern about future generations. Yet human impact upon the world was relatively small. Now, the very science that humbles us and removes our sense of responsibility for the world has given us greater power both to change the conditions of all life and to understand how we are changing it.

Having a sense of the future has always required an act of faith. But while the unseen was once the province of religion, it is now the territory of science, and an arena for human actions as well. We intervene in the chemistry of the atmosphere, the mechanics of heredity, the structure of matter, and we struggle to glimpse the paradoxical world of subatomic particles. Yet we still lack a convincing theory, or even a widely accepted hypothesis, that links such quantum phenomena to the world of everyday reality. We can, therefore, declare that our own lives are based entirely in delusion, which is arguable and possibly even true, but it does not help us make it through the day.

A sense of the future must incorporate the discoveries of science, but it should not devalue direct human experience. People's sense of their own meaning is an evolutionary adaptation, a reason the human beast has survived and prospered. We may be insignificant on the scale either of the universe or of the quark, but we do have meaning for ourselves. We can launch Voyager, which has given us a view of the earth from the edge of the solar system that shows a speck so tiny it is only visible if you are looking for it. But we cannot live our lives by taking such a God's-eye view of a universe in which we do not play a role. We cannot conceive of a world without ourselves. Our concern for other living things and for the many environments we inhabit comes from awareness of our dependence on them. We seek life, not death. We strive to preserve ourselves and our kind. Our minds' most compelling thoughts concern the survival of our bodies. We need and enjoy human society.

It is true that many contemporary problems cannot be perceived directly. People have no way of sensing atomic radiation. We cannot see or smell many of the threats to our atmosphere, and those that we can, we learn to ignore. Much of the technology on which the economy is based exists microscopically on silicon chips, and it keeps shrinking constantly, ever farther out of sight. Our fundamental understanding of human power to change the world comes from our technologically enhanced ability to find and measure things that we cannot sense.

Yet, as we shall see in later chapters, when people look at the future, they are far more likely to lose sight of the things they know viscerally than of the scientific and technological opportunities and menaces that may loom ahead. There is a great temptation to take a God's-eye view, rather than that of the extraordinary animal that we are. Thus, people propose visions of the future that rest on the assumption that abstract intelligence is the only worthy aspect of human beings, and that all other visceral and emotional impedimenta can be safely jettisoned once we are able to fashion an intellect-on-a-chip. A corollary to this thought is the belief that the earth can be used up, then discarded like an old Kleenex while disembodied human intelligence begins its spread throughout the cosmos.

And not all of these crazy ideas are confined to science fiction. Proposed technologies for personal entertainment, some of which are already in the prototype stage, are based on the idea that people want to escape the world and the society of which they are a part. Hell is other people; heaven is having it all yourself—and being in total control of your own experience. It is easy to see that products—both electronic and chemical—that allow people to escape to a world of planned surprises would be attractive in a world of increasing squalor and cruelty. Television and crack show that the market is there. Stanislaw Lem's vision in *The Futurological Congress* of an entire society drugged not to recognize its own collapse is chilling for its grotesquerie, but even more for its familiarity.

There are also futures which seek to mechanize every productive activity of society, and are unconcerned that it would render human activity essentially worthless. They see productivity in terms of units manufactured with no thought for the meaning of people's lives. In fact, it will be good news when machines take over still more laborious, dehumanizing tasks, but this is not an end in itself. Such a future must also focus on what people do and how they derive satisfaction. The current assumption is that the human role will simply be to consume the things that are being made, a future, in other words, in which humans will exist to give meaning to machines.

Such futures are not useful because they are not human. They have no flesh and do not breathe. We cannot project ourselves into these visions and imagine ourselves living lives that would interest us and make us happy. We should bear in mind that one of the wonders of the present day is widespread participation in the activities of the society and the enormous power wielded by the average individual. We should think before we surrender such privilege.

What we are talking about really is a form of enhanced common sense. It would augment what we know from our senses with what we can learn through our technology, but still keep its eye on human survival and the healthy environments and societies that promote it. Such a common sense would virtually have to be re-created. That's partly because we have been taught to mistrust what we see, smell, touch and feel. But the main reason is that those who live in technologically advanced societies feel themselves to be more dependent on their technologies than upon each other. We trust the sense; it's the commonness that gives us problems.

A sense of the future cannot be selfless, because only through our own minds and bodies can we understand others who live now and will live in centuries yet to come. But it is unselfish, because it implies a belief that there are some things worth making sacrifices for, even if all of those making the sacrifice won't necessarily be present for the payoff. The future is a generous concept, with an eye toward the well-being of generations yet unborn. And it is also a conservative idea, a belief that actions will communicate lasting values through time. In having a sense of the future, we place ourselves in the role of loving parents rather than clamorous children who know only their immediate desires.

During the last two decades, such altruistic ideas about the future have fallen into disrepute. The paradise and punishment inherent in such ideas have been understood to be powerful instruments for coercion, which powerful people can pervert for their own immediate gain. As we shall see, many of the promises of the future—limitless leisure, unending peace, enormous personal power—are very ancient. (So are many of the fears—including ever more efficient political oppression and the danger of surrendering your humanity to a machine.) The promise of heaven makes today's hard labor more bearable, and the principle of altruism toward unborn generations must be balanced against the needs of those alive today. Economic orthodoxy tells us that the value of the future to people today declines so rapidly that it is hardly worth including when calculating the choices that we make.

Moreover, the very idea of the future has itself been under siege. Some see it as a mere accident of grammar, a linguistic phenomenon which, while widespread, is not truly necessary. The future tense is an admission of alienation and a desire to change the environment. If we felt truly a part of our surroundings and harmonious with them, the present tense would suffice. Alternatively, its usefulness may be primarily psychological—as a compartment in which fears, anxieties, hopes and fantasies can be segregated so that we can get on with the immediate challenges of living. Our subjective ideas about the future are confused by the regularity of clock time, but we know that the temporal dimension is a rather lumpy thing, full of fits and starts. Physicists tell us that electrons seem to be able to move both ways in time. Some have suggested that the universe perpetually bifurcates into new universes in which every possibility is realized. For human beings, though, time seems to be a one-way street. The only way we know we can be affected by future generations is morally, through the obligation they impose to leave them a world in which they can live.

Still, the current discomfort with the future does not have to do with widespread acceptance of physicists' observations or philosophers' speculations. Rather, it is a result of people's tendency to see themselves not as participants in history, nor as members of a larger society, but as consumers of their own lives. We know that our time here on earth is a scarce commodity, and feel that, fundamentally, we live and die alone. Life's meaning comes from pleasures we enjoy as individuals. People are skeptical of sales pitches that urge them to forgo a pleasure in the hope that the sacrifice will benefit another, possibly someone they will never live to see. People are reluctant to take responsibility for their actions because they have difficulty understanding that they are actually acting. Individuals feel passive, picking and choosing among the packages of things, ideas, fantasies and values that are being offered to them. Many reside in what Lewis Mumford, in 1922, labeled "the utopia of the country house," an enchanted realm where, separated from society, culture and obligation, they can partake of the world without ever having to become involved. The popularization of the automobile, the democratization of suburbia that happened after World War II and the rise of television and other media made the utopia of the country house available on a scale Mumford could hardly have imagined. Still, the dynamic is the same. The society urges passivity, in order to turn its citizens into good consumers, and in so doing, destroys its own resiliency, its own capacity to live and to change. The only future it can provide is a "new, improved" product, claims which the consumers, by now jaded, seriously doubt.

Yet if we do pay attention to history, we can see that the consumer economy and the productive mechanism that brought it into being are little more than a century old. Moreover, they may be on the verge of breakdown as new technologies and other principles of animating the economy take their place. Whether we like it or not, we may be plunged back into society, back into history, back into the future again.

We have come to a moment when we have to think about the future. Indeed, we can scarcely avoid it.

The most obvious reason to pay attention now is also the least rational: number magic. We are coming to the end of the century, the beginning of a new millennium in the way we reckon time. Historians have demolished myths that the onset of A.D. 1000 provoked panic and apocalyptic expectations in medieval Europe. They weren't the clock and speedometer watchers we are. They hadn't even adopted Arabic numbers, so it was a matter of DCCCCLXLIX becoming M, which might be magical if it weren't so hard to follow. Few were literate then, and even fewer dealt with large numbers.

Still, the widespread belief that our ancestors went through a crisis at the outset of the second millennium seems to indicate that we expect a similar crisis at the beginning of the third. And if we expect it, chances are we are going to have it. Few individuals are likely to divest themselves of their worldly possessions and wait for the world to end, although some do expect the West Coast to fall into the sea and others are certain that fleets of spaceships are waiting at the other end of a wormhole in time, either to move humanity to a higher spiritual dimension or to have it for breakfast.

The ultimate origin of the fascination with the millennium is, of course, religious. Our counting is based on a calculation of the birth of Christ, which is apparently off by a few years, and the millennium itself refers to a period of heaven on earth. Indeed, for much of Western history, the future referred primarily to a time after worldly existence had ended. As the Hebrew prophets demonstrated and St. Augustine argued, it is possible to care about both an immediate worldly future and a supernatural future simultaneously, though it is also tempting to use a belief in the eternal to escape responsibility for the imperfect world in which we live. Current New Age millennialism is far too diverse to be simply categorized, though it appears that the escapist components are more visible and active than those that spring from the impulse to be actively involved in the fate of the world as it reaches a significant time. Up to now, those who have expected the imminent end of the world have been disappointed while those who have reverently engaged the challenges of their times have very likely found greater satisfaction. In any event, it is surely possible that the coming of the third millennium will lead to an upsurge in religious faith—both new and traditional—which would change current attitudes toward the future.

Even if you believe that the millennium is but a quirk of counting that has much more to do with the number of fingers on our hands than with any fundamental order of the universe, it can still be useful. It is a milestone, or more accurately an alarm clock that can force us to wake up and see where we are. It may be arbitrary, but if we decided decades in advance to have a crisis as 2000 approaches, we might as well just go ahead and have it. There may never be a better opportunity. Like a round-numbered birthday, the millennium invites both frivolity and fundamental stocktaking, the kind that leads people to change their lives.

Even as the coming of the millennium spurs us to fresh thought, it also has a certain mind-clouding effect. You wonder whether the world *seems* to be experiencing fundamental change because it's almost a new millennium or whether the calendar is mysteriously in synch with reality and is truly heralding a new world. A third possibility—that things have been changing under the surface and are only now becoming inescapably evident—is probably closer to the truth. Whatever history decides scarcely matters to those of us who are living through this time. It surely feels extraordinary. And passive as we try to be, the program we are watching will be regularly interrupted by news of the previously inconceivable. "What next?" people ask one another, and the future creeps back into the public consciousness.

Change is in the air, along with carbon dioxide and other so-called greenhouse gases that many scientists believe have already begun to warm the earth, and the state of the environment has emerged as one of the world's hot issues. The international order of the postwar era has been destroyed, though the thermonuclear weapons that were believed to have shaped it have not been. In the corporate world, small fish have swallowed up larger ones, and have dealt with this physical unlikeliness by laying off people and taking on debt. The hardware of the industrial economy falls into ruin, amid yet unfulfilled predictions that the new center of production and wealth will be inside the living cell.

These and many other major forces that are reshaping the world will be considered in subsequent chapters. For now, it is worth noting that these phenomena, earthshaking as many of them seem, are entirely man-made. Human power has been growing ever since the evolution of the species, but the rate of its increase has accelerated to the point that it may, in practice, be counterproductive. Mere men have the kind of power that could hitherto have been entrusted only to God. The challenge of our newfound might does not come simply from the weapons that can kill much of humanity and instantaneously degrade all life on earth. Nor is it confined to the most Faustian frontiers of science, where the search for the better mousetrap has been replaced by the artificial creation of the better, patentable mouse. There is power, too, in our thoughtless use of modern luxuries, such as the chemicals that seem to be responsible for making holes in the earth's protective ozone layers. And you do not have to be rich and powerful to make a difference. You can be poor and barely able to survive and yet contribute to global warming by burning a patch of forest. In the past, having a sense of the future might have seemed an act of hubris, because only a modest part of it was within human control. Today, it is a moral imperative, because we are remaking the future of our species and our planet.

Old stories about the thoughtless release of uncontrollable forces—Pandora's box, Aladdin's lamp, the sorcerer's apprentice—show an ancient fear that people will not be able to control the power they have. People have long known that most consequences are unintended. The ability to make a mess of things is not a new discovery.

But although man has never been a particularly innocent creature, his ability to make mischief has generally been localized, affecting only a house, a family, a tribe or a nation. Except occasionally in myths, human power has had boundaries. That has changed. While humans have been changing the weather for many years, we are beginning to know how. We can act on a truly global scale, but must also bear the burden of knowing a great deal about the consequences of our actions. In the cases of ocean pollution, acid rain, depletion of the ozone layer and the concentration of greenhouse gases, humanity seems to be pushing against the margin for error.

While we do not know the results of all of our actions, we do know quite a lot, and we are developing ever better tools of prediction and analysis. We understand, for instance, that the layer of ozone at the top of the atmosphere provides an important protection for people and other living things, and now we can determine how it is changing, and exactly how human habits are causing it to wear thin. The earth's chemistry is being monitored as never before, and though we cannot say with certainty in all cases how large a role human activities play in the changes observed, everyone is implicated. Everyday habits are bound up in the fate of the planet. Not since Adam and Eve were expelled from the Garden has the burden of knowledge been so severe. Yet the possibility for redemption remains. If people know what they are doing, they can stop and can take new steps to ameliorate the problems. That doesn't mean that the terror of moral responsibility can be somehow engineered out of existence. There are no purely technological fixes for fear, guilt or shame, but there are technological and behavioral responses to many of the situations which might give rise to such emotions.

We cannot throw up our hands and hate technology. We cannot afford to. Nearly all human beings are deeply implicated in technological civilization; we literally cannot live without it. But some of the problems come from misunderstanding. In the popular view, technological progress means doing the impossible, something that seems to have been accomplished regularly. But people have often misled themselves about how such successes were achieved and what they tell us about technology and ourselves. It is not a matter of man going to war with nature and triumphing, thus asserting rightful dominance over creation. It is misleading to speak of miracles, breakthroughs, godlike achievements. This is a Faustian vision of dominance, control and progress at virtually any cost. Sometimes critics bemoan technology and complain about the terrible things it is doing to nature. But this is simply a negative interpretation of the same myth—that human beings stand apart from nature and use their skills in ways that transcend the boundaries of the natural world.

This is an illusion. Technology *is* human nature. Like the white coat of a polar bear or the long neck of a giraffe, technology is an adaptation to the environment. Our brains, our hands and our eyes are believed to have evolved together, so tool use is part of our basic biological makeup. Technology is a very powerful adaptation, which has enabled us to inhabit virtually every place on earth, largely by altering the habitat to suit us. Sometimes, just as deer can overgraze and jeopardize their own survival, some technological activities have backfired and jeopardized, not enhanced, people's lives. The difference between these two kinds of self-destructive behavior is in degree, not in kind.

During the last two centuries, technology has become immensely powerful, largely because of the big boost made available by the exploitation of energy stored as fossil fuels. That era will eventually come to a close and society will be challenged to maintain a high living standard once that legacy runs out. In this context, the complex efficiency of living systems provides a model to which human systems of production, communications and survival might profitably aspire. The universe is gravid with possibility, and progress can be made in countless different directions. But advances will be perceived less as violent crashes through the barriers of nature than as interventions into complex systems. Moreover, by learning from and using these living systems, technology will become more lifelike in its own right. The distinction between the man-made and the natural world may never have been valid, but it will become harder and harder to maintain the illusion of a boundary.

Technology is not at war with the physical world. Rather, it is a realization of its potentialities. For example, it seems that people have always wanted to fly and they have imagined winged gods, angels and supernatural means by which people could take to the air. But the development of aviation was based not on miracles but on careful observation and understanding of the atmosphere and the physics of birds' wings. By crafting machines that take advantage of the inherent possibilities of the atmosphere, humans were able to transform themselves into creatures that can fly. We put on an airplane as we put on a coat; both are human devices that allow people to inhabit a little bit more of the earth.

The last two decades have brought no slackening of scientific and technological promise, and much that is commonplace now makes earlier dreams seem modest. Indeed, past technological ambition, which was often focused on making vehicles go faster or shooting larger payloads into space, seems fairly primitive and simpleminded now. Today's big science consists of such projects as mapping the human genome—a breaking of the chemical code that makes people what they are. If that happens, an attempt to rewrite the program seems the inevitable, though scary, next step. Today's scientific frontiers are inside the brain, inside the living cell. The likely breakthroughs include new kinds of artificial experience and ways of fighting off aging. These are technologies that, even more than the automobile, suggest whole new shapes for society. The questions they raise are deeply troubling, but the promise they hold is close to irresistible.

It's not exactly the old technological joyride, when speed and power were enough. And the impact of these and other technologies could be far more revolutionary. It would be dangerous to complacently accept every new technological development as an indication of human progress. Some will, no doubt, prove to be just the opposite. Technology often seems to have a mind of its own, but that's only because the rest of us are not paying attention. Once we have decided that neither material expansion nor technological elaboration can alone be the measure of progress, we still need some guide to whether we are going in the right direction.

Mankind's massive, technologically enhanced power over the environment has, throughout history, been disguised by a different strong, man-made force—the power of money. Indeed, in recent decades, as weapons have become so powerful and absolute in their effects, money has become the chief tool of foreign relations. To bomb your adversary is likely to be self-destructive. Better to be able to buy and sell him.

Because money plays so important a role in relationships among people, they tend to ascribe to it a reality that it does not have. It is the most fundamental and effective communications medium to be found in human society, a device for expressing values and creating comparisons among things that are, in themselves, incomparable. But though people know, intellectually, that money is like a language, and economics a kind of descriptive grammar, they tend to behave as if money had a value in itself, quite apart from the human and physical resources it expresses. That's understandable. Access to money can be the difference between health and starvation, living in a house or struggling in the street. Moreover, most tend to think of value in terms of the amount of money something costs, rather than think of the amount something costs as a momentary description of the scarcity and desirability of the object. Individuals save money for the future, thinking only rarely of whatever combination of physical materials and human expertise underlies the investment.

This explicable confusion becomes dangerous, however, when people try to think in purely money terms about issues whose implications transcend the grammar of finance and may transform the meaning of money and what it can buy. In late 1989, for example, the *New York Times* published an analysis of the economic impact of the possibility of the greenhouse effect and actions that might be taken to ward it off. While there is some uncertainty among scientists about whether human-produced gas emissions are, in fact, leading to global warming, and if so, how rapidly, there is little doubt that such a phenomenon would have enormous physical impact. In the United States, it would very likely bring massive flooding of coastal areas and the turning of much of our richest food production land into desert. Each of these might be expected to have an impact on the value of a dollar.

Yet the consensus of the economists interviewed was that Americans would be better off not taking any action to delay or prevent the greenhouse effect, because this would interfere with economic growth. If there is a strong economy, they said, it will be easier to pay for dikes and other massive ameliorative projects if the crisis comes. One's first reaction is probably to argue on humanitarian grounds: It is possible to imagine building dikes to save New York City, but what about the tens of millions who occupy the floodplains of Bangladesh?

But even on narrower grounds there are problems. The first is the assumption that remaking the society in a way that would reduce the emission of carbon dioxide and other greenhouse gases would be inherently unproductive. Indeed, it would probably make it more efficient in terms of energy, and ultimately more competitive. It might spur innovation in such underexplored fields as solar-generated hydrogen, which could provide a major new economic force. And even if every dollar does not have a payoff, economists have generally understood that the creation of public infrastructure—roads, water systems, rail lines, airports, power grids—is necessary for an advanced economy. Maintenance of the infrastructure we have not had to build—our soil, our harbors, our climate—would seem to make a certain amount of sense. The other major problem is the assumption that anything done with the money not spent on dealing with global warming would inevitably be more productive. What will people spend it on? If recent years are any indication, it will go for imported clothes, imported electronic equipment and imported cars. The wealthy might invest it in a house on the beach—which the economists would presumably consider a worthy investment—and then wait for the government to build structures to protect the asset from the rising sea.

By that time, of course, money will be telling a different story about the world. It will reveal that what once had been very desirable has become worthless, and things that had been taken for granted will be deemed essential for survival, and hence very expensive. Money catches up with reality quickly, but when people think only of the future behavior of money, they can squander the opportunity to keep and enhance their wealth.

The rhetoric of the future—the threats, curses, hopes and promises—is persistent and transcends any given time or set of challenges, as the next chapter will demonstrate. Humanity's sense of its own powers has always been a burden, even when they were negligible compared with those we exercise today. It is easiest now to find hints of the apocalypse in environmental concerns, perhaps because most people have long since wearied of paying attention to the enormous numbers of nuclear weapons already in the world and the prospect that they will spread and be used. A few years ago, many saw the confrontation between Communism and freedom as a moral issue of cosmic importance, and certainly both sides in World War II argued that the future of civilization depended on their victory.

The future is always with us. We must perpetually shoulder the burdens of our own knowledge and our own ignorance. Some challenges grow, others are faced or forgotten, but patterns of thinking about the future persist. In order to think seriously about the future, it is probably necessary to believe in two utterly contradictory premises. The first is that the lives of men and women go on as they have for century after century and that much of what seems to be a concern of this very moment turns out to be a perennial worry of the species. The second is that everything changes all the time, not simply technology but also behavior patterns that seem, at any given moment, to be both natural and immutable. A belief in the first position helps to put a lot of immediate concerns into perspective and sets down a humanist baseline against which possible change can be measured.

Stories written thousands of years ago still speak to us today, and indeed myths, scriptures and ancient tragedies deal with concerns that are more central and universal than those that deal more directly with the physical or social conditions of contemporary life. If you look to history for guidance, many of the challenges that appear new and unprecedented turn out to have arisen time and time again. Visions of despots using technological power to control their subjects' actions and thoughts were current a thousand years before George Orwell wrote *1984*. The question of whether history follows cycles, which has recently become a lively topic, seems to recur in cycles, over at least the last 3,000 years. The thought that the evolution of intelligence might pass from the human body to machines was developed by Samuel Butler in *Erewhon*, little more than a decade after Darwin first published his theory of biological evolution. Questions of what human society is for, why people work, how they are to live in the world, are perennial, addressed repeatedly through time and probably never to be resolved. Paradoxically, such a long view can also enhance the accuracy of predictions, simply because things that people in different times and different cultures have dreamed about for centuries are quite likely to be realized.

Such an ability to identify with previous generations helps us to identify with those who come after us. The problems of our future will reappear in changed but recognizable forms as the problems of their future. Still, we would not be fair to those people of the future if we were to say that because nothing changes and everything recurs, it is not at all necessary to pay attention to immediate problems.

The belief in endless and comprehensive mutability can also be derived from history, and it is useful because it greatly expands the possibilities of greater knowledge, choice and wisdom. It is a belief that gets us out of dead ends, and lets us vault over blank walls. It reminds us that many of the qualities and attitudes that are most pervasive in contemporary life are recent, can be changed and even have changed within our lifetimes.

If you were to sum up these ideas as "Nothing changes" and "Everything changes," there is not much hope for any sane integration of those thoughts. You would be as sensible as quantum physicists, one of whose fundamental premises is that matter behaves both as a wave and as a particle and that such behavior depends entirely on how one looks at it. The state of the observer matters. In ordinary language, however, you can begin to resolve the dilemma by recasting these observations as "Life goes on just as it always has" and "Everything about society changes, including people's sense of themselves." You don't want them to harmonize too well, because the tension between the two perspectives gives us a structure for assessing statements about the future.

It is possible to understand these two perspectives as referring to the changelessness of Homo sapiens as a biological entity through all recorded history and to the very rapid evolution of human culture during the same period. Such a distinction may be valid now, but it probably will not be for long, as genetic engineering offers the possibility of taking control of human evolution at the biological level. We may not choose to do it, but it is an unprecedented possibility. Humanity is like that, always facing unprecedented possibilities of our own making. That's why the future has been so thrilling and so frightening for so long.

And it's why we need a sense of the future—to keep an eye on life and try to nudge these incessant self-induced changes toward a direction we can recognize as progress.

Oracles, Prophecies and Utopias

If you have an awareness of the future, it means that you are able to see yourself as an actor in history, a participant in an ever changing process of human development. Yet if you go to the library and look up "future life" in the card catalogue, most of the volumes you will find will present visions of heaven, with a little hell mixed in. They are descriptions of a state in which eternal harmony (or discord) replaces incessant eventfulness. Most of them show that life can come to some satisfactory conclusion.

An awareness of human power, a belief that one's actions have consequences, is what has forced people over time to think about and plan for the future. Yet the act of looking ahead spurs a hunger to be unshackled from time and living in an ecstatic, enchanted, eternal present. For individuals, such a fantasy often takes the form of a religious promise of everlasting spiritual life, which is often related to a story in which the material world is destroyed in a fiery event of cosmic conclusiveness. On a social level, heavenly visions are secularized into utopias in which human life goes on but in which all the important decisions have been made in advance and people need no longer feel responsible for their actions.

It is, of course, possible to take another approach and deny the reality of human power, accept the forces that are stronger than those of human volition and surrender to harmony with the rest of the universe here and now.

All three responses—grasping human power, dreaming of escaping its consequences and denying its reality entirely—enter into the way people have always imagined the future. The balance of these responses changes from time to time and culture to culture, but all are constantly present, and each is in some sense correct. Individuals live brief lives and most of them have relatively little impact on the world, but through their participation in culture they partake of the knowledge and technology of past generations and help shape people of the future. The very act of nurturing children and teaching them implicates us all in a cultural evolution that has lasted for millennia and has surely reshaped the earth. And in practical terms, the desire to escape the everyday leads people to develop visions of how things can be better, many of which have been realized.

"In the long run we are all dead," said economist John Maynard Keynes, speaking for all who believe that our influence over time is limited and that the future should take care of itself. But he was responding to a much longer tradition of equating children with immortality, which thus entails responsibility for the future. The God of the Old Testament visits "the sins of the fathers upon the children unto the third and fourth generation." To be part of history is a terrible burden, one that people have ceaselessly longed to escape.

Still, an overview of people's approaches to the future over time must begin well before the evolution of historical consciousness in the contemporary Western sense. It comes, instead, out of what might be considered a protophilosophical impulse to understand how things work. Such thought deals not so much with causality as with connection, the belief that all phenomena are linked by patterns and forces that are not immediately apparent. Ancient oracles would look to the skies, throw dice or sticks, make sacrifices or simply look and listen for omens that were believed to be linked with the weather, success in battle, personal character or some other topic of immediate human importance. This search for portents reflects a belief that people's activities are part of a larger set of patterns that permeates the earth. A person who consults an oracle is not posing as a shaper of reality, but is, instead, looking for a bit of an edge in a world whose events are fundamentally preordained.

In retrospect, we call the hypotheses of association that proved useful for making the crops grow or understanding the behavior of animals the beginnings of science, while the rest are viewed as magic or superstition. It's worth noting that the quest continues, as scientists seek "a theory of everything," and that, at least at the subatomic level, phenomena that seem to have no relationship at all to one another do appear to affect each other.

Moreover, the ancient belief systems also persist. We do not seek relationships between the entrails of a sacrificed animal and the fate of a city, perhaps because we are dissociated from and guiltless about the slaughtering of livestock and the eating of their flesh. But we do continue to consult astrologers, patronize readers and advisers, look for stock market trends in the outcome of the Super Bowl. The *I Ching* is a perennial best-seller of Princeton University Press, which publishes that ancient Chinese book of chance, metaphor and advice in an anthropological context. Many of its buyers probably want their fortunes told. Today, most educated people at least pretend not to take such exercises seriously, and yet, for a time, astrological advice helped dictate the actions of a President of the United States.

Nevertheless, while the patterns suggested by astrology and most of the surviving oracular traditions have been shown to have almost no validity, the search for hidden patterns and unexpected connections remains a ceaseless and worthwhile human activity. Even worthless patterns can offer new angles for viewing the world and can thus serve as spurs to creativity. Many modern oracles call themselves consultants. They read computer printouts rather than entrails, and, as with their predecessors, their reliability is enhanced by the willingness of those in power to take them seriously.

> Sound the trumpet in Zion,
> give the alarm on my holy mountain!
> Let all the inhabitants of the country tremble,
> for the day of Yahweh is coming,
> yes it is near . . .
>
> Joel 2:1

The prophets of the Old Testament deliver a different message from that of the oracles, one that focuses on the importance of human activity and of the ability of those who heard them to do something about the dangers against which they warned. Their voices, the clarions of historical consciousness, remain fresh and vivid, relevant to our own time as they have been to countless generations since their prophecies were first made. Their subject is their people, the role they play on earth and how they should change the way they live.

"It is near," says the prophet Joel, echoing Isaiah, Ezekiel and Jeremiah, who wrote during the two centuries before him, and maintaining a tradition that would be carried on after him, through Daniel and into Christianity in the Gospels, Paul's Epistles and the book of Revelation. And later, the prophetic tradition would become the basis for yet another world religion, Islam. The prophets taught that human history—and especially the personal behavior and intentions of individuals now alive—has cosmic consequences. The prophets looked disapprovingly at what they saw in the world of their time, and they had visions of a time, not far off, when transgressors would have to pay for their sins while the righteous would be saved.

In our own age, we have the power to accomplish many of the most dire things they foresaw without the need for any supernatural intervention. We have become accustomed to the vocabulary of holocaust and Armageddon. Despite some of humanity's worst efforts, the world has gone on a lot longer than they believed it would. But the promise and menace to be found in the writings of the prophets persist. They are one important way in which we project ourselves in time.

We conventionally speak of prophets as people who can look ahead, but the biblical prophets were not oracles providing interpretations of the unfolding of fate. They were social and moral critics who deeply believed that what they and their contemporaries did would make an important difference to the fate of heaven and earth. They were looking at the here and now, and trying to show the way.

If we take a detached view of reality, the oracles' attitude is closer to the truth than the prophets'. The end was not so near, after all, and the people they addressed were not likely to affect the world's immediate fate. The ancient Hebrews did not have much impact on their own geographical region, let alone heaven and earth. The Egyptians, for example, who played so crucial a role in the history of the Jews, hardly mention them in their own chronicles. The Hittites, by disseminating iron technology, helped change the basic conditions of human life and the organization of the world. The Hebrews appear to be deluded underachievers by comparison. But in their own eyes they were the focus of the attention of a God who was first a sort of tribal deity but who later became the unique and universal God. Later, the first followers of Christ and Mohammed were heirs to this prophetic tradition and also emerged from the wilderness to become a global force. What distinguished the Jews, Christians and Muslims from their neighbors was the sense that they were part of an unfolding story, indeed the essential story of mankind. They affirmed that God was directly involved in the affairs of humanity, but that what individual men and women did would make a difference. They took a long view of history and placed themselves at its climax.

The future is, in large part, a story we tell about ourselves. It is an attempt to invest our lives with a meaning and a drama that transcend the inevitable decay and death of the individual. We want our stories to lead us somewhere and come to a satisfying conclusion, even though not all do so. Throughout history, people have given endings to the story. The bad ones that involve universal death and destruction are the easiest to grasp, because we have plenty of experience on which to base our imaginings. Even the prophets, who believed in salvation and cosmic harmony, at least for some, do not give a strong impression of what a harmonious conclusion would be like. God takes care of that. They concentrate on the preliminaries of fire, plague and bloodshed.

Still, the prophets do provide a sense of direction and the possibility of an ending. They speak to a desire to believe that life is taking us somewhere and that a resolution is just around the corner. To view human life as a great story, with suspense, climactic choices and dramatic endings, is, of course, artificial and even a bit perverse. The essentially literary form of this way of thinking induces people to look to a rapid resolution that has not yet arrived. That is the dilemma of many of Samuel Beckett's characters. Vladimir and Estragon, the tramps in *Waiting for Godot*, think that they're in a drama and that there will be a resolution, but the play demonstrates that dramatic narrative has only a limited value in understanding individual lives.

In contrast to the brief past and even briefer earthly future suggested by the Bible, other religious traditions have embraced endlessness. The Mayan calendars organized time in cycles of hundreds and thousands of years. Some of the religions of Asia find the eventfulness of life, so important to the prophets, either a curse or a delusion and see spirituality as a means of escaping the consciousness of history.

Moreover, one can make a case that Western historical consciousness, as embodied by the prophets, has been a plague upon the earth. It encourages the assertion of superiority over other peoples, thus leading to colonialism—whose ill effects include overpopulation, mass starvation and environmental degradation in much of the world. It creates a sense of alienation from nature, which leads to the many environmental nightmares that plague the planet. It leads to the belief that the world is only an intermediate stage of human spiritual existence, which can justify the development of weapons that threaten to make the planet uninhabitable.

Still, the voice of the prophets is one of our greatest cultural legacies, and one that is absolutely essential for dealing with the future. We don't pay much attention to the Hittites anymore, despite their impact on material culture. The prophets put their emphasis on people and the weight of their actions, and in so doing gave the actions of their own people an importance that resonates through time. The ancient Hebrews may not have mattered much to their neighbors, but they mattered a great deal to themselves, and as a result they had a profound, long-term impact on hundreds of future generations and hundreds of millions of people throughout the world. Similarly, the species Homo sapiens may not matter a great deal in the vastness of the universe, but human life ought to matter to human beings. True self-respect need not lead to megalomania in either case. More likely, it leads to humility in one's actions, because they are anchored by the knowledge that what you do has an impact far beyond your own circle or your own time.

Once, perhaps, it was possible for people to live lightly upon the earth, but the growth of technological civilization has rendered that impossible. There are too many people, too many inventions, too many consequences to even the most routine and unconsidered human actions. It no longer takes a religious imagination to envision worldwide destruction, frightening beasts, mysterious plagues. We

don't need God for that. We can bring all this destruction upon ourselves. The prophets' most lurid descriptions of worldwide destruction now seem believable, if a bit tame. Even the prophets' evocations
of monstrous animals have a certain resonance now that genetic alteration is a reality.

Thus the responsibilities we bear may be far greater than
those the prophets assigned, because we can observe our own powers
and measure their effects with great precision. Change is coming, the
prophets warned, and we can affirm. Tomorrow will be different from
today, and every day counts. Where once the imminent threat was
divine vengeance on sin, we today warn ourselves about an apocalypse of global overcrowding and famine. And where once there was
the promise of eternal spiritual life, there is today the promise of
longer, healthier, more fulfilling lives on earth. Cosmic threats and
the possibility of transcending the limits of life as we know it are
essential components of the prophetic tradition.

The danger of the prophetic tradition in these millennial times
is that too many will become preoccupied with its seeming impatience
with history and want to see the human story brought to a conclusion.
The prophetic books of the Old Testament and the book of Revelation
of the New Testament have the quality of wide-screen extravaganzas,
with many-headed monsters, battalions of trumpeting angels, blood
streaming through the landscape, black suns and many more mysterious and wondrous events. Even when they were new, such descriptions must have had a certain entertainment value, though it is
unlikely that those to whom the prophecies were addressed were as
passive and detached as we are today. Still, we are probably every bit
as uncomfortable with the idea that the world will go on and on and
on without us.

Another Old Testament voice, that of the Preacher in Ecclesiastes,
expresses another powerful strain in the Western sense of time and
the future. "Who knows what is good for a man in his lifetime," he
asks, "in those few days he lives so vainly, days that like a shadow he
spends? Who can tell a man what will happen under the sun after his
own time?" This existential complaint, the cry of toil and boredom
and futility, contrasts strongly with the sense of power and destiny
found in the writings of the prophets and in most of the rest of the

Bible. The Preacher sees existence as an eternal series of cycles that ends in death for individuals and lacks any promise of a satisfactory conclusion. But he does not welcome the cycles or seek to lose the self in some greater harmony, as a Hindu might do. Instead, he deplores his fate. He wants to believe in the cosmic drama of the prophets, but he sees little in his world to justify their vivid, extravagant expectations. He thinks that life on earth *ought* to be leading somewhere, that the narrative should be moving toward a satisfactory resolution. But everything he experiences suggests that it isn't.

He speaks of the dailiness of existence, of the incessant passage of the days and of the seasons and of the vanity of assuming that humans make any difference at all in this grinding, indifferent process. "What was will be again; what has been done will be done again; and there is nothing new under the sun." Life is just one damned thing after another, and though you can't predict exactly what will happen tomorrow, it probably won't be extraordinary, and it probably won't make any difference. As science has given us wider perspectives of time, space and the forces that have shaped both the earth and human life, Ecclesiastes' long and humble view of life is more literally accurate than the prophets' shorter, more dramatic stories. But his attitude is hardly one of blissful resignation. "Much wisdom, much grief, the more knowledge, the more sorrow." He yearns for the conclusiveness of the prophets, but he cannot find it.

These two conceptions of time—one finite and directed, the other infinite and cyclical—have coexisted in Western thought down to the present. It's easy to see why, because both describe aspects of human experience.

Things do happen, even in the lives of people whose lives are tied to routine. Those living in medieval times, for example, could see the progress of such extraordinary collective achievements as the building of cathedrals. These took shape on a different scale, both physically and temporally, than did the houses of the people and their routines, which were dictated by the crops and the seasons. Moreover, a repetitive existence can easily make you wonder whether there must be more to life than this.

Still, there is security in repetition. Who could live in a world that had to be discovered anew each morning? How could parents teach their children if their knowledge too quickly turned stale and irrelevant? In some respects, of course, we live in such a world, and parents expect to learn things from their children. But in a deeper sense, experience and wisdom have not entirely lost their value. Deep stability seems to coexist with rapid change. We can identify with the emotions of the author of Ecclesiastes even though it was written at least 2,200 years ago. Humans are still the same creatures they were then, with most of the same instincts and emotions. And society seems to have an inertial defense system to protect it from quick and possibly unwise reform. Today, it seems reasonable to view change as part of the routine. There is so much that is new under the sun that its newness becomes insignificant, no more shocking than the introduction of "new liquid Sunlight for dishes" or an all-new Perry Mason special. "Into the sea all rivers go, and yet the sea is never filled," says Ecclesiastes. And to the consumers the products go, and we are not filled either. We thoughtlessly consume energy that may melt part of the polar ice caps. The seas will be filled and will overflow our cities, our prophets tell us, but we do not listen because their warnings have become part of the ordinariness of life.

There is yet another ancient tradition that contributes to our cultural view of time and the future—that of the pastoral. This is a conception that is outside of time and outside of society, in which nature is benign, not like the sun beating down on the writer of Ecclesiastes, and man lives in harmony with it. Man is not driven by relentless cycles, nor does he look forward to escape. It is an image of equilibrium and wholeness. The pastoral is, of course, associated with classical antiquity and the myth of the Golden Age. The aesthetic and leisurely life that is depicted in pastoral literature is surely imaginary, an escape both from history and from agricultural routine. It is, nevertheless, tempting to identify the persistent recollection of an idealized pastoral time with the nomadic, preagricultural way of life that has characterized most of human existence. The domestication of animals that makes the pastoral life possible is an important step from hunting and gathering to an agricultural civilization. But it was the coming of agriculture that brought the greatest shock by tying people to specific pieces of land and increasing the importance of personal ownership of things. It permitted a tremendous increase in human population, but it also required an intensification of labor, and large settlements made social relationships more complicated. Thus, despite the benefits of agriculture, it is easy to see why people would look back to a simpler, less complex way of living. The pastoral is, in a sense, the first nostalgia.

In the book of Genesis, the immediate consequence of Adam and Eve's expulsion from the Garden of Eden is the necessity to labor to bring forth food from the earth. This is soon followed by the conception of Cain, the first farmer and the murderer of his brother Abel, the shepherd. The violence of Cain's crime seems linked to the coming of agricultural civilization, which followed the acquisition of knowledge and the concomitant loss of innocence. The murder sprang from Cain's envy of his brother, to whom God had shown greater favor. After cursing Cain to a life of toil, God still agrees to protect him. Today, we might say that you can't stop progress.

St. Augustine saw the farmer Cain as belonging to the city of man, the place of our temporal, earthly lives, while the herdsman Abel belonged to the city of God, beyond earth and time. Augustine, writing nearly six centuries after the time of Christ, knew that the end was not coming as quickly as the prophets and the early Christians believed it would. He called for the perfecting of the city of man, so that it could become as good as it could be. The worldly and time-bound are a gift from God, he argued, and human civilization embodies, however imperfectly, man's highest aims. Thus did Augustine admit social reform, as well as spiritual devotion, as worthy of the attention of believers.

Despite such important religious echoes, the pastoral tradition is primarily a secular one, deriving, as it does, primarily from the pagan traditions of Greece and Rome rather than the biblical tradition. The pervasive reappearance of the pastoral during the Renaissance speaks of a sensibility that is willing to recast even heaven in worldly terms. It is an affirmation of human goodness that, if left to its own devices and freed of the hobbles of civilization, could perfect life on earth.

The Utopian way of life provides not only the happiest basis for civilized community, but also one which, in all human probability, will last forever. They've

eliminated the root causes of ambition, political conflict and everything like that.

Thomas More, *Utopia* (1516)

Utopia is Arcadia with a program. The pastoral evokes a
changeless, idealized past, while utopianism proposes an equally
static, idealized eternal present. It is a different sort of escape from
history, one in which the eventfulness of human life ends not in hell-
fire and monsters but in a rational, self-regulating mechanism. The
boredom and endless hard work of which the Preacher complained is
replaced by toil that is efficiently organized and fairly shared.

Utopias need detachment either in place—on an island, in a
remote valley—or in time, so that they have the opportunity to establish their better way of doing things without the pettiness and inter-
ference of the outside world. And as Lewis Mumford noted, they
tend to need a change in elevation, to give them a variety of activities
and physical scales. Thomas More coined the word "utopia" from the
Greek for "no place," along with its homonym, "eutopia," which
means "good place." Plato's *Republic*, the ultimate ancestor of attempts
to imagine a perfect society, was set in a past nearly as remote as the
long-ago, faraway setting of the *Star Wars* movies. And More's Utopia, which is set somewhere in the Southern Hemisphere, chose to
isolate itself further by digging a channel that turned its land from a
peninsula to an island. (Public works projects are characteristic of utopias.) As believably unknown parts of the world have diminished and
belief in the possibility of progress has increased, utopias have tended
to inhabit the future.

The residents of utopias generally need a high degree of consciousness of what they want their society to achieve, something that
is rare in the real world. At the same time, they tend to be rather
apolitical creatures, because they are dedicated to a transcendent idea
and a universally beneficent system that makes faction and contention
not worth the effort. The residents are defined almost entirely in
terms of the society of which they are a part, and the rules that govern
how they will contribute tend to be very strict.

Like Arcadia, Utopia tends to be a rather dull place, no matter
how much their authors argue otherwise. Indeed, shepherds would
probably be much better company than the denizens of perfect soci-

eties, who tend to be a righteous, self-satisfied lot, armed with a ready answer for every hard question. Utopias are conceived almost entirely as a response to those questions the authors believe are most pressing. Such questions and answers dictate the shape of ideal societies and all their principal institutions. And although utopias have been written from many points of view—from Plato's idealism to More's Christian humanism to B. F. Skinner's behaviorism—it's very striking how alike they are. There's also a strong resemblance between the characteristics of societies imagined to be ideal and those that are intended to represent a world gone wrong. More's Utopians were watched almost constantly, and although their workdays were short, they rarely had a moment to themselves, just like the future Englishmen in Aldous Huxley's dystopian novel *Brave New World*, written more than four hundred years later. Likewise, some of the architectural ideas of the nineteenth-century French utopian Charles Fourier bear a striking resemblance to prisons that were being built throughout the world at the same time. One man's dream is another's nightmare.

When we think about the future, all of these traditions of thought come to mind at once. We hear the prophets saying that great changes are coming and what we are doing now will make a big difference. We hear Ecclesiastes, along with the voices of classical culture, saying that everything goes in cycles and nothing ever really changes. We hear the oracles telling us to look for the patterns of the universe and to plan our lives in harmony with them. We hear the utopians telling us that over the years we've fallen into some self-destructive habits, but through reason we can escape into lives of endless harmony. And we can even hear St. Augustine's sensible and elegant compromise, which tells us that we cannot expect heaven on earth but that it's worth trying to come as close as possible.

That makes nearly three millennia worth of futures that are so ingrained in our culture that we draw upon them without really even having to think very much. The future of which we are conscious, however, seems to be something else. It grows from an environment of doubt rather than belief. Most of all, it is technological.

Francis Bacon, in his unfinished utopian work, *The New Atlantis*, published in 1627, provides a bridge between the old religious and moral approach to the future and the more recent scientific one. He never quite gets around to telling how society works on his mythical island of Bensalem, but it is clear that this is not what interests him the most. Instead, he describes a society that began with the same set of religious scriptures as does European society—including the miraculous receipt of some of the Epistles and the book of Revelation even before they were written. But his islanders are not looking to the end of things, or to deliverance in another life. They are far more interested in understanding what exists and making use of this knowledge to improve the quality of their lives. They are drawn not to the fire of apocalypse but to the light that was the starting point of creation. Bensalem's central institution is a kind of priesthood of research known as Salomon's House or, alternatively, the College of the Six Days Works, referring to the six working days of creation described in Genesis. It is dedicated to "the knowledge of Causes and secret motions of things," and it has modified the entire geography of the island to serve as an enormous observatory and experimental laboratory.

The contemporary world is so dependent upon science and technology to sustain itself that one might say that we are all living on Bensalem now. Still, the kind of intellectual shift Bacon advocated—from Purpose to process—was truly basic. It had been going on before Bacon's time, and it tremendously accelerated after him.

The search for laws and secret motions drew people to once again consider all those cycles of which Ecclesiastes complained so bitterly. But now they were not seen as causes for despair but as principles of order that opened the understanding of the universe to human reason. In England during the eighteenth century, the processes and cycles began to be put to work. First waterpower and then the energy contained in wood and coal were mated with machines. The turning of the engine brought a new kind of cycle into the world that increased human productivity, even as it imposed disciplines on workers that were new and dispiriting. The farmer's enslavement to the natural cycles seemed benign compared with the industrial worker's bondage to the new mechanical regimen.

The idea that a continuous process could actually be a model of stability was an extremely powerful eighteenth-century idea. Adam Smith used it to create modern economics. It underlies the U.S. Constitution. And indirectly, in the form of the geological concept of uniformitarianism, it changed people's conception of time itself. Essentially, this stated that all those things—such as the running of rivers to the sea—that Ecclesiastes thought were accomplishing nothing are changing the face of the earth but are doing so very, very slowly. Change came not through the catastrophes described in the Bible but through incremental changes that happened on a scale of time so vast that it is, for the most part, imperceptible to humans. And the remains of plants and animals found in rock strata that had been deposited long ago suggested that those first six days were very long. Obviously some geologically significant catastrophes, most notably volcanic eruptions, do bring extraordinarily rapid and perceptible change. Still, they do so in the context of an earth whose age is to be measured not in a few thousand years, as the Bible seemed to suggest, but in a few billion years.

Within this new view of time, change was no longer a result of dramatic divine intervention but of ongoing processes. Such thinking reached its climax in the work of Charles Darwin, whose painstaking observation of nature ultimately led to the conclusion that man himself is part of the evolution of the earth and its creatures. His thinking also raised the possibility that man might be continuing to evolve. Consciousness of that process seems certain to change its outcome. The further evolution of humanity is one of the most profound issues of the future.

Even as the discoveries of science were proving that past and future were unimaginably extensive and humans but a latecomer to the earth, they were also providing the basis for new technologies. The onset of the industrial revolution is a familiar and often told story. Wherever it occurred, first in Britain, then in Western Europe and North America, it changed the face of the earth. Its requirements of energy sources, raw materials and means of transportation and distribution reordered the society. It changed economic and social values and gave a new shape to human life.

In *The New Atlantis*, Bacon mentioned the belief of his time that the earth was old and weary and not capable of supporting as many people as it once did. In fact, the old earth was carrying enormous reserves that lay untapped until the scientific and technological course that Bacon advocated was pursued. While the discovery of geologic time made it possible to understand that coal was really the remains of plants that had lived and died in the far-distant past, the release of that pent-up energy brought rapid social and material transformation. Time had slowed down, but change had speeded up. The future as we know it—driven by technology and inviting mankind to be either godlike or satanic—had been born.

Is technology enough to build a future on? In *Utopia*, Thomas More alluded to this nagging issue. His narrator mentions that Europeans have introduced the magnetic compass to the residents of the Southern Hemisphere. "They'd never heard of it before, and for that reason had always been rather frightened of the sea, and seldom risked going on it except in the summer," he reports. "But now they put such faith in their compasses they think nothing of winter voyages—although this new sense of security is purely subjective. In fact, this overconfidence threatens to convert an apparently useful invention into a source of disaster."

More was raising one of the key practical questions that face any technological society. It is the same question that arises when, for example, the space shuttle is guided by a computer program during an emergency because things are happening too rapidly for humans to keep track. More broadly, it is the question of whether humans have become too confident that technology will always be able to find unexpected solutions to problems into which people have blundered thoughtlessly. From the 1920s onward, our consumer economy has prospered largely by making people feel confident about technologically complex devices—automobiles, appliances, televisions, computers—that they don't understand. When they break, people feel betrayed. "It has always worked before," we say, but that doesn't make it work again.

The practical dimension of dependence on technology is but one part of the question. The other is spiritual. Are we to be more confident of the compass or the supercomputer than we are of ourselves? Are we to remake ourselves and our society in the image of the machine? Does the confidence the machine and its organization give us inevitably tempt us to become monsters?

Two rather ambiguous early-nineteenth-century heroes who are synonymous with the possibilities and discontents of industrial society are Goethe's Faust and Mary Shelley's Frankenstein. These icons of romanticism still pervade our vocabulary and our fears about the dangers of human power. We speak of them when we fear what we are doing, when we might not know enough about the consequences of our actions or when we feel that pride and arrogance, not wisdom, are in control.

"I've created a monster!" is a cliché of modern life, usually spoken by people with little awareness of the godlike powers they have arrogated. The prophets saw visions of monsters, most of them images of the evils of their world. The industrial age was only a few decades old when we started to think about making our own. Now, two of the most lively and promising frontiers of technology—genetic engineering and robotics—are in different aspects of the monster-creating business. The U.S. Supreme Court has ruled that organisms are patentable, and monster-making, though we don't call it that, seems likely to turn into a major industry.

The first monsters created by industrialization were probably the industrialists, the prideful ones who remade the world in the name of productivity and acquisitiveness. They, in turn, created other monsters—the displaced urban working class, the distant people who were victims of colonialism. Many of the problems of domestic and international politics in the latter half of the twentieth century have been the result of attempts to unmake these monsters.

"Selling out" is another cliché, one that contains the faintest of echoes of the Faust legend. The story of the gifted, ambitious but unfulfilled man who sells his soul to the devil is a very old one that first became prominent in the sixteenth century. There have always been ambitious people, but as the social commentator Marshall N. Berman has argued, Goethe's Faust represents a new kind of ambition. It is largely altruistic, it is comprehensive and it is utopian—in the sense that it is dedicated to a comprehensive vision of improvement. He is not a capitalist looking out for his own gain and remaking a little bit of the world in the process. Rather, he is making a whole new world according to the latest, most technologically sound principles. Berman calls this new kind of person the Developer, and he traces the type from the writings of Saint-Simon to such figures as Stalin and Robert Moses. He might have added the turn-of-the-century architect and urban reorganizer Daniel Burnham. His admonition "Make no little plans; they have no power to stir men's blood" could serve as the motto for the movers and shakers of the modern world. The 1939 Futurama was, in this sense, a Faustian work, more than a hundred years on.

But when we speak of selling out, we are talking about a betrayal of principles, whereas the sin of Berman's Developer is adherence to a principle. This seems to be a contradiction, but it isn't. What we are selling out are all of the little humanistic principles, the loyalty felt, promises made, dignity respected. These are the eggs that get broken in the name of the omelet. (The results of the Developer's activity are often like an omelet, spreading, undifferentiated and bland, compared with the integrity and easily perceived scale of what has gone before.) We sell out in little ways in hopes of realizing a larger vision. But by the time it is supposed to be realized, a new, more remote vision has taken its place and the endless process of betrayal goes on. Utopia is always just out of our reach, but in seeking it we will trample anything that is in the way. The utopian is a true son of Cain, the representative of a new mode of human life who is nevertheless compelled to spill his brother's blood in reaching the goal.

Seen from this perspective, utopians make everyone victims, including themselves, and their destructiveness is all the more pathetic because it generally grows from good intentions. Yet it is difficult to escape the utopian impulse, which sees in the reality of change the possibility of improvement. It partakes of the Old Testament prophets' sense that history is moving toward a goal, along with a faith in the power of modern technology and organization to realize long-cherished dreams. If we can go to the moon, we say, surely we can solve the problem of . . . whatever. Utopians tend to speak not as advocates but as interpreters of the inevitable. They don't say that they have shown one possibility for the future. Instead, they show us the future.

Yet one would not want to be without utopians. Just as we need prophets to question our conduct, we need utopians to focus on our goals. We know that the future is a process, but utopians can provide useful anticipatory snapshots to help us decide which way we want to go. The act of thinking about the future is, in a sense, a process of discerning the programs that are hidden within platitudes, evaluating them and, when necessary, replacing them with better visions carried in new, improved clichés. The point is not to escape from utopias, but to recognize them when we see them, and think twice before we decide to move into one.

The coming of the technological age was made possible by the release of two different kinds of energy. The first was that of the fossil fuels that ran the steam engines and other machinery of the industrial age. The other was human energy that seemed at once to have been harnessed and freed as modern forms of organization supplanted tradition.

The unchanging life of the village gave way to the chaos, squalor and possibilities of the industrial city, and people were quite willing to leave the old, generally static life for one of greater instability. As we read Dickens, Hugo, Balzac and the other great writers of nineteenth-century urban life, their characters seem subjected to more changes of fortune than anyone could possibly stand. But most people would probably choose a life in which both bad and good things are happening to them constantly over one in which it's likely that nothing will ever happen at all. If the people who gave up the traditional life for the modern regretted their loss, it was not until later. Being able to simply throw things away is a very powerful measure of freedom.

In such a society, it became possible to conceive of a tomorrow wholly different from today. One aspect of the French Revolution of 1789 was an attempt to change everything. Even the names of the days and months were changed, as if to dramatize the changing of time. Measurements that were based on the human body were eliminated, replaced by the metric system whose measures were related to what were believed to be the dimensions of the entire world. This change of measurement represented an enormous shift in meaning, a displacement of the human scale by a rationalized system, one whose frame of reference was derived through scientific inference rather than through any directly observable comparison.

In a world where change is constant, anything can be questioned, and very likely improved. Such a situation produces an explosion of utopian thinking. Instead of modeling an alternative world, complete with architecture and geography, as More and Bacon did, modern utopians typically show how their own place and time can be remade into something far better through the application of a few sensible principles. Sometimes these are social ideas. Often these ideas are linked to heroic public works, the application of the powerful transforming technologies to the earth itself. Technology, generator of the constant change that makes such radical thinking possible, is often depicted as the savior of humanity, the force that will permit people to be freed from backbreaking work and live a life of harmony and leisure. But contemporary utopianism is far more likely to be found in annual reports, television commercials, five-year plans, inaugural addresses, development proposals or *Popular Mechanics* than in literary creations. Writers, filmmakers and other creative artists are more drawn to dystopias, which make more compelling visions. To have a convincing utopia, everything has to go right, but only one or two things have to go terribly wrong to make a memorable nightmare.

There is an inherent contradiction between utopian visions and the fact of constant change. Utopian visions tend to require remaking the world and society in basic and even violent ways, but they promise an end to change as the ideal is reached. Thus they confuse the very turbulence and uncertainty that make their dreams realizable with the problems they hope to correct. Because we know that we have not yet arrived at an ideal society, we tend to dismiss utopian thinking as irrelevant. This is wrong. Utopias get built all the time. Post–World War II American suburbia was a kind of utopia, one that was promoted by the Futurama and many other similar events, and so were the widely spaced apartment towers that were supposed to put an end to urban congestion. Mussolini's revival of Roman imperial grandeur was a utopian idea, as was Hitler's thousand-year Reich. Television broadcasting was, at its outset, wrapped in a utopian vision of a society that would be better educated and hungry for cultural development. If the consequences of the utopia are not as happy as was promised, that doesn't mean that the idea was not utopian. And even though society keeps on changing even after utopian projects are realized, that doesn't mean that utopian ideas are irrelevant. They help to set a direction which can be very difficult to reverse. Utopians aren't only charming eccentrics. They may be armed and dangerous.

Where utopians part company with observable reality is in their assumption that, at some moment, society will achieve an optimal balance at some higher level and then stop. The prophets' view of a directed history is emotionally satisfying, but perpetually unproven. Ecclesiastes' view of the world's ceaseless, meaningless activity comes closer. Karl Marx embraced the endlessness of that view and incorporated it into a vision of never-ending human development. He saw the contradiction between the pervasive social and technological change that was making utopian visions conceivable and the static nature of the visions themselves. He chose to embrace the process of change itself as a progressive force. That is how he distinguished his ideas from those of other socialist thinkers—notably Henri Saint-Simon, Charles Fourier and Robert Owen—whom he termed utopian. Still, it is easier to paint a picture than to ride a whirlwind, and even many of those who have claimed to be Marx's followers have been more at home with utopian images than with his confidence in constant, generative movement.

From the time of its discovery by Europeans, America has been utopia's natural home. More located his Utopia in the Western Hemisphere, albeit in more tropical climes. But the very idea of a New World suggests a place where a much improved society can be established, even as it tends to devalue the lives of the people who already lived in the Americas. The founders of New England dreamed of a city upon a hill that could be an example of piety for all the world. William Penn sought something quite rare, a tolerant utopia. And though Americans consider themselves pragmatic, and celebrate mobility and change, the dream of becoming "more perfect," as the Constitution has it, permeates our national character. The Constitution, though it grew out of a political process rather than an individual imagination, is perhaps the world's most successful example of conceiving of a political system from scratch, and in adding the Bill of Rights, the founders foresaw the need to protect individuals *from* utopia.

The American landscape is filled with the remains of utopian communities, based on principles including the religious communalism of the Shakers, the productive socialism of Robert Owen, the crafts revivalism of William Morris and the single-tax principles of Henry George, among many others. Utopian romances were a very popular genre of nineteenth-century fiction and took much of the speculative role now served by science fiction.

Edward Bellamy's *Looking Backward*, published in 1888, is the most influential literary utopia America has produced and a good place to begin to look at the American search for perfection during the previous century. The book, a mixture of science fiction, economic reformism and romance, became a text for feminists and city planning reformers and the basis for a political movement. It concerns a prosperous Boston businessman who is, through mischance, buried alive and awakened in the year 2000 in a handsome city whose prosperity is based on cooperation rather than competition. We are not living today as Bellamy said we would, but his book has special resonance for Americans, in part because its voice is the familiar one of the hardheaded dreamer, the pragmatic idealist. Americans talk constantly about their dream, but they insist on being thought practical and realistic. We try to sound casual about landing on the moon. We chase rapture, but fear emotion.

The leaden style in which the vision is described was probably involuntary on Bellamy's part, but it serves the purpose well. He wanted to show that society could be very different, and a good deal better, without pain or disruption of any sort. He was carefully non-ideological, avoiding the words "socialism" and "utopia," even though what he was proposing was both. Specifically, he took note of the increasing concentration of American industry into giant trusts, such as John D. Rockefeller's Standard Oil and Andrew Carnegie's steel empire. He argued not that the trusts should be busted, as the Progressives later advocated, but that their concentration should be encouraged. After each industry resolved itself into a single massive organization, all would then be nationalized and run for the benefit of the nation rather than the investors in the company. All the members of the society would have to spend part of their lives working for such organizations, as members of an Industrial Army. Because everyone must serve, and economies of scale would make productivity high, the amount of one's life spent working would be relatively modest. That would mean that people would be able to spend most of their lives doing things that would interest them. (Such freedom from mindless labor is one promise that nearly all utopias have in common.) Some of the best members of the Industrial Army would be asked to stay on beyond retirement to serve as directors and elders of their industry, which Bellamy termed "government by alumni." Politics, per se, would wither away, presumably because all of the hard choices about the society's goals and values had already been made. Society would be ruled by managers and experts.

The rule by experts that Bellamy proposed is a characteristic feature of utopias, from those of More and Bacon to those of B. F. Skinner and General Motors. Saint-Simon praised engineers as "the priests of civilization." From his time to ours, society has placed tremendous hope in the possibility that the kind of thinking that built the railroads, the bridges and the crystal palaces or that placed Americans on the moon and invented the computer could be mobilized to solve some of the eternal problems of poverty, ignorance and crime. Utopian thinking is itself political, but it looks ahead to a postpolitical era, one in which the engineer's question "How?" supplants the deeper question "What?"

In Bellamy's utopia, as in most others, the rule of experts is validated by the happiness, prosperity, comfort and leisure that the entire society enjoys. That generally allows those who invent utopias to finesse the difficult question of the relationship between experts and the populace. What happens when the experts, who know better what is good for us than we know ourselves, try to make us do something that feels wrong to us? How much unhappiness must we put up with in order to be happy in the way experts think we ought to be? Can the experts actually *be* wrong? Utopias are rarely democracies, but their authoritarianism doesn't rankle because all the key decisions have been made in a manner that is satisfactory to its inhabitants.

Aldous Huxley's *Brave New World*, one of the most chilling critiques of the utopian impulse yet written, shows a society that is totally oppressed but is compliant because its leaders have mastered the technology of keeping everybody happy. In Huxley's novel, this takes the form of psychoactive drugs, extraordinarily elaborate games and various kinds of pornographic entertainments, a constellation of technologies that seem likely to be realized in mere decades, rather than the several centuries predicted in the novel. Even Huxley's "feelies," tactile movies, may not be too far off.

Bellamy is able to assume that his readers are unencumbered by any belief in aristocracy and will identify themselves first of all as economic creatures. This places him in sharp contrast to H. G. Wells, who a few years later in *The Time Machine* looked thousands of years forward to find that the British class system had produced a bifurcation of the human species and reduced the privileged classes to the food and playthings of the producers. Bellamy was confident that his readers would agree that nobody has an assured place in society and those who think they do are deluding themselves at the expense of those who must labor. He associates this condition with the egalitarian values that underlie American democracy, but it is probably equally a product of the way in which industrialization exploded earlier social relationships and remade them in its image. But unlike Marx, who dwelt upon the psychological effects of industrialization, Bellamy does not question or even deeply consider how the production system affects those who participate in it. He believed that industrial organization is not society's problem but its solution. He argued that workers were alienated, not from the jobs themselves, but from the fruits of their labors. Society's problems were, therefore, almost entirely questions of distribution.

Indeed, in Bellamy's turn-of-the-millennium America, buying decisions have replaced political ones. Subscribers to magazines would choose the editors, precisely because they are subscribers. Citizens would be subject to a relatively short period of compulsory production, after which they would lead lives dominated by cultivated consumption. The credit-card-wielding residents of his ideal world would not distinguish between their role as citizens and as consumers. This is prescient because the consumer society was only beginning to emerge, in the form of the introduction of brand names and packaged products.

Bellamy assumed that such a society would be efficient because people would realize that providing the good life collectively would be cheaper than selling off pieces of it individually. For example, the buildings he describes all have arcades and other features to keep pedestrians from getting wet when it rains, and he has a character observe, "The difference between the age of individualism and that of concert was well characterized by the fact that, in the nineteenth century, when it rained, the people of Boston put up 300,000 umbrellas over as many heads, and in the twentieth century, they put up one umbrella over all the heads." Bellamy was right about the increasing American tendency to measure democracy in terms of what its citizens were able to buy, but he did not understand that such a measurement made goods that are shared essentially valueless.

About twenty years later, Henry Ford would develop the

working model of the consumers' utopia when he rationalized the production process, prices and wages to the point that those who made his cars could also afford to own them. Jobs became less interesting but more lucrative, and the ability to buy the product became the worker's chief reward. This is the utopia in which many still believe we live, though it stopped working years ago.

Except for the internationalism of Woodrow Wilson after World War I, which was soundly rejected by Congress, the United States was far more concerned with economic growth than with building a new society during the first decades of the twentieth century. Our immense national resources and the engine of the consumer society made the country an increasingly important economic power. New communications and entertainment media, many of them supported by advertising, created an illusion of cohesion as nearly all Americans were able to share the same vicarious experiences. The proliferation of the private automobile was forcing an improvement and expansion of the nation's road system, and the upper middle class was able to move to homes in sylvan surroundings that at least simulated a house in the country.

Utopian thought really did not reemerge on the public agenda until it was absolutely necessary, during the Great Depression. President Franklin D. Roosevelt was not a utopian by nature, but he was determined to make things work. Facing a protracted and unprecedented economic disaster, he convened the first "brain trust" of largely academic experts, who were, in theory at least, the kind of skilled, disinterested technocrats who are a mainstay of utopian administration. Roosevelt conceived of new kinds of primarily economic "freedoms" that were never anticipated in the Bill of Rights. He established the principle that the national government would guarantee a measure of "social security" to its citizens. He refused to wait for economic cycles to run their course and attempted to intervene and bring about change. Perhaps the most striking thing about his administration was that, in the face of the Depression and the Dust Bowl, the populace remained docile. There was a tiny minority that wanted a workers' revolution, but there were far more who hoped for a refrigerator, and in fact, refrigerators sold quite well during the 1930s. Rising material expectations were maintained through a decade of economic adversity. Americans had dipped deep into their reserves of historical optimism, but they did not hit bottom.

The Depression had engendered a mistrust of the old, a mistrust of fantasy skyscrapers, of the classical edifices which had come to represent old money run amok. The remade society would be for the ordinary worker, one in which he could have things and be comfortable. The world's fairs held in Chicago in 1933 and New York and San Francisco in 1939 were largely about the dream of modern consumption. The center of all this modern living was the family's house, which had always been a powerful symbol in American life and which became an even more sacred object during World War II. Throughout the war, magazines, advertising and government propaganda presented the American home, typically in a small town or quasi-rural setting, complete with apple tree and a porch swing, as what our boys were fighting for. It mattered little that the picture did not correspond with the way most Americans were living. This was an urban, industrial country, and much of the urban housing was dilapidated, lacking in sanitary facilities and, partly because of the economic hardship of the Depression, horribly overcrowded. It seemed to housing advocates that by applying to good housing the same commitment and methods that had been brought to the war effort, the country could keep its economy on track and honor its commitments to its soldiers at the same time. "The American Dream," that persistent, though vague, expression of the country's utopian penchant, could be translated into a house full of appliances, a car, a television set and some children to whom the good fortune could be passed on. It was a materialistic vision, to be sure. But if Americans do not crave possessions only, they do crave possessions, which provide the easiest measure of well-being. For immigrants and the children of immigrants, being able to make money and to buy things is a particular expression of freedom, because it shows that through hard work and shrewdness it is possible to obtain comforts available only to the socially privileged elsewhere.

Roosevelt was an activist on two fronts. His administration linked the improvement of Americans' lives to the exercise of world power. The wartime and immediate postwar experience suggested that the more the United States asserted itself in the world, the richer it became. This connection was rarely stated quite so crudely, but it barely needed to be stated. This was the belief that underlay Henry Luce's declaration of "the American Century," and it was implicit in the Truman Doctrine, a wide-ranging commitment to intervene against Communism virtually everywhere. When Daniel Bell argued in 1960 that the postwar era had brought an end to ideology, what he was really talking about was widespread acceptance of a single, very powerful ideology—anti-Communist, managerial, technologically optimistic, generally supportive of a measure of governmental activism and confident that it offered solutions to many long-standing problems.

This attitude drew much of its legitimacy from the experience of World War II, when the country had been able to organize itself on a scale never before achieved, to produce large quantities of ships, airplanes and weapons, to mobilize the society and fight two different powerfully armed enemies in Europe and the Pacific. Our Industrial Army had triumphed. When the war was over, many feared that the demobilization would plunge the country into a new Depression, and there were proposals to convert aircraft plants and shipyards into prefab housing factories, and to retool other defense plants to make products for the new postwar home. The appliances did get built, and so did the houses, though not in factories. But the United States never truly demobilized. It merely turned its attention to another threat, that of the Soviet Union, which had drawn most of Eastern Europe into its sphere of influence as World War II ended. Far from bringing bad times, the end of World War II signaled the start of an economic miracle, the one that help propel those that came a bit later in Western Europe and Japan.

The material success of the postwar era is a familiar story, as are its shortcomings, particularly in the areas of racial and economic equality. But for a majority of Americans, the postwar prosperity was real, and they rarely came into personal contact with people for whom it was not. The dreams of the Depression and the World War II era were more than achieved, by any measurable standard. Of course, much that is important in life is unmeasurable. More possessions do not bring greater joy, and in fact, the extra bit of happiness brought by each new acquisition becomes very small very soon. And what of the next generation, the supposed beneficiaries of all their parents' efforts? They had not lived through the Depression and the war. They did not experience the reality of scarcity, the uncertainty that they would be able to afford a place to live or food to eat. They had not sacrificed for the war effort, or spent many years facing death in foreign places, nurturing a dream of home. (From earliest childhood, they had been threatened by the menace of Communism and the possibility of nuclear annihilation, but both of these were really impossible to conceive of in terms of their own experience.) For them, postwar prosperity was not a dream fulfilled, merely a place to start.

As the United States entered the decade of the 1960s, there was much about it to warm the heart of a good utopian. The country was in the midst of a physical transformation, one that changed the faces of the cities and allowed families to stretch themselves across the landscape. The previous decade had brought about the largest increase in real family income that had ever been experienced. The working class had virtually disappeared as menial jobs became fewer and fewer and skilled jobs paid salaries that pushed wage earners well into the great American middle class. At the same time, it appeared to some that the country's unprecedented affluence would provide the occasion for solving its oldest and most morally troubling problem, that of race discrimination, by integrating all into the good life. College education, once a privilege of a small elite, was rapidly turning into an option for all.

And the American people, far from being troubled by change, absolutely gloried in it. In 1960, they elected a President who had campaigned on the premise that the country—which had changed enormously by almost any measure during the previous fifteen years—was not moving rapidly enough. John F. Kennedy called for commitment and sacrifice to deal with those problems that still existed in the nation as a whole after a long period of private enrichment. These seemed soluble, in part because Americans had deluded themselves into thinking, for example, that poverty existed only in tiny, shrinking "pockets" and that segregation was a problem only in the South.

What was so potent about Kennedy, particularly for young people, was his suggestion that, while prosperity is fine, there ought to be something more to life. The nobility of his rhetoric of personal sacrifice was badly tarnished by the war in Vietnam that followed. At the time, though, the Peace Corps was more to the point. It was a conduit for those American energies that were not simply acquisitive, and not incidentally, a chance for young people to learn that their material comforts could not be taken for granted. In its early years, when the recruits were mostly inexperienced people born during the war, it probably had greater impact in the United States than it did in the places that were supposed to be helped. It was based on the rather arrogant assumption that one could solve the pressing problems of mankind simply by throwing enthusiastic young Americans at them. The belief was that they could remake the world largely through the strength of their own good intentions. Although it was specifically involved in helping with modernization, its utopianism was based more on changed consciousness than on superior organization. "Vigor" was one of Kennedy's favorite words, and he often suggested that the application of pure energy could succeed when other methods failed.

In his celebrated 1958 book, *The Affluent Society*, economist John Kenneth Galbraith argued that the United States had become a new kind of place—an affluent society—and its challenges would grow out of living with its economic success. Robert Heilbroner, another economist, was less sanguine in his 1960 book, *The Future As History*. "Whereas we may have begun as optimists out of conviction, we remained so out of conditioning," he wrote. "For looking back over the special circumstances which favored our national career and which shaped our national character, we can see that we were spared the one exposure fatal to a philosophy of optimism. This was the experience which Europe suffered, first by small degrees, and then in overwhelming assault: an exposure to the forces of history, not as the proponents but as the opponents of our volitions." Certainly, there were aspects of U.S. behavior that were not sustainable. Americans boasted of burning half the world's fuel and driving half its cars, as if this were evidence of nobility rather than the slovenly voraciousness of a pie-eating champion. And the Vietnam War, the catalytic event of the decade, would prove that American power was not unstoppable.

Yet the principal disagreements of this decade did not so much involve challenges to national volitions as they did an internal conflict over what these volitions should be. Liberals, bureaucrats, Cold Warriors and New Leftists alike shared Galbraith's premise that America had moved beyond the fear of scarcity and would be able to accomplish things in a new way. Heilbroner's prediction, that the United States would face forces more powerful than itself, was not really fulfilled until the 1970s and 1980s.

During the 1960s, and especially after the assassination of John F. Kennedy in November 1963, the postwar consensus broke down. The model of the future that had seemed so clear and so desirable for so long was revealed as limited in its scope and oppressive in its impact. But the consensus didn't just grind to a halt like an old car. It broke into several different movements, each with its own ends and its own energy.

Rarely in our history has the future been so directly addressed and strongly considered as it was in the 1960s. The conflict of the period can be viewed as a war between utopias, a bitter clash among the forces for improvement. At the heart of the dispute was a question that haunts utopian thinking: Do better institutions make better people, or do you need different people to make a good society? Utopians believe in the perfectibility of the way people live, and they devote most of their attention to the simple changes in organization that can allow human goodness to flourish. But no matter how well the institutions of a utopia are designed, the suspicion remains that people will have to transform themselves before the social and political transformations the utopia promises can come into being. This change is not gradual and procedural; it is a flash of insight that things can be much better if people change their attitudes toward life.

Buckminster Fuller, for example, strongly believed that circumstances change consciousness. He argued that by building a dome over the troubled city of East St. Louis, Illinois, all the city's problems would be solved. Nobody would have to worry about shelter, he said, and people could be confident of being able to meet their needs. What appears to be evil, Fuller argued, is only the fear of scarcity. He thought that perfection could be engineered, and transcendence was most likely to emerge from a 60-degree angle. Fuller's identification of structure and geometry with human transformation bordered on the mystical, which is probably why he had so many admirers who did not generally take a technological approach. Fuller could capture the imagination in a way that utopian ideas of an even more ambitious, but familiar nature—such as the great dams and power stations of the Tennessee Valley Authority—no longer could.

The emotional utopian might have replied to the builder utopian with a chant, a joint or some LSD, to demonstrate that a better life begins with a change of mind. Synthesize, don't analyze, the argument goes. Consciousness reshapes reality, and taking action helps reshape consciousness. This idea has its roots in the romantic tradition, and the bookish could point to Emerson, Thoreau and Whitman as distinguished American forebears. But it is really an anti-intellectual stance, and more people probably tried to arrive at new states of being through sex, drugs and rock and roll than through nineteenth-century writing.

The technocratic intellectuals Kennedy brought to Washington were not advocating either the building of domes or a revolution in consciousness, but they were also utopians of a sort. While they wouldn't argue that utopia already existed, they were confident that the situation could be perfected without the asking of any very hard questions. Kennedy's rhetoric was peppered with exhortations to sacrifice, but it followed a very centrist path, one that stayed close to the middle of the very narrow road of American political discourse. Indeed, those on the left had to appear even more bellicose than those on the right, so that they wouldn't be thought soft. "Leadership of the Free World" was the overwhelming national purpose. Kennedy had defeated Richard M. Nixon by only the narrowest of margins, but one could hardly say that the country was politically divided, any more than it had been under Dwight D. Eisenhower, Kennedy's predecessor. Eisenhower had, in fact, made a near-radical criticism of the prevailing political consensus when, in his farewell address, he warned of the rising power of "the military-industrial complex." At the time, though, this statement was little noticed. Most of the disputes in national politics did not concern basic goals, but rather questions of degree and of detail.

Moreover, even these seemed susceptible to solutions on a technical level, free of any conflicts over values or political accommodations. Just as universities had become part of more and more Americans' lives in the previous decade, the Kennedy administration made the universities an important part of government. It tapped specialists in a number of different disciplines, who believed that they had figured out how things really worked. Many were hired for middle-echelon jobs in various executive departments, while many more stayed on campus but received highly flattering telephone calls or summonses to Washington to contribute ideas or advice. Social scientists, who had long aspired to the rigor of the pure sciences, now sought to have the effectiveness of engineers as well. Economists believed that the economy could be "fine-tuned" primarily through varying government expenditure and tax rates. There was a whole class of "defense intellectuals" who were willing to apply their considerable brainpower to coolheaded consideration of Armageddon and other policy options. Sociologists had insights into poverty that appeared considerably more subtle than the big-city patronage system that had previously been the primary way in which government helped the poor. Architects and planners had developed a vision of the new city—freed of congestion, crisscrossed with high-speed highways, a grand mechanism of transportation and commerce.

Professional management had taken hold in the postwar era, and it promised to bring big changes in the way every branch of government analyzed its problems, priorities and options. Robert McNamara, Secretary of Defense to Kennedy and later Lyndon B. Johnson, was portrayed as the ultimate technocrat, but he was merely the highest-ranking and most visible member of a team dedicated to making the agreed-upon policies work more efficiently and more effectively than they ever had before.

One of the chief sources of their confidence was the cluster of ideas about systems, information and cybernetics that arose in the postwar era, largely as the result of wartime research on gunsights and the development of the digital computer. This thinking, which affected physics, psychology, biology, engineering, meteorology and many other disciplines, concerned the behavior of complex systems and the role that information plays in them. It was, in some sense, an updating and rethinking of the oracular approach, a search for patterns and connections. Systems, which can be anything from a protozoan or an ant colony to the earth's atmosphere or the New York Stock Exchange, are not seen as means to an end, but as entities which interact with their environments. They both act and receive information, much of which concerns the impact of their previous behavior.

This information about past activities that affects future behavior is called feedback, and it is graphically represented as a loop that interacts with many other vectors and loops within the system, which is generally seen as a closed circle. Feedback comes in two forms—negative, which, like a thermostat in a house, works against the direction in which a system is headed and pushes it toward stability, and positive, which accelerates the tendencies of the system. That positive feedback can lead to disastrous results is the lesson of "The Sorcerer's Apprentice." For example, the rising population of a species constitutes a positive feedback loop, because it increases the number of individuals that will eventually multiply. But a limited food supply leads to starvation, a negative feedback loop which depresses and helps stabilize numbers. One can add numerous other loops to this system—such as predators, weather patterns, disease—and come up with a model not only of how the system behaves but also how it might react to specific situations.

This is an admittedly crude caricature of a powerful set of insights which unified thought in many disparate fields. For the moment, though, it is most important to understand a few of its seductions and limitations. Chief among these is its concern for process rather than goals. This is an advantage for natural science, but though it provides some useful analytical tools, it is a limited approach to policymaking. It has the attraction of seeming postideological, as if society could somehow be managed without objectives or conflict. Moreover, the complexity of the system makes it possible to couch adjustments to it in positive or neutral terms. You can say, for example, that you are squeezing inflation out of the economy, rather than admit that you are throwing people out of work.

The predictive power of systems models is based entirely on the richness of the information and the precision of the understanding of the relationships that are built into them. In recent years, scientists have learned that seemingly tiny variations in input can produce grossly divergent results or even throw the system into chaos. Moreover, values and assumptions get built into the models in a way that those studying the output might not analyze. Anyone who has ever used a spreadsheet on a personal computer knows how easy it is to let the seeming exactitude of the results overwhelm the frailty of the assumptions that produced them. Confusing simulation with the real thing is one of the perennial modern dangers. It should also be noted that, when applied to politics, systems thinking allows for popular participation, but not necessarily democracy. The people constitute a feedback loop, but they don't change the nature of the system. "Beating the system" is even tougher than fighting City Hall.

The confidence that academics and bureaucrats placed in analysis of systems was more than matched by the suspicion it induced in those who opposed their policies. One man's efficient defense system is another's uncontrollable war machine. The entire society could be seen as a complexly interlocking system in which the largest corporations, the Pentagon, the media and the universities interact and support one another. Interlocking boards of directors, government-sponsored research, the cozy relationship between weapons buyers and weapons makers, all served as evidence of a malevolent, uncontrollable system.

The murder of President Kennedy, and the killing on live television of Lee Harvey Oswald, the suspected assassin, seemed to open the country to a whole new range of ugly possibilities. It is true that throughout the early 1960s civil rights workers were murdered and beaten in the South. The charismatic Black Muslim leader Malcolm X was killed in 1962. Killing a President is different. It was an end to the aura of stability that surrounded the postwar consensus. The assassination showed that change could come very quickly, and not always for the better. The killing of Kennedy signaled the beginning of the conspiracy boom, which revealed patterns of betrayal, odd connections, peculiar coincidences and intriguing questions lurking just beneath the seemingly smooth surface of American life. Stories that later surfaced about the CIA contracting with the Mafia to kill Fidel Castro with an exploding cigar (and the much later revelations of Kennedy's sexual liaison with Judith Exner, a crime boss's mistress) proved that you don't have to be crazy to be paranoid. This was in itself a change of consciousness, from a sunny complaisance to dark suspicion. That first assassination made others more likely, and they happened. The killing of John Kennedy was traumatic, that of Martin Luther King, Jr., in March 1968 was shocking, while that of Robert Kennedy the following June was almost expected. The stabbing of Andy Warhol was almost inevitable; people had learned that attempted assassination could be a road to celebrity. Television commentators wondered whether America was "a sick society" and talked of its violent history. They talked about the bloodshed in the Wild West rather than of the genocide committed against the American Indians, but the point came through well enough. There had been plenty of bloodshed on the way to freedom and prosperity and there would probably be more.

By the mid-1960s, Americans became accustomed to hearing the "body counts" from Vietnam, in which the enemy was always losing many more soldiers than the South Vietnamese or the Americans. How many of them could there be? people wondered. But there were always plenty more. The phenomenon of body counts showed that this was a different kind of war. Earlier, it had been possible to draw lines on maps to show where territory had been taken, but in Vietnam any advances made during the day had a way of disappearing at night. Counting corpses was the only way of keeping score, or at least of keeping score in a manner that suggested it might be possible to win.

This aspect of the war, which became apparent soon after the massive escalation of the conflict in 1965, dealt a serious blow to Americans' belief in their country's invincibility. How could the most powerful country on earth, the great technological superpower, be fought to a stalemate by such a small country? Even critics of technological culture, such as Jacques Elul and Herbert Marcuse, believed in its effectiveness, which was precisely why they did not like it. Elul argued that technology reorganized society in its image, enforced its order through oppression and rendered a change of goals impossible. This universalizing tendency of the technological society could explain why the United States had become involved in Vietnam, but it doesn't really explain why the United States wasn't able to win.

Those who opposed the war tended to do so for one of two reasons. Either they thought the war was wrong or they thought it wasn't working. While the two groups cooperated on some protests, and while many individuals might have held each of these opinions at one time or another, this was a major intellectual rift. To believe that the war should end because the United States wasn't winning implies that the war would have been good had it been fought successfully. Kennedy had promised in his inaugural address to pay any price for freedom, but many of those who had supported him decided that the cost would be too high. It wasn't that they were opposed to widespread American intervention. It's just that some investments are better than others. There were people in Johnson's administration who took this view from the very start of the war, many of whom stayed on in hopes of persuading him as the costs mounted.

Those who took a moral view broke with the postwar consensus. They argued that the United States had no right to wield its technological might in Vietnam or anywhere else. The United States was behaving as a colonial power that viewed much of the world as its de facto colonies, they said. It cloaked its imperialist aims in the rhetoric of world modernization—with the United States as both exemplar and catalyst. (The scholarly writings of Walt W. Rostow, a leading Johnson adviser and war advocate, provided a good basis for this line of attack.) Early in the war, this mode of opposition was usually based on the hope that the United States would live up to its basic democratic ideals, but as the body counts rose, even such retrospective optimism about American motives began to seem suspect. The sweet land of liberty gave way to the violent home of slavery. For some the enemy came to seem like heroes, a romantic vision of people fighting for their land and their lives against a soulless American war machine.

The Vietnam War overshadowed what Kennedy had hoped would be the great American crusade of the decade: putting Americans on the moon. This heroic effort was entrusted to the National Aeronautics and Space Administration (NASA), which appeared to be the very model of a soulless machine. NASA applied enormous technological and public relations expertise to making exploration of the cosmos seem routine. Its route to the stars was entirely by the book.

The American space program had gotten off to a slow start after the Soviets launched Sputnik in 1957, but Kennedy's pledge of a moon landing brought it into very sharp focus. What a goal! Even a small child could understand that this was an attack on a cosmic mystery, the gratification of a desire that has been felt by anyone who has ever looked into the sky at night. How wonderful to be alive at a time when such dreams can come true. The decision to go to the moon grew in large part from competition with the Soviet Union, but there is little doubt that there was something Promethean about it. The astronauts—and the rest of us watching at home on television— would transcend our earthly limitations, freed from the grinding cycles of Ecclesiastes, and take a new place in the universe. Some scientists argued that unmanned probes could yield far more data for the money than would the manned landing, and they were undoubtedly correct. But there is no substitute for the adventure of men taking risks to do what long seemed impossible and ultimately setting foot on very unfamiliar ground.

Kennedy did nothing less than promise the moon. Still, he knew when he made the announcement that such an effort would not require any great conceptual breakthroughs. It was an engineering problem, one that was far more susceptible to a technical approach, as it turned out, than fine-tuning the economy, erasing pockets of poverty or stopping the Vietcong. NASA was utopia in action, an exercise in engineered transcendence.

Success through sound organization and careful execution of procedure is the principal value that NASA represented. The Mercury, Gemini and Apollo astronauts were allowed a measure of personality, enough so that you could tell them apart, but they were without passion, at least as they were presented to television and *Life* magazine, which had the print rights to their experiences. They spoke in an utterly emotionless style and a peculiar, pilot-engineer vocabulary. Americans had to learn that when the situation was "nominal," things were going very well indeed. "A-OK" betrayed an emotional high. In the years since, many of those who have gone into space have said that they had powerful spiritual experiences there, though it is understandable that they might not have wanted or been able to share these with worldwide live audiences. In one case, an astronaut let his euphoria get out of hand and had a troubled landing, for which he was widely criticized.

It was, of course, simply a fact that one person, or even a small group, could not accomplish such an ambitious undertaking as going to the moon. Many people who were alive in the early 1960s could remember the daring of Charles Lindbergh, flying the Atlantic by himself in his little plane. The very first flight, the Wright brothers' short hop at Kitty Hawk, happened in 1903, not even one lifetime before. And yet the scale of challenges and of achievements had changed so enormously in the interim. It was progress, said television, magazines and newspapers. It was inevitable. It was a good thing.

"Progress" always seemed to be a trend from the small to the large, the intimate to the impersonal, the variegated to the monolithic. Future clothing was always going to be made out of a single material. Future worlds of the movies were always made of space age plastics.

In the 1968 film *2001: A Space Odyssey*, the object that appears on the prehistoric earth and on the moon to spur man to higher levels of intelligence and consciousness resembles a steel beam, the emblem of modernist architecture. Mies van der Rohe, who died the year the film was released, had used such elegant, minimal means to produce some of the great buildings of the century, but one might still ask whether such abstraction always represents an advance. The film itself offers an alternative imagery, the onrushing, disorienting, but exciting psychedelia that precedes the astronaut's climactic encounter with himself. In contrast with the static, cold, objective, reductionist imagery of the official culture of the time, psychedelia was a dynamic, intense distillation of pure consciousness, experience without any need for meaning. *2001* remains one of the most evocative creations of its era, largely because it contains and almost reconciles the two warring visions of humanity and its future.

2001 was far more than a technological toy show. It was finally about a view of the future that embraced and transformed technology. Its subject was the change of consciousness of the mind of man, which at the beginning induces the caveman to use tools (and to murder) and when it reappears on the moon prompts the shooting of a spermlike probe to Jupiter. From the film only, it is difficult to conclude precisely what it is supposed to mean, whereas, by contrast, the novel Arthur C. Clarke wrote along with the screenplay seems to reduce the impact by explaining far too much. Precision isn't necessary.

What was clear was the implication that there are breaks in history where there is a profound change in the human mind and history must begin again. For many, 1968 felt like such a moment. As the film argued, technology had taken humanity to this threshold of change, but was not, by itself, enough. Expertise was deadening, reform ineffective. There had to be a new way to think, to see, to be. The new kind of person that many felt would come into being would be an explorer of mind, body and spirit, a more authentic being who had not been trained—like an astronaut or an executive—to suppress the mysteries of life.

Such personal exploration did have its technological dimension. LSD, believed capable of opening the doors of perception, was invented in a laboratory. So was the birth control pill, which greatly expanded opportunities for sexual exploration. This kind of ecstatic idea of the future had its pretensions to primitivism, but it was, and is, rooted deeply in advanced, industrial culture.

Nineteen sixty-eight was a particularly apocalyptic year, marked by assassinations, worldwide student rebellion and a new level of violence, on the part of the establishment and the protesters. The antiwar movement took credit for Lyndon Johnson's decision not to run for reelection after his embarrassing showing in the New Hampshire primary election. But, if anything, Johnson's retreat launched a reaction against the new forces in American society. Across the country, police departments stocked up on Mace, an aerosol device that could incapacitate demonstrators and help cities maintain control of their mostly empty streets. The FBI was on the job, accumulating encyclopedic files on people involved in all sorts of protest and infiltrating many of the organizations.

The climax came in Chicago. After the killing of Martin Luther King, Jr., in March, there had been widespread rioting, and much of the city's West Side was destroyed. Mayor Richard J. Daley had ordered the police to kill or maim all looters, and when criticized for doing so, threatened to publicize the addresses of his critics, so the looters could attack them. Despite such official toughness, there were several major arson fires each week in Chicago that summer, and often-violent racial confrontations at about the same rate. Daley declared that the Democratic National Convention, which could be expected to draw major antiwar forces, would be the place where America would draw the line against the forces that were destroying the society. For weeks before the convention, Chicago police were warned that LSD might be put into the drinking water and were briefed on the offensive tactics of such small, but memorable movements as the Yippies and Up Against the Wall, Motherfuckers. The result was what was later to be termed, by the commission that investigated it, "a police riot." Many of the confrontations in the city parks and on Michigan Avenue outside the headquarters hotels were seen on national television. "The whole world is watching!" the demonstrators chanted, but the police seemed not to care. They were not there to control a potentially disorderly situation, but to try to defeat everything that the demonstrators represented.

A lot happened after Chicago, too. Richard M. Nixon, whose election was, in part, a result of the convention clash, continued the war, and even stepped up the bombing. The draft was changed to a lottery system, which probably reduced the antiwar constituency a bit. There was Woodstock in the summer of 1969, an event that seemed to evoke nostalgia even while it was happening. Four students were killed by National Guardsmen at Kent State University. The women's liberation movement absorbed the rhetoric of heightened consciousness and showed that it could work. The Supreme Court legalized abortion. Earth Day in 1970 seemed to portend a new era of environmental consciousness.

If 1968 was a turning point in the nation's emotional life, 1973 was an even more significant date in the material sphere. The first Arab oil embargo was a turning point in the national consciousness, a moment when it was discovered that American volitions were at the mercy of others, indeed others who had long been the target of racist contempt. Arabs had earlier been viewed as comic figures, but now they seemed to be in charge. A wave of panics over shortages swept through the country. For a few weeks people were hoarding toilet paper, and supermarket shelves emptied, and after that raisins and tennis balls also disappeared.

The evidence for 1973 as a turning point is more than anecdotal, however. In many areas—including real personal income, unemployment, grown children living at home, energy prices, productivity, child health, population below the poverty line—where trends had generally pointed toward economic growth and personal expansiveness, the numbers took a turn. The material progress that had been taken for granted for nearly three decades was suddenly cast into doubt. The days when a man could earn enough at a factory job to provide a middle-class living standard for his wife and several children were gone forever. The pie had stopped growing, which made it more difficult to provide more for those who had long been excluded. Antipoverty programs, many of which had survived the coming of a Republican administration, were quickly cut back.

This was also the year of Watergate. The burglary happened the year before, and Nixon's resignation happened the year after, but this was the year in which it began to be clear what happened. Cubans with bags of money, a President who bugged himself, Howard Hughes, an enemies list, Martha Mitchell on the telephone—it was all too much to be true. One piece of the story was that the fear of the challenges of the 1960s had pushed Nixon and his lieutenants to precisely the kind of behavior about which the protesters had darkly fantasized. Watergate outdid the imagination. And although it had considerable entertainment value, it certainly cast a pall over the public life in this country. "The system works," said President Gerald Ford as he took office. We had just seen how.

Yet the unfolding of Watergate and its aftermath was marked by extraordinary political docility. Several reformist Democrats were elected to Congress in 1974, but there was no cultural impact of the kind that one might have expected only two or three years earlier. Americans followed it, like a soap opera, by now accepting that their nation's fate lay outside their control, in a netherworld populated by thugs, admen, émigrés, corporate lawyers and a sometime writer of spy novels.

There are some ways in which the 1960s have never been undone. America is far more tolerant of childless couples, single mothers, working women and other unconventional ways of living than it was before. There is still a significant amount of communal living, though lower-key and more conventional than the most publicized experiments of the time. The 1960s push toward redemption through direct action faded out of the political arena, but it has continued in religious and spiritual forms.

The technocracy, too, is still with us, although, until quite recently, those who are trying to create it have kept out of sight. Just as many of those 1960s glass boxes have donned plastic pediments and granite veneers, so the technological society comes at us under the mask of entertainment. And its effort is to appeal to people as individuals, not as part of a larger society. Once, they convinced us to build roads. Now, we have to drive to feel free.

But the hunger for the future—either technological or transcendent—seems to be gone. The fear of scarcity that was reintroduced into the society from 1973 on has made Americans lose their appetite for tomorrow. The American habit of optimism, which had persisted through the Depression, did not entirely disappear; people just expressed it with their credit cards. But the shortages and reversals, which were not all that severe, did cause people to stop thinking of a collective future and start looking out for number one.

This drove the techno-future into hiding, and it just about killed any alternative visions. Unfortunately, most of those that emerged during the 1960s assumed that material circumstances could be ignored because they would not be a problem. People had spoken of the "postscarcity society." They called for a change of priorities, but had not really addressed the issue of how much people ought to have and what they, and the government, ought to do to make sure they get it. After the oil shock, the counterculture reaction was to advise people to move far away, learn to grow things—and take guns.

Since the great cultural war between the opposing armies of progress, the only claim to utopia has been made by those who think we live there already. Nostalgia and self-absorption have replaced vision, and few have been interested in looking beyond the next quarter. Only in the late 1980s, when a series of environmental disasters captured public attention, was there a tentative look forward. Worry about the directions we are taking has also spilled over into concern about the schools, family life and investment in the public realm. The main voices heard so far have been prophetic ones, shouting warning. These tell us we cannot proceed as we have been. But prophets by themselves are not enough. We need oracles to tell us of patterns that are larger than ourselves. And we need utopians, dangerous as they are, to paint the pictures that will replace a vision of progress shattered into two hundred million pieces.

3 /	How Many People,
	How Much World?

Generations of well-fed children learned their first lesson in world affairs at the dinner table when they failed to eat what was put before them. "Think of the poor starving children," their parents exhort—depending on the moment and their politics—in China, India, Poland, Africa, Bangladesh, Vietnam, Armenia, Guatemala, Haiti or wherever. This argument rarely induces children to clean their plates, and the bravest among them suggest that the remains of the dinner be wrapped up and sent to these other, less discriminating children. Still, the message slips through: We have more than we want, but the world is full of those who are less fortunate.

There are several conclusions that children can draw from this fact about the state of the world. One is that they are overfed while many others are starving because the others are somehow lesser human beings who do not deserve such a privileged life. Another is that there will be a lot of people trying to take away what they have, so it's important to fight to get as much as they possibly can. And the third is a feeling of generosity, a sense that the plenty can be shared and that others need not starve so that some can eat.

Having enough to eat is a fundamental human anxiety, an animal passion that can burst through the veneer of civility at the slightest provocation. People wearing dinner jackets and long gowns can turn instantly into a pack of hyenas fighting over prey the moment that they realize that the buffet table does not hold enough food to go around. Indeed, while tribes that survive by hunting have developed elaborate rituals for the sharing of the kill, those who face the least scarcity often react the most savagely to the threat that there will not be enough. "If there is not enough for all," they ask, "how can I be sure that there will be enough for me?"

Residents of the developed world know that there is a relationship between our plenty and others' scarcity, but the connection is not clear and direct. We can't simply wrap up what we don't use and send it to them, and figure that the problems of inequality will be solved. It is, of course, precisely because we are well fed that we can afford to think about the long-term future. And when we wonder about whether there can be enough to go around, the question is not wholly unselfish, because we do have something to protect. Nevertheless, in a world where people are confident of their own survival, there is at least the potential for altruism.

It is possible to imagine a future in which the things that sustain people's lives—food, energy, shelter, medical care—will be in increasingly short supply. But it is not a pleasant prospect to contemplate. It is a world of perpetual personal insecurity and endless conflict, one where energies that people could devote to increasing human possibilities are spent instead in an unproductive struggle to protect what they already have. There is reason to worry that we might be moving into that kind of a world. It is not possible, however, to imagine real progress in a world where there is not enough to go around, or even in one where there is enough but people choose not to see it.

If the answer is that there cannot be enough to go around, self-preservation becomes life's only goal. It portends a world in which the abstract, ideological struggles of the Cold War era will be replaced by innumerable squalid, visceral struggles by nations, and groups within nations, to protect what they have and grab what they want. The question of whether there will be enough for you is not an inquiry into the state of the world, but rather a speculation about your personal strength. In a global context, will you be able to impose your will on others, and to let them starve, if need be, to make sure that you will survive? It is the question that gives rise to fortifications, armies, warships, imperialism and other persistent phenomena of human history. A belief in plenty adds to human interaction and adds to the inventory of possibility. The conviction that there isn't enough encourages hoarding, raiding, warfare and the use of wealth to protect itself rather than to increase itself. As the resources are used up, the perception of scarcity becomes an increasingly accurate description of reality. When people are preoccupied with how little life offers, all they will be able to see on the horizon are threats.

Thus, one of the key issues of the future is whether we see the world as a place of scarcity or of plenty. Do we foresee ever more people crowding into a finite world, heading toward a day of reckoning in which millions will die until the carrying capacity of the planet is reached? Or do we concentrate on trying to find practically infinite possibilities within the limits of the world in which we live. The prophet of scarcity points to many grim statistics and extrapolates them into catastrophe. The believer in plenty points to history and celebrates humanity's genius for social, technological and spiritual innovation. Both propositions are fundamentally unprovable, yet they must be dealt with. The possibility of scarcity helps us focus on the need to innovate. The hope of plenty keeps us from being immobilized by the fear that there will not be enough.

Facts alone do not tell us whether the future will offer scarcity or plenty. Our measurements are flawed, and our resources are as much products of human imagination and activity as they are of the physical world. But it is necessary to count heads to try to determine how many people the planet can expect to accommodate in the next half century, and figure out how resources can be stretched to provide enough for all. We need to consider the prospects for the poor, who are becoming ever more numerous. And equally we need to examine the demographic trends and values of people in the developed world, where there are fewer mouths to feed but far larger appetites.

During the 1980s, a new and shocking phenomenon appeared in the United States—large numbers of homeless people living in streets and public places. Rapidly, Americans became accustomed to seeing their fellow citizens stripped of dignity and bereft of hope, living their lives in public places. They shivered on sidewalks. They filled railroad stations and made it more difficult to use public libraries and automatic teller machines. Public facilities and monuments to civic and patriotic ideals were mocked by the presence of some who were clearly excluded from society's benefits.

People learned to walk a little faster and not inhale to avoid smelling the homeless. They learned to notice the lumps of rags and papers on the street, so they wouldn't walk into them, while simultaneously learning not to notice the man or woman at the bottom of the heap. The public realm, already besieged and shrinking before the homeless problem became severe, became even more undesirable, more a place to be avoided. The wealthy learned to move through this squalid cityscape in womblike, dark-glassed limousines, and even the middle class learned to be grateful that their homes and cars and such nonpublic places as shopping malls allowed them to live their lives without confronting the unpleasant realities of streets, public places and mass transportation. Avoiding the homeless and the places where they are became just another part of adjusting to a tough world.

The homeless comprised only a relatively small percentage of the population, but polls showed that they were visible and troubling to a majority of Americans. Their presence belied Americans' generally accurate belief that theirs is a land of plenty. But rather than spurring outrage and public action, the presence of the homeless only heightened a sense of hopelessness and general decline. Politicians, the news media and most others began to speak of the homeless not as the result of some miscalculations of public policy but as an intractable and possibly eternal problem. Homelessness came to be spoken of as a disease, in terms that suggested that it wasn't really their fault that they were homeless, but that it wasn't anyone else's either.

The presence of the homeless heightened people's sense of scarcity. They provided an affirmation that everything could go wrong and one could fall right out of the society and be given up as crazy and useless. Yet America in the 1980s was still an extremely affluent society, still the wealthiest nation in the world with an economy twice as large as its nearest rival and living standards that are, by most measurements, unequaled anywhere.

The homeless were not inevitable, nor is the phenomenon inexplicable. The clearing of skid rows to build large high-rise office buildings and the restoration of rooming houses as single-family residences and condominiums helped cities with their tax bases, but those who lived in such places were left out of the calculations. The cutting of public housing subsidies, combined with widespread corruption in the agencies that administered them, also contributed to the problem, as did what seemed to be the liberal reform of cutting the population of mental institutions—unaccompanied by services to help those freed to cope with the world. Now the problem of homelessness is difficult to eradicate, but its origins lie more in the overheated real estate climate of the 1980s than in any fundamental threat to the American dream.

But seeing the homeless seemed to confirm people's fears that there is not enough to go around. And while many tended to blame the homeless for their own fate, their presence was seen as an indication that the country had to tolerate a situation that had hitherto been viewed as endemic only to the world's very poorest places. We had gone from Oz to Calcutta almost overnight.

It is easy to conclude that if so wealthy and powerful a nation as the United States is doomed to have its citizens living on the streets, the prospects for human dignity must be in rather short supply all over the world. Urban office workers who must run a gauntlet of beggars each morning and evening are likely to conclude, at least subconsciously, that their own prosperity must come at the expense of others. Pathetic, ragged people with outstretched hands may at times elicit generosity, but in the long run breed callousness and cynicism. In a world of shrinking possibilities, you have to grab all you can get and fight to keep it. It is no accident that the growth of homelessness coincided with the rise of another new type: the self-absorbed, conspicuously consuming yuppies. The yuppies were associated most prominently with financial manipulations and corporate takeovers, activities that did not add to the sum of plenty but sought to aggressively redistribute it—and then cash in. This attitude grew directly out of a slowed growth in average personal income during the 1970s and 1980s. Those who had to trim their personal expectations were reluctant to make any further perceived sacrifices for the good of the community. Together, the homeless and the yuppies were a message from America to itself. They seemed to show that life is inherently unstable, that no one should expect gratitude for service in war or devotion to a company, that the strong and ruthless prosper and the weak deserve nothing.

"We have more will than wallet," President George Bush said in his inaugural address, in a memorable phrase that captured the nation's emotional state, though it was not very close to the truth. While America no longer dominates the world to the extent it once did, it is hardly an economic basket case. American consumers are still the target of businesses everywhere, because they have more money, freedom and power than anyone else. What has changed is that their belief in the inevitability of general improvement has given way to fear that they are losing ground in their personal lives. The homeless are a reminder that sometimes everything can go wrong. Moreover, their presence changes the character of public space and makes the private domain even more desirable. People retreat into their private fortresses and show little desire, or political will, to provide for a common future.

Such pessimism makes Americans doubly reluctant to address similar issues beyond its borders—even though its living standard is dependent on products and resources from all over the world. Still, questions about the adequacy of the world's resources and its entire environment are very real. The accelerating human exploitation of the physical world, combined with the explosive growth in humanity's numbers, poses a serious threat to our expectations, if not to our lives. Someone born in 1950 entered a world in which there were 2.5 billion people. By 1987, there were twice that many people, 5 billion. Current UN projections state that even if population control programs continue to expand worldwide and to increase their effectiveness in the coming decades, there will still be another 3 billion people on earth by the time our hypothetical baby boomer reaches 75, and that the world population will level off at 10 billion later in the twenty-first century. Such unprecedented numbers mean that we cannot be reassured simply because there has always been enough before. Indeed, there has been a tremendous acceleration during the last three decades in droughts, floods and other phenomena which tend to be labeled "natural disasters," though they are largely the result of human stress on the environment. Already, people's lives are becoming increasingly precarious. In thirty years, we will be living in a different world with billions more people. Can there be enough then?

Over 90 percent of the people who will be added to the world's population between now and 2025 will be born in what are now underdeveloped countries. That number of new poor is larger than the total population of the world in 1950. It is difficult to see how such countries will support their populations without economic growth. But such development will place a severe strain on the world's resources and particularly on the environment. Each resident of the United States, for example, makes a claim on the world's resources equivalent to several dozen residents of sub-Saharan Africa. Industrial development has increased even faster than population: fiftyfold in the last century, with about 80 percent of that happening since 1950. The United Nations has estimated that annual increase in industrial production now equals the total production of Europe just prior to World War II. We make what used to be decades of demands on the earth each year. Economic and technological development, which appears to be the only hope for staving off human disaster, will mean that each of these newly added people of poor countries will need to use proportionately more of the earth's resources. Is this possible? Can the earth and man's evolving technology support the people it has, and those it is soon going to have? Is life going to become worse for most of the world's people, or is it still possible to think in terms of human progress and hope for a better life?

Demography may not be destiny, but people's numbers, ages and geographical circumstances surely provide a strong foundation for speculations. And though the finite amounts of materials and available high-intensity energy sources do not constitute an absolute limit to human achievement, they will have to be used carefully and effectively if a 10-billion-person world is to be something better than a hell on earth.

The world has never been more interdependent than it is right now. Yet tremendous inequality exists in the world, and there are many indications that the differences are not narrowing but growing wider.

The wealthier countries have the power—both political and economic—to protect what they have and protect their ability to get more of what they need from the poor countries.

The countries that have the money to buy things will simply be able to outbid others, who might actually need them more. The developed countries will be able to get the materials they really need by corrupting the governments of the places where the resources are. Many of the problems of some of the world's poorest countries were caused by colonialism. They might be better off if they were left alone to figure out their own paths toward economic and social development, but this surely won't happen in the face of threatened economic collapse. The image of a sinking ship is almost too benign. Not all the passengers will go down together. Those in first class will be breathing much longer, largely at the expense of those below them.

We may well be at a crossroads in the way the world works. The end of the 1980s brought the collapse of Marxist-Leninist political ideology and a widespread outbreak in demands for personal freedom, rewards for economic initiative and the end of the all-inclusive state. It appeared to be a sudden and shocking ending to an idea that has shaped the lives of a substantial portion of the world's people for decades. The conflict between the individualist West and the collectivist East ceased to be the world's organizing principle.

We are moving from a world characterized by different ideologies of modernization and social development to one in which the most important differences concern people's ages, expectations and access to resources. The East-West confrontation, between planned and market economies and collectivist versus individualist societies, was bitter and dangerous. The apparent failure of the planned, collectivist alternative grows from the inescapable conclusion that the individual freedom to innovate creates more possibilities than the effort—always prone to corruption—to distribute a limited resource.

Now that this conflict seems to have subsided, however, it seems rather abstract and bloodless compared with those that loom on the horizon between rich and poor, old and young. This is a consequence of partial development, much as was seen in Europe during the nineteenth century. While developed countries have experienced declining birth and death rates over a long period of time, the poorer countries have benefited from medical advances that have reduced death rates and child mortality while birth rates have declined only slightly.

On a global scale, the richest, most powerful nations are characterized by declining youthful populations and increasingly long-lived elderly, while the young dominate the poorer countries in Africa, South America and parts of Asia. In 1984, 35 percent of the world's population was under 15 years of age while 6 percent was over 64. The figures for the United States were 22 percent and 12 percent, respectively, for Europe (excluding the Soviet Union) 22 and 13 and for the Soviet Union 25 and 10. By comparison, 44 percent of Mexico's population was under 15, 49 percent of Iraq's, 47 percent of Libya's, 48 percent of Nicaragua's, 45 percent of Pakistan's. None of these countries have an over-64 population of more than 4 percent.

In the rest of the world, though the rate of increase is slowing, the number of people is continuing its tremendous increase, and populations will still rise even if family planning programs keep improving their effectiveness, which is not a sure thing. Population control is a very sensitive and mysterious business, intimately connected with people's sense of themselves. The rather coercive population control program in China taps a key human resource—the meddlesomeness of old women and their ability to make life miserable for the transgressing young. It is difficult to know whether a freer political regime would be able to enforce so restrictive a birth policy. In looking at the global picture, it is easy to conclude that population should be controlled, but having children is an intimate, highly personal act, potentially one of life's greatest satisfactions. It is possible to provide incentives for people to make use of family planning services, but attempts to force contraception, sterilization and abortions can probably not be sustained in the long run. China's success in lowering fertility has made an enormous difference in global population projections, but it might be reversed if the political climate became freer. An extensive population control program once lost an election for Indira Gandhi, and recent projections show India surpassing China as the world's most populous country sometime in the next half century.

Development has been said to be the best contraceptive, and birth rates decline dramatically as incomes rise and better medical care assures that most infants will survive to adulthood. Brazil, a middle-income country that is essentially without a family planning policy, has recently experienced a massive and unexpected decline in the fertility rate, far more dramatic than that of some countries where population control is a national policy. This drop has been attributed to television soap operas, few of whose characters have large families. Brazil has apparently reached the threshold at which the security that children provide their parents is not worth as much to them as the comfort, opportunity and freedom they have to forgo.

The consequence of not having children is to become a middle-aged society. That's a feature that the United States shares with Europe, Japan and the rest of the developed world. In terms of age distribution, the population of the United States is among the world's oldest. It is a bit younger than Europe, older than the Soviet Union and about on a par with Japan, but tremendously older than most of the rest of the world. A world that is divided between youth-dominated poor countries and substantially richer maturing ones seems likely to be a volatile place. Countries whose populations are dominated by teenagers are likely to be characterized by energy and impatience and the pursuit of crusades that are not entirely rational. One reason the mutually destructive struggle between Iran and Iraq was able to go on as long as it did is that both countries could draw on large numbers of committed young people to fight. Military technology continues to become increasingly sophisticated, with computer-controlled weapons guaranteed to be lethal. But most of the world's wars—in Ethiopia, Sri Lanka, Afghanistan—tend to be low-tech and bloody.

The older, developed countries will have to deal with the younger, poorer ones whether they feel charitable or not. It may be a matter of self-defense. Mexico's population has recently been increasing at a rate that would statistically lead to its doubling in twenty-eight years, and several of the countries of Central America are growing even faster. For people in the United States, such population pressures are not likely to remain foreign policy problems for long. Immigration is the issue over which those who fear scarcity are ever battling believers in plenty, and the United States alternates between attempts at exclusion and opening the gates to floods of energetic new-comers. Each new wave has brought social upheaval and ultimately greater prosperity. It seems likely that some from the world's multitudes of young people will replace the children Americans refrained from having.

The likelihood of continued dramatic population growth does not, by itself, guarantee shortages and conflicts. It only indicates that there will be accelerating demand for the world's resources. The key question is whether these will prove sufficient.

Is there enough?" sounds, at first, like a factual question, one that can be answered by studying information on such crucial matters as agriculture, energy, mineral resources and technological approaches. All of those are very important, yet none of them, or not all of them together, really give a satisfactory answer. In the end, the answer one finds is as much a matter of one's attitude toward life or one's religious faith as of a compilation of material factors.

The problems emerge almost immediately. "Is there enough?" rapidly becomes "Enough for what?" Because many of the crucial factors studied underlie an industrial economy, the question seems to imply that the way of life to be found in North America, Western Europe or Japan should be the model for everyone else. Perhaps the world is large enough to encompass a number of different ways of living. But who is to decide? Industrial civilization produces many goods and methods that make life less difficult. It has been shown that people will take them whenever they get the chance, though they may not fully understand or accept the social changes that come along with the conveniences. While contemporary American or European life-styles may not be the appropriate target for all the world's people, they suggest a general direction that would require immensely larger expenditures of resources to attain.

One can, instead, take the question another way and ask, "What is enough?" This leads to an attempt to assess basic nutritional needs, minimum standards of public health, of education and economic opportunity. This is the notion of absolute poverty, which has been applied in various countries by the World Bank. The effort is to seek ways to help people to reach a minimum standard so that their survival will not be in doubt and they can help themselves. That standard is very difficult to define in material terms, because cultural expectations differ. Two people with the same access to food, materials and energy might have very different views of the quality of their lives and their hopes for the future, colored by the attitudes of those around them and their own personalities.

For example, according to the UN nutrition standard, the world currently produces about 20 percent more food than is required to provide an adequate, primarily grain-based diet to all the people now on earth. We might expect that people in the United States and Western Europe would find this to be a grossly inadequate diet, but so would most people in South America, whose expectations are much lower than those of wealthy countries but higher than the UN standard. If the diet standard were improved only slightly to include some animal protein, there is only enough food in the world to allow 80 percent of its population to meet this standard. Of course, such averaging masks inequality. Even in the United States, there are people who are malnourished. Worldwide, about one person in five has diet deficiencies that are defined as hindering either one's ability to do work or one's normal physiological functions.

This state of affairs, as unsatisfactory as it is, represents substantial material progress. Though there are areas, particularly in Africa, where people's nutritional levels are declining, a higher percentage of the world's people are getting adequate diets today than ever before. Never in the history of the world have so many people been so well fed. This is the result of decades of sustained improvement in agricultural productivity and the technologies that make it possible. However, there are two pieces of bad news in this picture. Much of this technology is energy-intensive, wasteful of water and destructive of soil, so it may not be possible to sustain it to feed the world's rapidly increasing population. And while there have never been so many adequately nourished people on earth, there have never been so many hungry ones either. There are about as many malnourished people in the world today as there were people on earth at the close of the eighteenth century, when Thomas Malthus wrote his famous treatise arguing that people would reproduce at a rate that would lead to starvation.

Material standards of sufficiency can quickly take on a life of their own. They are the lifeblood of bureaucracies, which would far rather deal with abstractions and categories than with real people and their problems. Standards can stigmatize. They can spur people to misrepresent their situation in order to qualify for aid. And they almost always underestimate people's abilities to cooperate and do things to improve their own situations.

This last point is very important because all resources have a human component. People's ability and desire to make use of something in the physical world is what makes something a resource. Many of the deepest disagreements various specialists have about the future are rooted in a difference of opinion about the relative importance of the physical and human components of any resource. For example, the center of the North American continent is the earth's richest and most productive granary, the source of nearly all the world's food surplus. The nutrition of Americans and Canadians and of residents of about 100 other countries—including such giants as China, the Soviet Union and Japan—depend to some extent on the productivity of the North American interior. The world's hunger for copper, manganese or even petroleum waxes and wanes from year to year; the need for food is the ultimate hunger and it never goes away. By any standard, the North American heartland is one of the world's most important resources.

Defining what makes such a physical phenomenon into a resource is more difficult. Certainly, it begins with physical circumstances. Its climate, forbidding as it often is for human occupation, is well suited for the growing of cereal grains. Centuries of prairie growth enriched the soil, and it did not take much imagination to see that this vast natural grassland could be turned into a man-made grassland of wheat and corn. But while most people would concede its essential suitability, physical circumstances by themselves do not constitute a resource. Commitment to develop it and an efficient system for doing so are perhaps equally important. Once the Indians had been systematically dispossessed and exiled to reservations, the heart of the continent was unencumbered by patterns of aristocratic ownership or by generations of families breaking their holdings into smaller and smaller plots in order to assure each child an inheritance. The settlers, self-selected for ambition and willingness to work, had the opportunity to tap a resource that seemed infinite. Most of the developing world lacks this sort of freedom to create a resource. In many areas, especially in South Asia, the land is densely settled by people who use it very intensively to survive. In other areas, there are large landowners who produce for the export market with little concern for the needs of indigenous residents.

And today, though the actual frontier has been closed for about a century, many still see the American agricultural resource as essentially infinite. That is because technology took up where the frontier left off and allowed continued increases in agricultural productivity. Both the amount of grain produced per person and the amount produced per acre have shown a steady upward trend. The largest increment of this productivity came from the application of energy to the land, in the forms of fuel for farm equipment and of chemical fertilizers to supplement or replace the land's natural virtues. Irrigation is another expensive human intervention that has enormously improved the productivity of the land. The North American grain regions are thus a human artifact, triumphs of investment and organization. It is a natural gift but also the triumphant realization of a set of powerful abstractions, ideas that can change the world.

Indeed, many discussions of the future of food virtually ignore the land itself. Conventional wisdom among agricultural economists is that there has been a historic trend toward ever greater productivity on the American land and there is no reason to predict a decline. They don't point to the specific innovations that will make the resource practically infinite, but they have confidence that they will come along in time to do the job. Belief in the infinity of the American agricultural resource is what prompts dreams that the United States can replace petroleum with fuels made from corn and sugar beets, even though Brazilian efforts to replace petroleum with sugarcane were technically successful but economically disastrous.

The conventional wisdom may be right and the size of the American agricultural resource might be practically infinite for quite a long time. Today's highest hopes lie in biotechnology, which promises to perfect plant strains that can survive on less water and will have the capability of fixing nitrogen and fighting pests, thus eliminating chemical additives that create pollution and use dwindling petroleum supplies.

On the other hand, there are indications that some limits have already been reached. The amount of land being irrigated in the United States actually shrank during the late 1980s, in part because underground water supplies were being depleted. In other words, the water was being mined, like oil, rather than harvested. That means that some of the gains produced with the basic resource of water were illusory and that some land may not be able to be farmed until, over an extended period of time, the aquifer is recharged. Soil erosion is not as large a problem in North America as it is in many countries, but it is still quite substantial. Soil depletion is outrunning soil formation, a foreboding trend. About half the fertilizer applied each year is intended to undo the effects of erosion, which claims about 3 billion tons of American topsoil annually. The products of biotechnology will most probably provoke greater efforts at soil conservation because they will be intended to augment natural systems rather than to provide a concentrated dose of nutrients, as do chemical fertilizers. The soil and plants will have to produce on their own.

The decade of the 1980s had a series of hot, dry summers that brought dramatic declines in North American grain production and in 1988 reduced the U.S. harvest to less than what was consumed domestically. (All exports that year came from older reserves.) Each of these drought years was viewed as an aberration, but some scientists believe that this upward trend is consistent with theories about global warming produced by the release of carbon dioxide and other greenhouse gases into the atmosphere. If this is true, the resource is being redefined, and depleted, by human activity, most of it not directly related to farming.

Attempts to express the quality of people's lives in numbers can lead to dangerous confusion of means and ends, which often gets in the way of thinking about the future. Few people dream about being able to consume more barrels of oil each year or more pounds of copper per capita. They think instead about getting where they want to go, staying cool in the summer or getting in touch with the people they need to talk with. There is usually more than one way of meeting such needs and more than one mix of materials, energy and planning that can accomplish that. Yet, too often, we think of a life that is less wasteful as one that is less rich.

One way to deal with this dilemma is to redefine some terms and question our accounting procedures. The economic indicators that define growth are biased toward waste and consumption. They deal with the number of tons of coal burned, the number of tons of copper mined, the number of kilowatts of electricity used. The association of such consumption with the well-being of the individuals in the society and their personal growth is tenuous. It is easier to put numbers on the production of goods and services and the consumption of resources than it is on those activities that promote human growth.

The gross national product, the purported value of all the goods and services an economy produces, is the most widely used tool for comparison. But it almost always contains serious distortions. One extremely important factor is the valuation of the labor of women, which, because it often takes place within the home and outside of the cash economy, is significantly undervalued. Moreover, when women enter the cash economy, they are typically paid lower salaries than men. This raises two issues, one for the underdeveloped world and one for the developed. There are strong indications that higher salaries for women produce dramatically lower birth rates. Education and economic opportunity for women may be the most effective population control program that can be invented. But it causes another distortion. The nurturing and training of children can be viewed as an important social investment, one for which developed societies have rarely had to account because they kept women in the home through social expectations rather than economic inducements. Custodial care of children has emerged as a growing industry which is part of the gross national product. But parental participation in child raising shows up on the social balance sheet only as a loss of potential personal income rather than as an activity that can have a strong impact on the country's future economic wealth and social harmony.

Similarly, rural and informal economic activity tends to be undervalued in comparison with urban activity. Growth has long been seen as synonymous with urbanization, and history suggests that it is. But the runaway urbanization that afflicts many of the world's poorer countries appears to stem in large measure from government policies that discriminate against people in the countryside. It is striking that while the United States, the European Economic Community and Japan have large, expensive and often irrational programs to subsidize their farmers, developing countries, which need more people on the land and fewer in the cities, do precisely the opposite. One reason is that urban activities generate more money transactions and are thus overvalued as a measure of economic progress.

We typically measure well-being in terms of money, a complex political and economic phenomenon that does not always have a direct impact on well-being. Dieters know that the amount they spend on their food has relatively little relationship to the health of their bodies. Dollar outputs can be equally misleading. As the gadfly economist Hazel Henderson has argued, such things as prison costs and pollution cleanups show up as increases in the gross national product, while constructive activities such as parental nurturing and resource conservation do not. Those with very little money almost always suffer from inadequate housing, bad health and short life expectancy, but in the richest countries, where most of the consuming is done, the correlation is not nearly so great.

Henderson and others have suggested that a number of different measurements should be used to assess how well the society is doing, of which energy, because of its centrality to the economy and its environmental implications, is probably the most important. The trouble with energy is that it tends to be expressed in such terms as trillions of joules, quadrillions of BTUs or metric ton coal equivalents, all of which are difficult to relate to. Another possibility is to look upon the society's energy usage as a dieter would and replace the dollar standard with a measure that is easier to relate to—a Twinkie standard.

Our bodies convert food into energy to sustain our lives. Modern society converts several sources of energy, the most important of which are coal and petroleum, into a wide range of goods and services that help sustain its life. Even our food production, until quite recently a way of harvesting energy from the sun, is now heavily dependent on fossil fuels for fertilizer, farm equipment, transportation and marketing. Our bodies are a great deal more efficient in their use of energy than is industrialized society. When they are given more energy than they can use immediately, they store it in the form of fat. Carrying too much of this fat around undermines health. Our industrial system tends to burn things incompletely, releasing a lot of undesirable chemicals into the air, and it gives off its other excess energy in the form of heat. This, too, undermines health, as we have recently become all too aware. But we know that when the body processes too many calories, it has a problem, whereas when the society at large, in its far less efficient way, processes too many calories, we call this progress.

A Hostess Twinkie, the filled sponge cake snack that represents the quintessence of junk food for most Americans, contains about 73 large calories. (Counting energy expended in fertilizer, manufacture and fueling of farm machinery, transportation, processing and marketing, each Twinkie probably consumes about ten times that many calories of energy for its production, but we'll leave that idea aside for the purposes of this discussion.) Although it would be very unhealthy—if not maddening—to live this way, about 36 Twinkies each day would provide the basic energy requirements of a normal adult, according to the UN standard. This would have to be supplemented with protein and small amounts of minerals and vitamins. The body does not live on energy alone, and neither does industry. But we do know that if we go very far beyond a ration of three dozen Twinkies a day, we are not doing ourselves any good and are probably causing harm.

If we look at the energy consumption of different countries of the world and convert it to large calories, according to the standard formulas, and then to Twinkies, we get a sense of the enormity of our energy demands. Not surprisingly, North Americans are the gluttons of the world, with Canada and the United States each consuming about 2,400 Twinkies worth of energy each day for every man, woman and child in the country. West Germany weighs in at 1,386, Sweden at 1,206, Japan at 903 and Italy at 719.

What's striking about these numbers is how little they are related to other statistical or subjective standards of well-being. Nobody would argue that Frenchmen live better than Romanians, even though Romanians are 17 percent ahead on the Twinkie index. You might expect that countries that export a lot would use more energy, but Japan uses less than most developed countries and Hong Kong uses less than half as much as Japan. And Hong Kong is also a year ahead of the United States in life expectancy and is one of more than a dozen countries with a lower infant mortality rate, both of which might be expected to be measures of well-being. Chile and its neighbor Argentina each have the same life expectancy at birth, 70, yet Chile scores only about half as high on the Twinkie index as Argentina. You might say Canada needs to burn more energy to stay warm, but how do you explain chilly Sweden's ability to make do with half as much energy per person?

Two factors that help explain the high consumption per capita of the United States and Canada are their relatively low population densities and wide-open spaces, though Australia manages on about 35 percent less. There are 34 countries in the world whose per capita energy production is less than 36 Twinkies per person. These countries, mostly in Africa, South Asia and the Caribbean, are also among the hungriest places on earth. But it is also worth remembering that until little more than two centuries ago, all of the countries on earth would have had Twinkie indexes of zero, because they were not using fossil fuels, but, some deforestation aside, were living off current energy income.

For the nations near the top and the middle of the Twinkie index, there is no relationship between rank and measurements of health, literacy or even general prosperity. Indeed, according to these 1986 statistics, East Germany was using 42 percent more energy per person than West Germany, and achieving a far lower standard of living and lower environmental quality in the process. Many of these measures of social well-being are at odds with dollar, mark or yen measurements of the economies as well. But we already know that money does not buy happiness. The Twinkie index has a more direct meaning. Just as we know that when we eat too many Twinkies, the effects will show up around our waists, when we consume too many Twinkies worth of fossil fuels or uranium, the effects will show up in our water and air, and perhaps eventually in our flesh and bones as well. The Twinkies may well be metaphorical but the health implications are not.

The implication of this discussion is not, however, that we need to deprive ourselves in the name of some principle of collective health that will constrain our freedom and happiness. Comparing the effectiveness of our body in its use of energy with the wastefulness of society at large could be a source of hope. It shows how much technological improvement is possible in this world. Now that the most advanced technology is beginning to become increasingly subtle and moving toward engineering at the cellular and molecular level, it is almost inevitable that the body, not the automobile plant, or even the computer, should be recognized as the highest of high tech. Human beings have invented machines that have tremendously augmented both their muscle power and their brainpower. In a world where energy was cheap, the addition of brute power seemed a good measure of progress. Now we are moving to a different standard, in which technology is being challenged to work more efficiently to achieve well-focused multiple goals, while doing as little harm as possible. Already, telecommunication is helping to replace a certain amount of transportation. Materials engineering replaces mining and the expensive transportation that accompanies it. Some already imagine submicroscopic machines capable of working at the atomic level to remake the world to human specifications. It's probably possible for society to go on a diet and feel a lot better besides.

Statistics alone are inadequate for understanding the dangers of scarcity and the prospect of plenty. It is also important to consider some of the subjective factors. If you are not constantly preoccupied with where your next meal is coming from, if you needn't worry about having a place to sleep, if you feel part of a family or community that will help you when you are in trouble, you probably have enough. Other people are not always competitors. If they feel an identification with your interests and needs, they can be a source of plenty. The ability of people to identify with one another and work cooperatively so that all can survive is probably humanity's most basic source of plenty, though it is one that is frequently devalued in quantitative assessments of the world's resources. Indeed, people's dependence on their families is often seen as a major problem, because it induces people to have many children in the hope that they will be loved and provided for in old age. This does contribute to overpopulation, though it is likely that psychological isolation induced by the consumer society wastes at least as much of the world's wealth.

The sense of having enough is neither static nor objective. It implies growth, of a personal, though not necessarily economic kind. Having enough is the confidence that, despite difficulties, life is worthwhile and will continue. Many who are well off by any measurable standard do not meet this definition. They have a sense of scarcity—both material and psychological—which the amassing of assets can do nothing to assuage. Such a sense of threat and deprivation can exist on a social as well as an individual level, and its inevitable result will be scarcity.

The conviction that there is enough has always been more a state of mind than an analysis of the proven reserves of any resource. Even the existence of visible deprivation does not invalidate such a belief. "The poor you will have with you always," Jesus said. He was not counseling callousness, but rather trying to keep his disciples' eyes on the big picture of a godly community and the promise of salvation beyond mortal life. He spoke of a universe of plenty, in which the poor represent a challenge to faith that can be overcome through charity. He said the injustices suffered in this life would be more than compensated for in the next. Religion devalues material reality, almost by definition, and in so doing opens possibilities for all to transcend their apparent earthly limits. A religious person does not have to count and measure and worry where the next barrel of oil is coming from. Progress is always possible, because beyond this world there is another where there is no need.

This religious idea of divine plenty has coexisted through the centuries with the idea of natural plenty—a sense of the vastness of the earth and the richness of its offerings. The profusion and complexity of life remain awe-inspiring. Rain forests teem with species that have never been identified, plants that have never been cultivated, miracle drugs whose powers are unknown—even as they are cut down in the name of development. And as often as not, new scientific discoveries show how much more there is to know. But natural plenty is diffuse, like the sunlight and the rain, life-giving but not in itself a force for improvement. Human beings have always sought to direct and concentrate the power of nature. From the flint blade to the laser beam, human progress has been defined by the ability to cut through the natural, to concentrate its power, to focus it into an expression of human will.

During the last two centuries, Western society has replaced faith in religious and natural plenty with the promise of technological plenty. By now, nearly all the world has been converted. It has made life richer, longer, healthier and more comfortable for more people than the earth had ever been able to support before. Nearly everyone on earth is implicated in a modern system of communications and production. Technology is so powerful a force in the world, people have little choice but to take it into their lives, and most people seek its benefits.

During the last twenty years, the notions of natural and technological plenty have been challenged. Technology, the argument goes, is a far from reliable savior. It has provided ever faster and more wasteful ways of using up the natural plenty and allowed people to reproduce at a rate that the earth cannot sustain. Now, those scarce resources have been used up, and there will be nothing to replace them so cheaply or conveniently. Growth was a false god, development an illusion. The only issue is whether mankind will come to a soft landing through rational acceptance of contracting horizons or whether the world will degenerate into chaos, futile and destructive wars of plunder, and mass starvation.

This argument, essentially a refinement of that made by Thomas Malthus nearly two centuries ago, gained wide currency in the early 1970s. Malthus argued that because population grows through a process of doubling and redoubling, while agricultural production grows only through addition, mankind will tend to reproduce itself to the brink of destruction. This did not happen, the neo-Malthusians argued, because the development of industrial processes, and particularly the use of such fossil fuels as coal and petroleum, added a tremendous shot of energy to the environment that allowed an increase in human productivity even greater than the increase in the population. Even improvements in food productivity, which appear to involve more effective use of the land, have really been heavily dependent on petroleum and high energy usage, something else that cannot expand as rapidly as population. Besides, there were three underpopulated continents that could be settled.

But these were opportunities that came only once in the lifetime of our species, and we squandered them on fast cars and Christmas lights, rather than husbanding the resources. There is always the possibility that there could be some wondrous technological breakthrough that could change all these equations, but at the moment it seems clear that the general trend is toward enormous problems. Computer models simulating the complex interactions of population, energy, mineral resources, arable land and other factors have demonstrated that things are running out and the human race has fallen right into Malthus's mathematical trap.

According to the authors of *The Limits to Growth*, the influential Club of Rome study published in 1972, the collapse will happen sometime in the second third of the twenty-first century. Paul Ehrlich, in *The End of Affluence*, published in 1974, predicted that unmistakable signs of collapse would be apparent by the end of the 1980s, which he said would be a time of shortages and worldwide depression. The extreme pessimism and seeming precision of such threats made them seem powerful at the time, but their failure to come true at the moment predicted seemed to undermine their entire argument. The real cost of petroleum actually fell during the 1980s, helping to fuel a consumption binge that might better not have happened. The world production system proved to be far more flexible than the doomsayers predicted, and the growth in global consumption of several key commodities stopped in the mid-1970s, as recycling and new man-made materials took their place. One bitter result of the world's unexpected resiliency was that the value of raw materials from some of the world's poorest countries declined, worsening their debt problems and lowering per capita income.

Still, the neo-Malthusian argument is not wholly invalidated by its failure to produce catastrophe on the schedule its most pessimistic adherents specified. As we have seen, population remains on a collision course with the planet. Moreover, these earlier computer models were rather naïve in their assumption of a world in which the impact of their predictions would be felt uniformly. In the real world, the symptoms will first be localized. One could argue, for example, that the disaster-prone character of Bangladesh, in which enormous numbers have perished because of flood and famine and people's survival is threatened by soil erosion, demonstrates that one populous corner of the world has reached beyond its limits.

The most shocking thing about *The Limits to Growth* was its argument that it was already too late to avoid disaster. It projected that even if population control succeeded, productivity rates increased and materials recycling became widespread, the world was still headed for demographic collapse. Its attack was not on people's behavior within the economic system but on the system's goal: economic growth.

Growth is, of course, at the heart of economic thought—either capitalist or Marxist. It has the same role in the consideration of material plenty that divine grace has in the Christian idea of spiritual plenty. It is the mechanism of distribution that makes hope possible. Growth offers the promise that people can become better off without making other people worse off. Growth has always been seen as the way in which conditions in the world can be improved. And while it's true that millions of people have suffered from actions taken in the name of economic growth, it has also brought longer lives and richer expectations to most of the world's people. In material terms, a faith in economic growth amounts to belief in the possibility of improvement. It is difficult to conceive of a society that does not have such a faith, but it would almost certainly be a very cruel one.

For the neo-Malthusians, such a belief in the infinite expansion of material possibility is out of touch with reality. Specifically, it seems to contradict two of the fundamental principles of physics, the First and Second Laws of Thermodynamics. The first states that matter is neither created nor destroyed but can be transformed into energy. The second states that these processes tend toward a state of greater disorder, or entropy. If you consider the economy from this point of view, growth is an illusion. It is a function of the velocity of transformation, something that has expanded rapidly since the onset of industrialization but which cannot do so indefinitely.

The earth's chief source of energy is the sun, and its principal mechanism for capturing and transforming that energy is green plants. This is the planet's income, as it has been for millions of years. But for the last two centuries, man has remade the planet and himself by living off of savings—fuels like coal, petroleum and natural gas that represent millions of years' worth of solar energy stored in the remains of plants that lived more than 300 million years ago. The transformations we call the industrial revolution could not have been fueled by firewood, waterpower or other current energy income (though wood is still the primary energy source of the majority of the world's people). It needed an extra jolt of power from the earth's long-term reserves. It also required the exploitation of minerals. Because many of the ores that are easiest to use have already been expended, further materials development, or even recycling, depends on the use of larger and larger amounts of energy. And as the process continues, large amounts of our material resources will degenerate into an unusable state, and in the form of trash, toxic waste, air and water pollution, pose a threat to the healthy working of the basic system of green plant energy capture. And the heat released in material transformations is yet another generally unrecognized source of pollution. Seen in these terms, economic growth works against the long-term interests of mankind.

This argument between the seemingly unfounded hopes of economists and the harsh limitations of the material world began in the nineteenth century. Up to now, the economists have been right and projections of imminent doom have proven, at least, premature. The discovery and exploitation of new resources combined with techno- logical innovation have created new possibilities within the physical limits. This has been the dominant theme of human history, and if we are to survive, it is how we will do so.

Still, the facts of human survival and increasing material pros- perity up to now offer no cause to feel complacent. The standards of comfort and consumption that are taken for granted in North Amer- ica and Europe could not be sustained in a 10-billion-person world. There aren't enough minerals in the ground, fish in the ocean or rain- drops falling from the sky to make that happen. Human ingenuity is in a race with human fertility, and during the next half century, they seem likely to run neck and neck.

The difficulty of making things continue to work as they do now is apparent from nearly all statistics, regardless of the ideology of those who gather them. The World Bank and the Worldwatch Institute both point to diminishing worldwide petroleum reserves and the slowed growth or reduction of acreage under cultivation throughout the world, even though the first has a growth-minded ori- entation and the other tends toward a neo-Malthusian analysis. But while it is possible to agree on measurements of things, it is much more difficult to quantify human possibility or happiness. Those who take a purely economic point of view believe that people are small- minded and self-ish, but are perpetually saved because unexpected advancement happens at predictable intervals. Those who stress lim- its rarely take into account either changes in technology or the evolu- tion of human values.

The one point on which most of the material pessimists and their more optimistic counterparts tend to agree is that no global col- lapse has happened yet. People are already starving in great numbers and living miserable lives, yet most of the experts in the contentious fields of agriculture, nutrition and materials supplies agree that there is, at the moment, enough to go around. The problem is distribution. This sounds as if it refers to matters like the well-publicized difficulty of flying or trucking emergency shipments of grain to remote parts of Ethiopia, but it's a great deal more complex than that. Distribution is more a political and philosophical issue than a logistical one. Distri- bution of food is inseparable from distribution of land and distribu- tion of wealth.

For example, many people in the world's poorest countries concentrate on growing crops that bring cash on the world market rather than food to feed themselves. The land exists to support its owner rather than those who live on it. In some instances, agricultural exports have continued even when a country was suffering from famine. The productivity of farmers' private plots in the collectivist agricultural systems of China and the Soviet Union also suggests that the fruitfulness of a piece of land depends on the commitment of the person who farms it even more than it does on presumed economies of scale. Meanwhile, charitable redistribution of food seems to lead the recipient to become addicted to aid and channel production into less crucial areas, as has happened in Egypt since the 1970s. Food is an area where the marketplace seems to work best, but in which nearly everyone involved—governments, landlords, food shippers and processing companies, the urban population—does everything possible to subvert the market. The problem of distribution goes to the very heart of the way societies are structured, and tackling it means changing nearly everything.

The issue of sharing the wealth proves to be inseparable from that of creating it. People who feel that they have something coming to them are less likely to take initiatives to change their lives and the world than those who know that they face a struggle. But a society with too many people who know they will never make it is likely to become unstable and threaten the wealth it has. This is both an economic and a philosophical question. Your answer is likely to be shaped by your view of human nature itself. Which of the seven deadly sins do you fear more, avarice or sloth? Which is more creative, Social Security or social insecurity? Who is more offensive, a millionaire who pays few taxes or a welfare cheat? Americans will generally come down on the side of freedom and opportunity, and hence insecurity. At the same time, they support some protection against economic catastrophe that does not threaten incentive to work or public morality. Within that context, it is not at all easy to find an acceptable way to help people who are in trouble.

Those who are able claw at one another to get all they can, while those at the bottom are simply abandoned. In America, there are soup kitchens and shelters for the homeless. In a no-growth world, the poor would simply die by the millions.

The neo-Malthusian scenario is either a recipe for despair or an incitement to riot. Its uselessness as part of a positive vision of the future has caused it to fade from popularity among those who concern themselves with population and resource issues, yet the warning it sounds is real. The challenge is to find a way to permit widespread growth within the earth's physical limits.

Perhaps the most important attempt to imagine a way to accomplish this was the work of the World Commission on Environment and Development, an independent body set up by the United Nations in 1983, which issued its report, published as *Our Common Future*, in 1987. It called for the widespread adoption by both the developed and the undeveloped world of the principle of sustainable development, which "meets the needs of the present without compromising the ability of future generations to meet their own needs." This requires a stronger link between economic activity and the physical environment, and a reversal of the accounting by which, for example, a country's sale of a nonrenewable resource is viewed as pure income rather than as a possible loss of future productive capacity. Still, the report argues that sustainable growth, driven in most countries by the demand of their own people to live better lives, is possible, and that the economic performance of many poorer nations during the 1960s and 1970s, combined with the ability of developed countries during the late 1970s and early 1980s to decrease the energy and resources required for each unit of production, gives some reason for hope. Most of the report is, in fact, an attempt to define absolute needs, assess how well these are being met in different parts of the world and propose improvements. In case after case, the conclusion is that the challenges are extremely difficult, though not necessarily insurmountable.

The changes required are not, however, of the sort one could expect the existing world economic system to effect automatically; sustainability is not a result it is designed to produce. In other words, the intention to be fair to the future would have to be an explicit goal of people, businesses and governments everywhere. This in turn raises the question of why people should attempt to protect the possibilities for those who are not yet born while remaining indifferent to those alive today. The commission's conclusion was that most of the benefits of more rapid economic growth should be channeled into efforts that reduce inequality, largely by increasing people's ability to participate in the economy. Most of the specific examples cited by the commission assume a market system and a freely trading world, but it would certainly seem to require a political reorientation, particularly in many postcolonial countries that have continued to be organized more as plantations than as communities. The idea that economic growth should be driven by and benefit the country's citizenry is a novel one in much of the world.

The commission's report is the work of an international committee with diverse political ideals and economic interests. It is thus able to be very specific about certain narrow policy strategies, though it cannot bring about the widespread change of worldview that would be required as a context for such policies. What is the mechanism that would cause elites to distribute their land more equitably, that would cause developed countries to forgo cheap sources of raw commodities or that would spur an unprecedented level of economic and technological cooperation? In other words, is there any force pushing the world's nations to view themselves as part of a larger community?

The report is itself a response to two beliefs that could conceivably help forge such a community. The first is that the problems of an increasingly populous, increasingly unequal world cannot be met without some kind of widespread economic development. The second is that development as it has been practiced during the last two centuries has placed unprecedented stresses on the chemical and biological systems that make human life on earth possible. If you put these two ideas together, you have to conclude that the wealthier countries cannot afford to allow the poorer countries to make the same mistakes they did. If the developed countries choose to cut back on carbon emissions to stave off the greenhouse effect while China industrializes by using its enormous coal resources, there would be no gain. There is little hope of outsiders stopping China's modernization. There is a worldwide interest in either working some technological miracles with coal or making renewable resources such as solar energy both cheaper and more effective. The results would transform the developed world along with the rest.

The difficulty with such thinking is that it portends a managed world. State economic planning has proven a political and economic fiasco. It is easier to mobilize people with a vision of improvement than with the threat of disaster. The beginnings of such a vision began to be apparent in the political upheavals with which the 1980s ended. Different as the situations were in Czechoslovakia, South Africa, China and all the other places where political transformation was accomplished, begun or suppressed, there was a common rhetoric of human dignity. Leaders spoke of the need for people to have some power over their own lives, to be free from repressive systems and crippling ideologies. In every case, some sort of economic development is being sought, because the inequality of access to material goods helped spark discontent.

Americans tend to believe that such people will quickly settle into lives in which they exercise their freedom by choosing between Coke and Pepsi, and perhaps they will. But it is also possible that these experimenting peoples will produce leaders with other visions of progress, in which fair relationships among neighbors and among generations play a larger role. People are willing to make some sacrifices out of prudence, but it takes galvanizing ideals to tackle the enormous challenges facing the world's newly liberated peoples. They may change the world's moral climate. They can hardly afford not to.

The United States has been looking upon the world's transformation virtually as a spectator. What is happening is, more or less, what the country's leaders have always said they wanted, but apparent victory in the Cold War has brought not joy but a crisis in identity. As the people who put more demands on the earth than anyone else, Americans will have to change if the world is going to change. We have to take our own measure to see how we will live in this increasingly difficult world.

The United States is no longer a brash adolescent nation but rather a maturing society that has experienced failures as well as victories. A young person might look ahead with unrealistic hopes and little sense of the costs or the perils involved. A more mature person might be more aware both of limits and of strengths and be able to use opportunities more effectively.

The United States may well come through this middle-age crisis successfully, but it will require a change of self-image. Americans have, throughout their history, viewed themselves as a young people. Once, this was literally true. The people who settled the West were largely in their teens and 20s, and the Civil War was one of those bloody sacrifices of teenagers to which youthful nations seem prone. Most immigrants to the United States throughout its history have been in their teens and 20s, and even these people often looked to their children to become Americans and show them how to do it. While other countries might revere the wisdom of the old, Americans have looked to the freshness and enthusiasm of the young to tell them what the world will become.

Now, the members of the great postwar baby boom are either in or facing their 40s, and the next-largest generational group is not the boomers' children but their parents. During the 1970s and early 1980s, Americans were literally hostile to children. Voters were demanding that budgets for schooling be frozen or diminished. Movies and popular novels depicted babies and small children as targets of demonic possession and destroyers of people's lives. Magazine articles pondered whether it was responsible to bring children into a crisis-prone world, and the world population explosion was also cited as a reason not to burden the planet with one's issue.

The boomers' antibaby backlash grew, in large part, from a rejection of the values current in the society when they were growing up. The most important of these was clearly the subservient and seemingly mindless role assigned to women. Motherhood was a trap into which many newly liberated women refused to fall. But the reluctance to have babies was also part of a delaying action—boomers don't like to admit that they've grown up. They spent their childhoods hearing that they were a special generation and, during the late 1960s, began to urge each other to be young forever. Though people often claimed that abstaining from having babies was a way of doing a favor for the earth, the postponement of the next generation brought with it an apathy toward the future.

Now there is a general sense that a turning point has been reached. Education has returned as a political and intellectual concern and child care is a mainstream social issue. Babies are cute again. Teachers' salaries are rising. The presence of an often delayed and rather underpopulated next generation signals an end to the luxury of self-absorption in which boomers have been able to indulge since childhood. The consequence of at least one of their decisions is running around the house and asking all kinds of difficult questions.

These belated parents have to extend their horizons from the more or less immediate to the world in which their children will live.

Baby boomers at virtually all economic levels are living more expansively, if more vulnerably, than their parents. But they have behaved, at times, as if they believed their prospects were narrowing. Certainly, the failure of their paychecks to grow as rapidly as they expected cast a pall over their sense of progress. Such negative perceptions may have exaggerated and distorted reality, but they represent a kind of experience on which people base their ideas about what will happen in the future. It is even possible that their inclination to borrow to achieve higher levels of consumption hindered investment needed for productivity gains that would have given them fatter pay envelopes. But if we're using more now and enjoying it less, there is at least the theoretical possibility of using less and enjoying it more.

If you view the populace exclusively as consumers, and follow past demographic profiles, change is not in the air. One market research firm advised its clients that because the bulk of the population will be middle-aged and older during the 1990s, they should not attempt to introduce new products with unfamiliar names. Anything they did that was new should appear to be a variation of something familiar. Liquid Tide and Cherry Coke represent the forefront of innovation. The 1990s, said the report, will be a decade of risk management for most of the population. People will be filled with uncertainties, so they will look toward something familiar to give them confidence. Similar thinking pervaded the financial markets during the late 1980s as enormous values were suddenly ascribed to familiar brand names. The population is settling down, say the marketers, going back to basics, looking for substance, reveling in nostalgia. In the 1988 presidential election a variation on this strategy was used: George Bush was represented largely as a spin-off from a familiar and beloved product.

The leveraged buyouts and purchases by foreigners of many of the icons of American life is but one indication that the continuity of which the marketers speak is largely an illusion. It is a mask for a culture in flux. Family relationships are metamorphosing so quickly that greeting card companies have to struggle to remain abreast of kinship patterns. A lot of birthday cards are sent to stepparents, though it is still not quite certain how such a card should address them. The broken home has given rise to the blended family. People jettison their biological families and try to fashion replacements from among their friends.

It is, in fact, quite tempting to see the weakening of corporate loyalties and synchronized work schedules—which have given rise to telecommuting technologies—as a special case of the distending and redefinition of family ties. In each case, bonds are looser, expectations less clear, improvisation more important. Many of the changes involved in both cases are extremely unsettling. But it is equally clear that many people have greeted middle age with the decision to change their work and personal lives.

The society's mid-life crisis is more than demographic, more than economic. It is visceral. It is bad knees, the result of years of jogging to stay in youthful shape. It is illnesses turning to "conditions," limitations of health that will probably last the rest of a lifetime. For women who chose not to have children, it is an awareness that the body imposes a deadline for such choice. It is an intimation of mortality, a reminder that nobody gets out of life alive. In a culture that has long celebrated youth, and in a generation that has maintained its own youth long past the time when the pretense was convincing, such an apparent failure of the self can come as a cruel shock. There is a temptation to conclude that the best is gone, that all one can do is live with decline.

Another response, albeit a novel one for Americans who now constitute the mainstream of a middle-aged society, is to learn to appreciate maturity. According to current life expectancy statistics, 40-year-old Americans have about half their lives ahead of them, and if any of the aging-suppressing medical technologies now under study succeed, their lives might be both longer and more productive. A long-lived society would have to embrace some of the values that we now view as youthful—such as a willingness to entertain new ideas—so that it could reanimate itself without large new infusions of the young. Even with our current life expectancy, it is foolhardy for the middle-aged not to think about the future, because they will be living there.

The idea of a future that comes to someone with a middle-aged body is likely to be different from that of a child or an impatient young adult. A concern for the body—its fitness, its beauty, its health—has been one of the chief preoccupations of the last decade. Indeed, acting to change and preserve their bodies has been the principal way in which people have dealt with the future. But the aging body gives a different message than the younger one. It provides a reminder that we don't start fresh on the future. There are limitations set by biology. There is sickness and health, and the constant awareness that much that is vital to our very existence is out of our control.

This sounds like a process of irreversible decline, a very negative perspective for a look ahead. But such an attitude ignores both the ability of the human intellect to find ways of changing physical circumstances and the ability of culture to communicate knowledge, values and ideas across time. If left purely to our physical resources to survive, most middle-aged people would be dead by now. The physical decline of what we now call middle age is real, part of our basic biological programming. Some people have always lived into their 70s and 80s, but hardly as a matter of course. And even today, there are 22 countries in the world with a life expectancy under 45, and 57—including a substantial portion of the world's population—where the life expectancy is under 55. You can't take those numbers at face value, because infant mortality is an extremely important factor, but it is nevertheless true that middle age is a cultural, even technological phenomenon. It represents a victory of agriculture, medicine, public health and civilization as a whole.

Middle age is getting longer, and already demographers have begun to speak of the young old and the old old, 80 and over. Salesclerks are accustomed to waiting on septuagenarian women who reject garments because "it makes me look like an old lady." In Japan, which has the world's highest average life expectancy, 78, old age doesn't begin officially until 70, and other nations may have to follow suit to keep their pension schemes actuarially sound, even if no youth-prolonging drugs are introduced. Thus, although most middle-aged people feel the tug of their bodies reminding them of old patterns of youth and aging, middle age is a triumph of mind over primitive destiny.

Thus the middle-aged body, as we know it today, combines physical and mental vigor with the awareness of mortality. Marketing wisdom claims that the result is a desire to cut one's risks and a general aversion to the new. And it is true that one might expect the middle-aged to be a bit less impetuous than the young. But they are also under pressure to make something of their lives, and they have the knowledge and experience to get things done. This could give rise to a sort of conservative adventurousness, a willingness to change old habits in order to make things work better.

The increasingly explicit acknowledgment by both sides in the longtime East-West conflict that their military strategies cannot lead to victory for either side, while the cost of those strategies has contributed to domestic decline, might well be a bit of middle-aged wisdom.

Finally, all the developed countries will have to find a way of living with a world full of children, most of them not their own. They will have little choice but to cooperate with the rest of the people in the world. Together, they will have to derive a mature definition of development, a set of goals that the rich and poor peoples can share without turning the planet into a toxic waste site.

So how does one answer the big question of whether there can be enough?

The laws of physics tell us we cannot accelerate our use of energy to infinity, but they do not tell us we have reached the end. Studies of the availability of commodities, arable land, energy and other material questions give plenty of reasons to worry, but they are fundamentally inconclusive about what the limits are and when they will be reached. The population statistics are frightening, and they make it seem certain that there will be tremendous migrations and international convulsions within the lifetimes of many people living today. Such increase cannot go on forever, and there will surely continue to be famines and other localized environmental disasters, which provide warnings and portents but will not necessarily mean that the end has come. There can never be enough if your economy is based on convincing everyone that they can never be satisfied. Many Americans believe that their economy can prosper only by inducing people to purchase things they do not need. To proceed blindly along the current path, assuming that some unforeseeable new technology will appear in time to avert disaster, seems utterly irresponsible.

Yet there is really no choice but to affirm that the world still offers enough to let everyone live and grow—if not necessarily to waste and reproduce ceaselessly. Only if people have faith in the world's plenty can they afford to take risks, to be generous and imaginative and create more for themselves and others. Belief in plenty gives people the freedom to be brave. And given the world's many problems, humanity is going to need courage to survive.

4 / The Use of Technology

If it is difficult today to come to terms with the future, the problem is not that there is any shortage of confident and authoritative forecasts. Indeed, there seem to be far too many contradictory inevitabilities. Detailed descriptions of possible or unavoidable tomorrows fill books, newspapers, magazine articles, television programs, advertisements, movies, video games, annual reports and scholarly papers, and each of them says something different. The economist quoted on page 21 of this morning's newspaper expects to live in a different world from the scientist on page 3, or even the marketing executive in the adjacent column. Politicians envision a different future for each audience. Tomorrow is running in all directions at once, toward boom and bust, heaven and hell. The future doesn't fit together:

We can look ahead to a time of unparalleled material comfort and personal freedom. The future will be a time of enormously efficient technology in the service of despotism.

We will swelter in a hell of our own making. We will shiver through a resumed ice age. We will turn outer space into a garden, while the contents of only one asteroid will be enough to keep earthly industry running for decades. We will harness the sun more efficiently and move easily into a postpetroleum age.

Continued disarmament agreements will eventually lead to the disappearance of the technology to produce thermonuclear weapons, and the ability of a country to enable its citizens to achieve personal satisfaction will replace military might and economic aggressiveness as the measure of national strength. National strength will itself become an outmoded concept, as international information networks and the need to solve global environmental problems turn people into world citizens. Terrorists will find ever more effective means to hold the world hostage.

The accelerated depletion of energy resources will continue to spur world tension as oil-rich countries seek to convert their resource into global power, while developed countries fight to maintain their supplies and their comfort. Something will come along—fusion power perhaps—that will allow personal energy consumption to expand even more rapidly than it has in the past.

Our lives will be longer and more satisfying. Population pressure will reverse the worldwide decline in death rates and the trend to longer lives. Robotization will render most human labor superfluous, setting the stage for a slaveholding society based on contemplative leisure, like that of ancient Athens. Robots will become so intelligent that they won't have anything much to say to us, beyond the sort of conversation people carry on with their dogs and cats.

A few people will do the interesting work of society, and the rest of us will be allowed to drop out of the bottom of the system to lead lives of futility mitigated by sedation, much like the underclass in today's large cities.

As civilization continues its slow collapse into brutishness, kindness will become ever more rare and generosity will be suicidal. The world will have too many people to feed. It will finally have enough people to achieve planetary enlightenment.

Everything will be the same, only better—or worse.

Not all of these things can come true. Some probably will. Even a few of the directly contradictory ones might be realized for different people in different places, and it seems very safe to predict that everyone's future will contain some combination of the good, the bad and the unimaginable.

From a technological point of view, every one of these predictions is, if not a sure thing, at least conceivable on the basis of what we think we know today. But the technology alone does not determine the outcome. In many cases, the inventions and methods on which the optimistic forecasts are based are identical to those that provoke other prognosticators' nightmares.

The profusion of divergent, yet conceivable futures can be confusing, but it need not be debilitating. We often speak as if technology is in the driver's seat and the mass of humanity is simply along for the ride. But the existence of so many technologically reasonable futures is an affirmation of a basic human freedom—the freedom to use technology for our own ends. Technology's role in the future is essential, but it is not decisive.

Technology has its origins in the way people respond to their environment and change it so that it suits them. It involves the making of tools, the extraction and refining of resources, the release and direction of energy, the selective breeding of plants and animals and all of the changes in human organization that such innovations have required. For most of the world's people, including everyone in developed societies, technology is a matter of life and death. If we were to eliminate every technology developed during the last five hundred years, several billion people would probably perish, and others would live lives of much diminished possibility (though the planet as a whole might be in better shape).

There is little danger that we are going to eliminate technology from our lives. It is one of the fundamental attributes that define the human species, as powerful, basic and unavoidable as language. Like language, it is both universal and subject to abuse. And just as one sentence leads to another, to form an argument or frame a view of life, so does technology lead from one invention or mode of organization to another, gaining persuasiveness with each step. Yet while it would be absurd to argue that all sentences will inevitably form the same argument and that they will inevitably lead to a happy conclusion, we persist in believing that technology forms a single path to progress. People understand that although language has the power to mislead, they cannot live without it. The same is true of technology, though it is not so widely acknowledged. It seems less human, more pure. And for a pursuit that is entirely materialistic, the idea of technology seems to demand a tremendous amount of faith. Even those who forget fundamental physical laws, in forecasting, for instance, the unlimited acceleration of energy production, tend to respect the rather more superficial logic of the machine. Criticism of virtually any technological behavior is likely to get one branded as a resister of progress, a prophet of a new dark age. The secular religion of technological progress is free with anathema, something that prevents what is purportedly one of the most rational, pragmatic fields of human endeavor from being considered dispassionately.

While it is likely that some technologies that are now either obscure or unknown will have a greater impact than those that dominate current discussions, it is even more likely that we are already aware of most of the machinery and techniques that will dominate the next half century. What we don't know is how people will actually make use of these innovations. Despite its aura of inevitability, technology is a cultural phenomenon. Predictions from three or four decades ago were more often than not correct about the technology we use today, but they seem to have been laughably out of touch about the lives into which the machinery fits. Technology gives us the computer, but it was the meeting of technology and lifestyle that produced the personal computer and the laptop. Predictions made during the 1950s confidently projected the nuclear family, itself a relatively recent innovation at the time, into the twenty-fifth century. Yet this vision of family life did not survive the next decade. Some of what brought about its demise was technological—the birth control pill, for instance. Some of it was about the failure of technology to deliver on its promises—women had to go to work to provide the expanding comforts that Dad alone delivered before. But mostly, what made the predictions wrong was a change in the way people wanted to live their lives.

We cannot help but see technological possibilities through the lenses of our own time. But it can be useful to view them from the perspective of sustained historical trends, while keeping in mind that trends do not, and should not, continue indefinitely.

The continuing development of worldwide information networks and instantaneous communication is seen by boosters as the basis of a dynamic new kind of economy and by critics as the generator of a wholly transparent society, in which privacy will disappear, lives will be monitored and dissent suppressed. More recently, people have come to see computer networks as the repositories of a parallel universe that may be more seductive than real life. We have already experienced collision between these realms, as when computers programmed to respond to the stock market have panicked in a distinctly nonhuman way, wiping out a lot of financial wealth in the process. The growth of information networks raises knotty political problems in guaranteeing fair access, and even free societies will be forced to find ways of policing these new environments.

Such changes in communications seem likely to reinforce the tendency during this century for technology to make possible physical isolation even as it works to homogenize society. For three decades after World War II, American culture was suffused with the promise of the joyride, the belief that modern life consisted of moving ever faster, ever farther. We would develop the means to obliterate time and space, it was promised, though we rarely dwelt on the possibility that it would result in making every place the same.

Gridlock and crowded airports have given the lie to the dream of going everywhere effortlessly. Still, the dream of the joyride persists in the parallel world of electronically based information. We cannot be everywhere, but we can see it all on television. We can plug into the global brain and carry on conversations and instantaneously acquire knowledge from virtually anyone in the world—anyone, at least, who has a computer and modem and has figured out how to use them. Some predict that the future of travel consists of places in every town where you will be able to don helmet, boots and gloves and project yourself into the body of a robot in some distant place—the moon perhaps, or Venice. In a booth in Tysons Corners, Virginia, or Irving, Texas, or Troy, Michigan, you might have the vicarious, yet visceral experience of sitting in a café in the Piazza San Marco, hearing the café's string orchestra play "Somewhere My Love" and looking across the square at all the other robots serving as alter egos for other people in similar booths. Perhaps the robot at the next table in Venice is having and communicating the experience to the person in the booth next to yours. You'll probably never know.

Other advances in electronics can be expected to continue the trend toward ever more vivid and varied forms of vicarious experience. Computers will be able to generate alternative realities so real and so engaging that sending robots to Venice will not even be necessary. Real estate development will be devoted to creating places that people have already experienced and enjoyed as artificial realities, much as Walt Disney World does today. The only point of reality is to validate and provide a new dimension to the total entertainment package.

Mortality remains a problem. Currently available drugs that stave off baldness might well be the precursors to other drugs that reverse hormonal and immunological reactions that constitute the aging process. Other drugs will enhance memory and sexual performance. People will be able to stay young, at least until the moment at age 110 or so when everything springs apart, like an overwound watch. And then, it might be possible to download your mental capacity into a robot and achieve immortality in communion with the machine.

Some of the drugs that will slow aging will be the product of genetic alteration, a technology with much larger consequences. It will be possible to design new plants that can resist pests, make better use of natural resources and provide specific nutritional benefits. It will probably be possible to engineer human genes to eliminate biological and mental disorders, to make our progeny smarter, taller or blonder or to redesign the human body for habitats in space or beneath the sea. We may be able to reconstitute entire organisms from their genetic materials, so that we can go to the zoo to see the dinosaurs.

Robots, which already play a role in many manufacturing processes, will continue to proliferate. Their flexibility will make custom work as inexpensive as mass production. Increasingly, robots will be fitted with computer capacity that will enhance their ability to make judgments based on incomplete information, and thus to "think" in a humanlike way. On the far more distant horizon is the prospect of miniature robots, barely larger than viruses, that would become, in effect, a new form of life, able, for example, to make limestone from seawater in such an organized way that they could build whole buildings all by themselves.

Some of these technologies will unquestionably be important in our immediate future. Most of them are part of the present. Their engineering challenges are largely understood, if not totally solved, but the challenges they present to society are far greater. All are universalizing, linking each to all while subverting the power of smaller communities. Such devices would allow individuals to direct large amounts of power, but at the same time they would subvert privacy and autonomy. They would mean that less and less of life will be left to chance, but they would also lessen people's opportunities to make their own decisions. Such technologies would exacerbate the paradox of modernization: Expanded powers shrink the meaning of human action.

These technologies collectively define the vector of progress, the directions in which those who pay attention to such things tend to believe we are going. Do they all lead toward happy results? Not too likely. But ignoring such technologies and their consequences will surely not make the results any sunnier.

You can't stop progress" is an American truism. It can be a statement either of aggressive optimism or of despair. There is something poignant about it, because it is spoken at moments when something real is being sacrificed in the hope that something greater can be gained. This does not always happen. Still, Americans' willingness to forsake the familiar in search of improvement is a basic piece of the national character, part of the myth by which we define ourselves. The ability to throw everything away and start anew is a very profound kind of freedom, one that will have to be redefined for a more crowded world, but one we'll probably never give up completely.

In the first few centuries of American life, the word "progress" was associated with the moral travails of John Bunyan's pilgrim in a book that, at least up to the time of Abraham Lincoln, was widely read. In the late nineteenth century, progress became associated with material improvement, and was the province of engineers, not divines. And yet, the idea of progress has never wholly lost its religious aura. Indeed, we still live with a version of the Puritan paradox that individuals must struggle to make progress even though, in the larger sense, progress represents the unfolding of the inevitable.

It is reassuring to believe that you are swimming with the inexorable currents of improvement, though there is also the threat that if you try to fight the tide you will drown. Throughout this century, most Americans have grown up believing that the future will be shaped by new stuff—products and processes that will continue the trend toward personal power, speed and convenience. Those who make such products spend vast sums of money to convince people that what they are offering is the inevitable next step. The idea of leaving familiar surroundings and building a new life has shrunk to getting rid of the old car or the old computer, in favor of a new, improved model.

Progress and technology are nearly inseparable in our vocabularies, and they dominate most considerations of the nature of the future. There is little question that technology plays the most dynamic and, in a sense, the most predictable role in determining the future. The belief that there is a clear direction to history and a single path for human progress remains compelling, not least because it allows people to be consumers, rather than makers, of their own time. The association of technology with progress suggests to many that the course of technological development is somehow out of control and that society's only choice is to keep up or fall behind. In thinking about technology and the future, it is important to remember that technology is a form of human behavior, while progress is a judgment about that behavior. Every technological act does not lead inevitably toward what our descendants would consider progress.

Society is undergoing a crisis in its faith in technological progress, prompted by environmental crises, spiritual yearnings and the end of the technological stalemate that was the Cold War. People are at once disillusioned with and intensely dependent upon technology. It is the source of both problems and hope. We can no longer look upon it as a magical savior, but there is little doubt that it is an important way in which people help themselves.

The geopolitical changes that have taken place during the last few years also challenge our understanding of the role of technology in our society. The 1990s have the sense not so much of a century or a millennium drawing to a close as of the aftermath of a heroic and tragic half century that has come to a dramatic ending with the sudden demise of Communism. This period spans the technological optimism of the Depression-era world's fairs; the often belated awareness of Germany and Japan as military threats; the mobilization of the American economy, backed by international brainpower, to repel this threat; the development of nuclear weapons and the polarizing of the world under this military technological threat. Obviously, not all these dangers have passed, and they will remain to influence the new sense of the world that is only beginning to take shape. But attitudes about what makes a nation strong are changing to take account of a world in which the most powerful weapons render their owners impotent.

For people in the United States, the country that dominated this extraordinary half century, the task of coming to a new understanding of power and technology is particularly great because it points toward a recognition that those factors that worked in the past to make us very successful may no longer work. In fact, the outlook may not be so bleak. It is possible that we have been misunderstanding the basis of our success all along.

The contemporary American view of the role of technology in the culture was largely shaped by World War II and its aftermath. That war, as well as the Cold War that followed, appears to validate claims, both optimistic and pessimistic, about the autonomy of technology. The war brought a concentration of American technology which not only produced weaponry but accelerated the development of devices, such as the computer, that have shaped life ever since. Moreover, Americans tend to believe that a technological breakthrough, the development of the atomic bomb, was the decisive blow in that war. Nuclear weapons have surely shaped the years since then.

In recent years, the postwar arrangement of the world has broken up. The immediate cause of this change was probably the inability of the Soviet Union's economy to sustain the country as a military superpower and multinational empire. But the realignment was also forced by the economic power of nations that were not trying to be superpowers. A demographic reality is at work: Most of the adults in the developed world are too young to remember World War II. George Bush is very likely the last of ten U.S. Presidents for whom World War II was a defining event, and the war he led against Iraq has been widely viewed as a vindication of decades of investment in military technology. Still, the breakup of the post–World War II order in the world will present many problems, but it also offers opportunities, one of which is to rethink the role that technology plays in shaping the world and shaping the future.

Throughout history, war and technology have been closely linked. If we view technology as a fundamental human attribute, this connection is hardly surprising. To ask whether technology is inherently warlike is the same as inquiring whether people are inherently warlike. There is plenty of evidence to say yes on both counts, but in neither case does the answer tell the whole story. While we are generally willing to concede human achievement outside of the war zone, we often limit our discussion of technology to those things that are most clearly aggressive and represent highly focused power. For example, the material from which prehistoric and ancient peoples made their spear points is considered a defining characteristic, while their pottery vessels merely provide additional description of craft or art. Warlike technologies are associated with movement and the breaking of barriers, whereas, as the French architect and thinker Paul Virilio has written, civilization happens behind walls that have been designed as barriers to the expansive, penetrating, unruly character of military conquest. The walls themselves constitute a technology, and they demonstrate the ways in which aggressiveness taxes even those who choose not to be aggressive. But in our minds, technology tends to be defined by the masculine attributes of focus and projection, while the more feminine characteristics of containment and protection are merely commonplace. Missiles penetrate bunkers.

Thus, we speak of technology in terms of the release and application of power, and depend on some other civilizing force to both organize and blunt the power, channeling it in directions that are more useful or at least benign. The U.S. Constitution and the Bill of Rights, drafted just as the industrial age was catching on in Europe, can be seen as a very elaborate set of brakes to prevent the country from being mobilized in any single direction.

In modern times, wars have provided the impetus for developing new kinds of machinery and processes. For the last half century, our society has been shaped by the technological legacies of World War II. Most of these were based on research done before the war began, but the war made their development urgent and focused the attention of scientists and engineers in an unprecedented way. The results include the computer, jet aircraft, advanced rocketry, game theory, information theory and cybernetics among others.

Nuclear weaponry, the most significant military technology to come from World War II, is in a different class from everything that came before. The bombs dropped on Hiroshima and Nagasaki and the far more destructive bombs that followed them, affirmed that there is no wall, no armor, no set of brakes, no physical defense that can control damage from such weapons. There is only self-control, something that has been in short supply throughout most of history.

There have been efforts to turn these into normal weapons by building different sorts of walls. The program begun in the United States in 1961 to encourage families to build nuclear fallout shelters was an effort to make nuclear war survivable. Compliance was minimal, however, and the shelters probably wouldn't have worked. Ronald Reagan's formulation of the Strategic Defense Initiative as an impermeable shield in space was intended to restore the security the United States once enjoyed when oceans were a barrier and bombs couldn't set the world on fire. Its combination of high technology and nostalgia was a characteristic expression of the 1980s.

The physicist and space scientist Freeman Dyson once speculated that it might have been better for the world, in the long run, if Germany had succeeded in building atom bombs during World War II. "If Hitler had nuclear bombs, their use would neither have changed the grand strategy of the war nor lessened our determination to fight it to a finish," Dyson wrote. "What would have changed is our postwar perception of nuclear weapons. We would have seen nuclear weapons forever afterwards as contemptible, used by an evil man for evil purposes and failing to give him victory. The myth surrounding nuclear weapons would have been a myth of contempt and failure, not a myth of pride and success."

Dyson's argument that the victorious Allies would probably not have taken this repugnant technology as the cornerstone of their postwar strategy is weakened a bit by the historical fact that both the Soviet Union and the United States made extensive use of German rocketry and German rocket scientists in their weaponry and space programs. Still, his fundamental point remains compelling. Technology does not exist in isolation but within a context of values, myths and expectations. Poison gas, for example, has not disappeared from the face of the earth, but it is viewed as something of an outlaw weapon, one that poses dangers to would-be users and encourages a cowardly kind of warfare. Dyson argues that the only way in which nuclear weapons will ever be abolished is if those who have them decide that they are more trouble than they are worth. It would be a conservative response, made in the name of preserving something people feel is more important. Dyson hints that one constituency for the abolition of nuclear weapons might ultimately be the military, because the bomb has rendered the skills of warfare obsolete.

The United States, whose Constitution is designed to create a limited government that is, nevertheless, capable of responding to dangers, began development of nuclear weapons in response to fears that Germany would do so. This helped set a pattern of innovating out of fear, which has led in turn to the belief that we should develop virtually any military technology we can imagine because if we fail to do so, somebody else will—and will use it against us. Thus do we commit to doing repugnant things because we, as Americans, or as "the Free World," are morally superior to others who might make use of the same idea. We are justified in being first with the worst. In this way of thinking, technology is for the fighting of wars and progress means the development of better ways to win. Sometimes this battle may be waged by economic means as well as military ones. But even though the eighteenth-century economic theory that underlies the capitalist system holds that the pursuit of selfish interests will result in a form of international harmony, the belief remains that technology exists to enable our side to win.

The impact of thermonuclear weapons has been to freeze the two great nuclear superpowers into positions of both preeminence and impotence. There has been no warfare between the United States and the Soviet Union, although each has been drawn into long, unsuccessful wars with much weaker nations. Both of the nuclear superpowers have spent most of the postwar era building up nuclear arsenals and perfecting missiles, submarines and other delivery systems that cannot be used in any way that could achieve victory against each other. Meanwhile, the race has drawn so much of the superpowers' money and scientific and engineering talent that the losers of World War II have been able to prosper, precisely because they were largely demilitarized.

Perhaps the first lesson we can derive from the Cold War is not so much that the United States won it as that the Soviet Union lost it first. The United States never focused its capabilities or wealth so narrowly on military technological development as did the Soviets, and it began from a far better position. Still, military research and development has consumed the attention of many of our most able engineers and scientists, not to mention hundreds of billions of dollars in public expenditures which might have been used in other ways. It is not surprising that many recent military inventions have had problems, because they were made not for actual use but as technological trump cards to prevent the Soviets from being confident of their capabilities. Usefulness is the prime test of a technological artifact. In the real world, what doesn't work is discarded. Weapons made for what is understood to be an act of ritual suicide are likely to be highly elaborate, but they are unlikely to lead civilization in any rewarding directions.

The real winners of the Cold War were those who were not allowed to participate, the losers of World War II. Germany and Japan were forced to have a broader view of technology and to channel their talent and money into meeting widespread needs and desires. While the reunification of Germany excites some long-range worries, recent polls have shown that Japan has surpassed the Soviet Union as the country Americans most fear. The Soviet threat is military and is seen as receding, while the Japanese threat is economic and is believed to be on the rise. Both tend to be discussed in a warlike way, and in both battles, technology is viewed as the weapon that will bring victory. We have come to view chip gaps and the threat of Japan's national research efforts in much the same way we used to fear missile gaps and Soviet military buildups.

The martial metaphors seem a bit ridiculous when applied to the current situation, because Japan's apparent aggression has taken the form of supplying the American market with more desirable, higher-quality products at better prices than U.S. companies do. The Japanese have advised us to stop whining, and give up buying if it makes us feel so bad, though they are probably counting on our not taking this advice. Yet there is a kernel of justification in our feelings of grievance. Americans can understand head-to-head military competition. But we find something insidious about a people that values common interests more highly than individual desires—even as it enriches itself by selling consumer goods to the rest of the world. This very effective behavior might raise questions about the future of America's consumer-driven society in an era when its productive capabilities do not match its desires. But most frequently, the Japanese example is used by those who argue that the purpose of technology is international dominance.

Nearly everywhere, the military has lost its dominant role in defining security. Many nations are turning their attention to making sure of their economic security, which depends, among other things, on reliable food supplies, on access to energy and on political stability. These interact with environmental security, which has been a particularly strong force in Western Europe, but which has also come to the fore in the United States and Canada, and in such places as Poland, where up to one-third of the soil has been made toxic by water and air pollution and the careless disposal of industrial wastes. These different goals sometimes come into conflict. For many countries, energy security means oil tankers, which means oil spills and the necessity of naval power to protect sea lanes. Current nuclear power plants pose safety hazards. But their dangers must be weighed against the possible contribution of conventional power plants to global warming.

Solar power, whose principal environmental problem is that it would take up a lot of space, tends not to be taken very seriously, largely on the grounds that it is diffuse and somehow passive. The vector of progress does not point toward harvesting the energy that falls on the earth each day but aims instead at releasing enormous forces, through nuclear fusion or improved fission reactors. Because our industries, government agencies and universities are so deeply invested in following technological directions that were shaped by the Cold War, there is a strong military flavor to the options most often mentioned for dealing with other problems. Yet while those who drafted the Constitution recognized the need for military capability, they believed that security *from* the military is also vitally important.

Yet even as we realize that the Cold War view of technology has not worked in the interest of either of the countries that were its strongest adherents, we are still faced with the knowledge that World War II did play a large role in producing many of the inventions and ideas that have shaped our world ever since. We cannot turn back history and give Hitler the bomb, which is probably fortunate. But we still need a useful myth to explain the phenomenon of World War II and postwar America that will help keep us out of trouble now that this half century of our history is over.

Perhaps we can begin by recognizing that all of the technologies that are viewed as products of the war had their origin before the war in the civilian sector. This is particularly true of computers, which grew from more than a century of thought and experiments.

Jet aircraft, radar and many other innovations, both large and small, were also speeded, though not created, by wartime needs. To pick a minor but well-known example, the wartime work of Charles Eames in designing plywood splints for wounded soldiers helped make Eames familiar with new glues and synthetic rubbers and led directly to his famous postwar, multiple-contoured furniture. But his work with splints grew in turn from his prewar experiments with plywood furniture.

The war focused energies, as life-and-death struggles will. It brought people together to work on projects who might not have come in contact otherwise. It forced people to identify specific goals and helped remove obstacles to their attainment. It speeded up innovation just as it speeded up manufacturing.

Moreover, the Allied powers benefited from a significant migration of scientific and engineering talent from Central Europe, which became a not-so-hidden cost of Germany's anti-Semitic policies. Political and intellectual freedom in Britain and America proved to be a powerful draw for those whose ideas and expertise played a major role in winning the war. America's successes came not through the creation of a military technology bureaucracy but by directing the capabilities of a diverse, though Depression-crippled economy and mobilizing a growing pool of academic talent. Military establishments are more often impediments to decisive innovation rather than their sponsors.

This high-end technology was supplemented by creativity among the rank and file. The long, difficult supply lines, particularly in the Pacific, spurred soldiers to improvisations that were scarcely high-tech by any standard but were extremely useful. Empty 55-gallon oil drums were used for everything from making bridges to constructing solar-heated showers. The Quonset hut and the jeep were simple, ubiquitous, easy to understand and repair and infinitely adaptable. For hundreds of thousands of soldiers, such materials and machines were essential to survival. The proliferation of home workshops in the immediate postwar years suggests that many enjoyed making and modifying things themselves.

The wartime practice of improvising to survive was reflected during the immediate postwar period in which improvising to make art became popular. Jackson Pollock dripped and splashed paint on his canvases. Jazz musicians began incorporating long improvisatory riffs. Allen Ginsberg wrote poetry as a passionate outburst rather than a well-wrought artifact. Eames designed a house, and when the materials were delivered, used them to build something quite different. Television was new and live, and seemed to be in a state of continuous improvisation. There was even one talk show that lasted as long as the conversation was interesting. An open, experimental and extremely matter-of-fact modernism—one that accepted and employed but did not idolize technology—was in the air.

But these seeming harbingers of a golden age appeared in a period of growing darkness, as fears grew that the country that had just been proven the world's strongest and ablest was being subverted from within. It was a time of blacklisting and political demagoguery. New careers were being built on the nation's feelings of insecurity, while J. Robert Oppenheimer, the hero of the effort to develop the bomb, was stripped of his government security clearance. The very atmosphere of freedom that had helped make our triumph possible was suppressed, if only for a time. The demobilization that some had feared would bring a new depression never really took place, as the Soviet Union replaced the Axis powers as the nation's enemy. The Soviet development of the atomic bomb led to a technological stalemate, as both sides spent billions of dollars developing weapons and military capabilities that could never be rationally utilized.

This account caricatures a rich and complex history, but its shift of emphasis may aid in putting the war and its aftermath into perspective. Rather than seeing the war as a generator of technology from which we have benefited ever since, we can see the war as a challenge that led engineers and scientists to temporarily focus their efforts and narrow their concerns so that the war could be won. It did, however, produce one technology that will forever change the rules of warfare, and which had the effect of prolonging the immediate postwar confrontation between the United States and the Soviet Union until quite recently.

The era of World War II and its aftermath was unquestionably a triumphant time for the United States, but even so, the end of this half century can liberate Americans too. It offers a release from the crippling, technology-based illusion of a two-power world and an opportunity to deal with problems and opportunities at home and throughout the world that were obscured by this limited vision.

Under the circumstances, it is not surprising that the fiftieth anniversary of the 1939 World's Fair became the occasion for some examination and even more nostalgia. The fair embodied a future that seemed to fit together, and moreover, the future that was predicted seems largely to have been the one that happened. The future, or at least America's piece of it, was headed in a single direction. America's great corporations would provide benign expertise, its citizenry would respond with blind confidence and the country would emerge from the Depression by following the vector of progress.

It is very attractive to believe that it is possible to foresee the future and then to participate in its realization. Technology is the facet of the future that is most amenable to forecasting because it is derived, in large part, from scientific research. Moreover, it has tended to follow pure discovery by at least one human generation. In this view of things, it is only a matter of time before the revolutionary insights of scientists become the commonplace world of the next generation of engineers, who contrive ways to turn cosmic discoveries into household conveniences. This is a bald, simplistic statement, but this view underlies much of what can be found in the financial pages and most other popular writing on the subject. Moreover, it is not wholly untrue. Scientific discoveries in both electricity and physiology can be seen to have converged to give us the telephone. Lasers, a phenomenon created as part of the study of optics, led to clear sound from our phonographs and crisp computer copies. By viewing the subject wholly in retrospect, and not paying attention to the many courses not followed and the many scientific discoveries left unexploited, it is possible to see a clear evolutionary pattern in our scientific and technological culture.

Such a pattern seems a powerful tool for thinking about the future, because it appears to overwhelm the other chief determinants of change—human values and material and environmental resources. Technology is seen as a way around all physical limitations. And while it may be impossible to know what people will want thirty or fifty years from now, the evolutionary thrust of technology at least indicates what they will get. And because technology helps shape cultural values, the products and processes available will largely determine what people will want.

This deep-seated, generally understated core of belief remains prevalent, particularly in American culture. The identification of technological change with biological evolution is particularly pervasive. We are encouraged to view technology as something that has taken on a life of its own, that is moving inexorably in a single direction. The only question, we are told, is whether we will be on the cutting edge of progress or will be left behind.

Intentionally or not, much of what enters popular consciousness about the future confuses means and ends. In the case of the 1939 Futurama, for instance, General Motors was seeking to promote an end—an automobile-based society—for which it was eager to supply an important part of the means. (Visitors to the exhibition, as taxpayers, would have to do the rest.) GM's sales job met little resistance because the public was certainly ready for it. The automobile does seem to fulfill deep-seated human desires for mobility, speed, autonomy and potency that far predate the arrival of the horseless carriage. By 1939, the idea of the high-speed-highway society had been around for nearly two decades and the pioneer examples were already being realized.

Such propaganda about the inevitability of a particular technology or technological transformation of society is, at bottom, an attempt to short-circuit the consideration of how the technology meets our goals and what safeguards should be developed to ensure that it does. In effect, those who argue for technological autonomy are trying to bypass the political process by assuring that their program will be so well accepted that it will be noncontroversial. Americans are mistrustful of politics; we would rather hear about the future from a car salesman than a candidate. We assume that the burden of adjusting to the future will fall on us as individuals rather than on the society as a whole, and most of us probably believe that is as it should be. But by making a particular future seem inevitable, and by making the transition to it a personal responsibility, we avoid discussion of larger goals and values and play into the hands of those who would like to see the society take a particular route.

In recent years, people with technologies to promote have turned this predisposition for trying things out into a kind of bullying. Rather than offer an attractively inevitable future, as did the Futurama, they push people to accept change as a by-product of fear. They demand that we jettison our beliefs, catch the wave, brace for the shock. The future is coming at us in thousands of new ways, at a speed that is only accelerating. One recent book deplored increased study of the humanities because, it argued, such thought hinders progress. We are urged not to think about where we are going, because those who do will only be left behind. Changes are believed to be coming like those rapid, relentless electronic critters that threaten the players of video games. And as in the video games, it's the threat you lose sight of that will nuke you, vaporize you or just gobble you up in the end.

The video game does seem to sum up much of the experience of late-twentieth-century life. It is a solitary activity, played with a machine that will inevitably defeat the most expert human player. The universe of the game is highly circumscribed and abstractly violent. There is no real way to win the game. The best you can do is defer losing it. This can serve as a reflection of the overloaded, tension-fraught lives that many people live in the last decade of the millennium. And most of the techno-bullies argue that instantaneous communications, computers and an ever accelerating pace of change will only speed up the game and threaten the players who can't keep up.

There is one more part of the game that should be examined, however. The video game begins with the insertion of a coin. When you do that, you have accepted the game. The mechanism by which one accepts the larger game of the hectic life and threatening future is not nearly so clear-cut. It is not easy to opt out of the game, particularly at a time when the society at large is quite willing to abandon the slow players and the nonplayers to lives of misery and squalor. It's tough to stand outside the game, especially when you think you might do all right if you join it. So you do join the game, and wonder whether you are serving yourself or merely the mindless, grinding logic of the game itself.

We should resist such bullying, and should also remember that, in thinking about the future, good intentions can be just as misleading as bad ones. Much discussion of the future combines technological extrapolation with social and political wishful thinking. The person doing the predicting looks at current technological trends, and at the recent basic scientific research that could give rise to technologies, and mixes them up with a set of values which, though they might be admirable, are not intrinsic to the technology being considered. Most often, the promise is that the technology will help ameliorate social ills even as it brings greater freedom and greater individual power.

This is the tradition of the technological utopia. Its most pervasive contemporary manifestation is the paradigm of an information age made possible by a global, computerized, interconnected network of intelligence, both human and artificial. Even though such dreams, if realized, would in turn create very complicated new problems, the goals themselves are not the major shortcomings of such ideas about the future. Their greatest weakness lies in their assumption that such technologies would inevitably lead toward such goals. The values that underlie the visions have gone largely unexamined.

Yet, even in recent memory, many different social programs have sprung from similar technologies. The recent enthusiasm for the electronic cottage—a vision of people physically isolated but plugged into the entire world—bears a certain resemblance to the 1970s environmentalist-libertarian dream of self-contained, solar-powered autonomous houses that would be able to secede from the central power grid. At that time, central power meant frightening nuclear plants and massive, polluting coal- and petroleum-fired plants, and on a more general level it was identified with big business, big government and the tendency toward international involvement, as in Vietnam. Today, some of the same people are rhapsodizing about how we can work for transnational business behemoths in the privacy of our own bedrooms—and still be plugged into the global nervous system.

During the 1930s, Frank Lloyd Wright, among others, saw the automobile as the technology that would make possible an integrated life closely attached to the land, in which government would play a very minor role. Two decades earlier, advocates of national electric power grids predicted that they would bring about the decentralization of production, even down to the household level, and free the nation of the blight that comes with industrialization. It is easier to imagine widespread home production of goods than it is to conceive of a rural nation of information manipulators, but otherwise current claims for the great promise of an information network strongly recall those for a power network. All are elaborations of a persistent American dream of a great green nation without the problems of cities, an antiurban bias that was powerful in American life even before the coming of industrialization.

Obviously, not all of these dreams of decentralization are identical. And it's worth noting that most of them have been realized to some degree. Electric power grids did decouple industry from energy sources and sent manufacturers nearer to their raw materials, or more commonly, cheap labor. The automobile did result in a political shift that took power away from metropolitan centers and brought people closer to their lawns, if not to the land as Wright conceived of it. The fraction of data manipulation that can be done at home may mean that those cities that function as management centers have reached their peak of office building density and will gradually begin to shrink as many of the most routine and most creative tasks are done elsewhere. Yet none of these technological innovations has brought so much satisfaction that the dream of decentralization has ceased to be a powerful force.

There are a few other notorious utopian claims that have been tied to many generations of technology. "Power too cheap to meter" is a promise that has been used nearly as often as "the check is in the mail," but it stays alive to describe the next energy technology. Currently, it is associated with nuclear fusion, though those who advocate solar collectors in outer space that would beam energy down to the earth have flirted with it too. The idea that people in the near future will be able to have lives of leisure is also a perennial promise that has been associated with everything from steam power to robotics. Up to now, economic vitality has tended to make people busier, while slowdowns have brought not leisure but idleness and want. Countless products have promised an end to household drudgery, but they have resulted primarily in higher standards of cleanliness, at least until the mid-1980s, when overworked Americans started letting their houses get dirtier.

When visitors looked at the wonders to be found in the Futurama and other predictions of the 1939 World's Fair, at least some of them might have wondered how much all these things were going to cost. Making ends meet was a real concern in Depression-era America. But the future did not have a price tag. Those who are trying to sell us something forward-looking rarely dwell on how much it will set us back. And now, we have a greater understanding that there are larger costs, ones that are borne by the whole country or the whole world. Costs that are purely monetary and have to be paid up front are the easiest to understand. But there are also costs that are not so evident, in the form of wasted resources, environmental degradation, social injustice and lost human talent. And there are monetary costs that are inherent not in the purchase of the technology but in the habits it induces, much as the low price of a compact-disc player or a Barbie doll masks major disbursements ahead. Contemporary housing and land development patterns, which lock people into complete dependence on the automobile and often lead to the waste of valuable agricultural land, induce such expensive long-term behavior.

Things that seem to be technological inevitabilities are often derailed when their costs and likely benefits are weighed. Back during the ascendancy of speed-demon technology, widespread supersonic air transport was believed to be just around the corner. The European Concorde was built, though its proposed U.S. and Soviet counterparts were not. The Concorde once seemed a harbinger, but it now seems likely to be a historical curiosity. The Concorde and supersonic transport in general represent an approach to air travel opposite to that which has been adopted. Instead of being able to go from point to point at terrific speeds, passengers now accept having to pass through several intermediate points, frequently changing planes, within a complex route network. This seems a step backward from the relatively more luxurious earlier days of passenger jets.

But such route structures permit airlines to use their planes more efficiently, which in turn has allowed them to offer many reduced fares and change air travel from an elite to a mainstream activity. U.S. government deregulation of air travel in 1978 resulted in a 74 percent increase in passengers during the following decade, and now three-quarters of all Americans have flown, compared with one-third before 1978. Now the hub-and-spoke organization of airline routes that resulted from airline deregulation has been adopted throughout the world. The costs of this are that flying is less comfortable, slower, less reliable and probably less safe. The advantage is that it is more widely available.

This example shows that there is far more than one kind of progress, and more than one kind of cost. In this case, a measure of new convenience for the many has undercut the quality of service available to those willing to pay for the best. It has also increased pressures to provide expensive new airports and passenger facilities.

Perhaps the monetary, environmental and political costs of these will constrain the growth of air travel and force people to look at such alternatives as high-speed rail links.

Technology follows the paths of desire, and the apparent trajectory of any particular technology is a less reliable predictor of the future than is the desire itself. When viewed from an engineering and design perspective, virtually any technology has a logical next step of sophistication, power and effectiveness. Yet when such seeming inevitabilities are weighed against other opportunities and obligations, we often forgo that apparent next step. Those who are advocating particular technologies are acutely aware of the many choices that have to be made. That's why they so often argue that society has no choice but to adopt their way of doing things.

Still, belief in the autonomy of technological development is something the most committed optimists and the most implacable pessimists have in common. Enthusiasts see technology as a new, and very likely improved, kind of natural force. But unlike other natural phenomena, which can be altered by technological innovation, this one must be allowed to go forward. To do otherwise is to stand in the path of history, and anyone who does so will be crushed. Many of those most critical of technological civilization make much the same assumption. Jacques Elul, representing the most extreme position, argued in 1963 that it was by then too late for people to try to regain control over technology because it had already transformed our values and expectations and developed ways to force people to accept its control.

If technology is not a new kind of natural force or a means of challenging God and the universe, what is it? The most obvious and ultimately the truest answer is that it is a vast tool chest, capable of assisting in a wide variety of human purposes. But that seems to fly in the face of our own experiences. Most people have far greater experience in accommodating to the demands of technology than they do in finding ways of turning technology to their own purposes. During the last forty years, television can be seen to have first reconfigured people's living rooms, then their leisure time, and ultimately redefined the terms of American politics. Computers have revolutionized work life, devalued skills and helped throw many people out of work. They have also contributed to a more general sense of lost control. When the computer is down, everything important grinds to a halt, though many are probably also reassured by such a demonstration of fallibility.

The issue of control is an important one. It is the key to the distinction Lewis Mumford made between tools and machines. Tools are things that people are able to use freely to serve their own purposes. Machines, by contrast, remake the world around them. They force people to modify their behavior to serve the purposes of the machine. They also beget other machines, which serve to feed or process the output of the first machine but also have human and environmental effects of their own. This proliferation of the machine and its redefinition of human purpose determine the vector of progress, at least as technological optimists define it. Answering the needs of the machine has a way of seeming far more objective than answering the needs of this person or that group of people. Besides, the argument goes, if we deny the logical development of technology, we are only providing the opportunity for others to surge ahead and leave us in a position of diminished choice. It is best to acquiesce to the demands of the machine so that we may be first in line for its benefits. In this argument, the nature of the machine as a tool to accomplish some specific purpose is lost. It is best merely to keep the machine running.

This is the fundamental premise of American consumer society, a phenomenon defined not by the Constitution or the Bill of Rights but by the invention of machinery and processes of mass production late in the nineteenth century. People have, of course, always needed to eat and to have clothing and tools to help them survive. Some powerful persons have always been able to amass great quantities of possessions. The industrial revolution enabled a far larger portion of the populace to acquire things. Machinery and the burning of highly concentrated energy sources were able to meet pent-up human desires, but it was not until late in the nineteenth century that anyone tried to change human behavior in order to keep the machines running. The historian James R. Beniger fixes that moment at 1882 when Henry P. Crowell installed a new machine to produce oatmeal from raw grain. Crowell's problem was that this single machine was able to process twice the U.S. demand for oatmeal. Few people felt the need for oatmeal, so Crowell set to work creating the desire. He decided not to sell it in bulk but to package it, with a picture of a Quaker on the box, and to promote and advertise it as a brand. Within the next few years, Crowell invented virtually every method, including box-top premiums and health endorsements, still used to sell cereals.

The transition to a highly capitalized, highly productive manufacturing system forced Crowell to innovate, and it forced others to follow suit, particularly in the food industry. This took place at about the same time the industrial system embarked on the deskilling of jobs, removing the satisfactions of craftsmanship. The satisfaction of doing a job disappeared and had to be replaced by the pleasures of what can be purchased with the paycheck. Three decades later, when Henry Ford's innovative industrial methods redefined the working man as a car buyer, the prerequisites to the consumer society were in place. Such manipulation of demand in the immense American market was one of the chief forces that built American industrial might in the first half of the century, and that of Japan, Korea, Taiwan and other emerging economic powers in recent years.

Perpetual dissatisfaction with ourselves and our lives is not simply a by-product of the mass-consumption society but rather its mainspring. We work harder to have more, and when we succeed are confronted with whole new universes of wants and worries. This pattern so pervades our lives that it is easy to forget how recent an invention the consumer society is and why it arose. The American consumer society continues out of sheer momentum, even as the productive system that made it necessary has atrophied.

The engineering of mass-production machinery is inseparable from the engineering of human desires. In Ford's case, the desire for personal transportation existed before Ford found a way to manufacture it at a price large numbers of people, including his relatively well-paid workers, could afford. In fact, Ford was slow to adopt the techniques of advertising and styling because he did not have to create desire for the Model T. His achievement was to create the system that produced the car. In this case, the engineering of the machinery and the process was far more important than the creation of consumer demand.

By contrast, Crowell, with a machine that was unexcelled in producing a commodity people didn't want, was forced to invent ways to induce demand. Ford responded to demand by developing a technological system. Crowell responded to a technological achievement by creating a consumer system. In a sense, then, Ford can be seen to be in the toolmaking business, while Crowell's less obviously mechanical achievement made him a pioneer of the machine-driven society.

This contrast, while it does suggest that machine creation need not require more sophisticated engineering than does toolmaking, is ultimately misleading. Ford's operation was a prototype for the producer-consumer economy that has driven America's economic success for most of this century. Moreover, the automobile industry served as the very heart of the industrial machine. Ford did answer a very strong, already evident desire, but the industry he began rapidly took on a life of its own. It became a vast machine that redirected tax expenditures to build roads, that changed people's idea of domesticity and convenience and ultimately remade the American landscape. Its proliferation has been largely responsible for changing the chemical composition of our air, a disturbing trend that is difficult to reverse because of the patterns of settlement and habits the automobile has induced. We have so much invested in the world that the automobile production machine has induced us to make that the car feels like a more basic part of our lives than the land we live on or the air we breathe.

Investment is, in fact, the key distinction between a tool and a machine. It is a measure of how much has been sacrificed for the means of accomplishing a specific task. This determines how much of a return must be expected and influences all decisions about future directions. We think, for example, of a chisel as a tool. It is sufficiently inexpensive that most people can afford to purchase it for use only on comparatively rare and appropriate occasions. But it is possible to imagine an instance, perhaps in some remote and relatively undeveloped part of the world, in which a chisel would be seen as a means of greatly improving one's life and thus worth a considerable sacrifice of property or labor. Someone who had staked so much of his wealth on purchasing the chisel would not be able to use it as an occasionally useful tool. He would seek occasions to use the chisel, perhaps to protect his investment, possibly to convince himself he had not been unwise. This simple, basic tool has thus become, in Mumford's terminology, a machine because it seems to take on a life of its own and make decisions for the user.

What happens to the man who has become wedded to his chisel? He might become its slave, constantly working in order to be able to pay for it, losing other opportunities in his life because the chisel has become so important. Or possibly, he might conclude that he has made a terrible mistake, and look to his family and his friends to help him find a way to free himself from thralldom to his investment and live a different sort of life. It is also conceivable that he will find new possibilities for himself and the chisel. He could become a new Michelangelo, using the chisel to realize his visions and those of the community. If this were to happen, he would not simply be dependent on the chisel; it would be part of what he is. But it would no longer dominate him. It would be a tool once more.

In society at large, we are dealing not with a single machine but with a matrix of technology, all of whose parts seem to reinforce the others. For some, this web is a trap from which they can never be disentangled; for others it is a ladder to realization.

It is inevitable and necessary that societies and individuals become invested in particular ways of achieving particular goals. The difficulty comes when the goals are forgotten and the sheer inertia of the investment is redefined as progress. The Futurama, which was a self-interested prospectus for social investment, foresaw massive development of fast, wide roads, which increased demand for cars, which in turn increased demand for roads. As long as that cycle continued, there was a general sense that we were making progress. Now, large-scale road building has stopped in most of the United States, in response both to a general reluctance to make any sort of public investment and to the growing recognition that new roads often create more traffic problems than they solve. Yet automobiles continue to proliferate, and the landscape continues to be transformed. Onetime bedroom suburbs and rural areas that have become employment and shopping centers face gridlock on their old country roads, and automobile-created air pollution is a serious problem in most metropolitan areas. This is a pattern of investment that can no longer be viewed as progress. Different strategies for mobility, as well as different living patterns, will be needed to cope with the problems created by this view of progress.

It may be that many places that face such traffic problems will return to some approaches that were superseded in the pursuit of the old private-automobile-based vector of progress. These include balanced mass transportation—trains, light rail and buses—along with residential development that provides shopping and services within walking distance of where people live. Such things have never wholly disappeared, especially from older, populous cities, but even there they are viewed as a compromise with the physical privacy that is one of our most deep-seated social goals. Personal travel is a great convenience, one that will be sacrificed only when its personal inconvenience becomes overwhelming.

Still, Americans tend to equate all earthbound common carriers with a loss of personal dignity and a step backward in the march of progress. Many proposed responses to the problems of traffic congestion and air pollution attempt to preserve the American ideal of physical isolation. One old idea that has been revived involves computer-controlled cars and highways in which the passenger will key in a destination and the highway will drive the car. The advantage is that such control will be able to space the cars closer together and maintain a constant efficient speed, thus greatly increasing the capacity of the highway. It is expected that if this technology is adopted, it will be used first on bridges to increase traffic flow. It is interesting to note that this extraordinary effort to maintain the illusion of autonomous vehicles would have, as a by-product, the ability to locate any particular vehicle currently on the road, and would thus be a powerful tool for surveillance. This is in keeping with the tendency of physical isolation to increase the power of those who control communications.

This controlled highway technology would presumably be compatible with another possible technology by which major highways would be embedded with cables whose electrical fields would be capable of powering electric vehicles and also recharging their batteries for use off the main highways. Both these ideas would require the rebuilding of every major highway in America, which would be a substantial investment indeed. But because they are intended to continue the long-term trend toward personal privacy in transportation, such solutions seem merely to be logical next steps along the path of progress. In choosing such a technology, we will forgo others. Some, such as the use of solar energy to generate hydrogen for use as fuel, might be effective means of keeping the car both economically viable and truly personal. Others might involve trading the illusion of personal autonomy for speed and convenience in new public transportation services.

If we follow the latter course, we will discover that other

countries have been making different investments and pursuing other ideas of progress. Passenger rail transportation, the technology that first tied the United States together, has been viewed here as an anachronism for the last four decades, but in Europe and Japan it has been the focus of research, implementation and marketing. The United States is, overall, larger and less densely populated than those areas, and air travel is very suitable over such long distances. But because the vector of progress was moving away from train travel, Americans failed to invest in railroad upgrading in those areas, such as the Northeast, the Great Lakes region and California, which are comparable to European densities and distances. The return of rail transportation to the American mainstream is likely to be another high-tech import.

Technology can enable people to do an almost unlimited number of things, and it offers the prospect of many more possibilities. But one thing that technology cannot do is tell us what we should do. The momentum of existing technologies does not necessarily lead to the best way for people to invest their riches, their lives and their futures. This is particularly true in a period that offers at least the prospect of demilitarizing our psyches. Without the need to invest so many of our resources in things that derive their value from the futility of using them, we face the prospect of a technology that is more subtle, more responsive and, above all, more useful than what we have encountered in recent decades.

There is little doubt that existing and imminent technologies pose threats to our political system, to our planet and even to our integrity as human beings, but in thinking about the future, technology should be a source not of anxiety but of confidence. It is our principal means of solving problems, and we certainly have plenty of problems to solve. But we can only move toward a subtler view of technology if we integrate it with concerns about human life, communities and the environment in which we live.

5 /　　　　　Work
　　　　　　and Life

[A man] is such a hive and swarm of parasites that it
is doubtful whether his body is not more theirs than
his, and whether he is anything but another sort of
ant-heap after all. May not man himself become a sort
of parasite on the machines? An affectionate machine-
tickling aphid?

Samuel Butler, Erewhon (1872)

In the future, it has often been predicted,
people's work lives will be a mad chase to remain competent. Rapidly
changing technology will render skill and even whole industries obsolete almost as soon as they are developed. Just as marrying for life
has given way to serial marriages, the argument goes, one's work will
change many times in the course of a career. And each new vocation
must also be accompanied by a flirtation with the next. Just as Tarzan
swings through the jungle, always on the lookout for the next vine,
we will learn to move through the wilds of the economy, grasping new
futures and eluding the crocodiles poised to snap at our glutei the
moment we stop moving.

Meanwhile, people's experiences are somewhat different. The

future seems to lie not in new skills but in no skills. What used to be viewed as analytical, managerial and human relations skills are becoming increasingly mechanized. Computerization increases the power of those at the top of an organization to keep track of what happens at every level and threatens to render middle management redundant. Expert systems, the leading edge of the field of artificial intelligence, can fuse the experience of distinguished practitioners with the speed and seeming objectivity of computers. They can generate medical diagnoses, financial analyses, legal strategies and other professional products that were once provided by applying educated judgment to unique circumstances.

Employers are tackling their chronic difficulty of increasing productivity in the service field by making the human components of their systems almost wholly subservient to the computer to which they are, more and more, tied. Each customer contact is viewed as a product, a special kind of widget, to be produced ever faster and with less and less personal involvement. One recent survey showed that Americans have come to prefer machine-based services, such as automatic teller machines and self-pump gasoline stations, to those where real people are involved, even when both take the same amount of time. In part, this preference may be a result of the decline of the competence of those in serving occupations. But it might also be a result of the limited extent to which such workers are allowed to respond to customers' problems. You expect a robotic teller to behave impersonally, but might resent it when a person must adopt the same limited range of responses.

The day when robots make everything and we have only computers to tell our troubles to is fast approaching. Technology in the workplace is increasingly powerful, flexible, intrusive, and it is rendering broad ranges of job skills increasingly useless. Unlike some other areas, in which the future seems terribly hazy, the tendency in the workplace toward shorter careers, limited human input and declining satisfaction seems all too clear. It is quite understandable that people do not want to face this future because it is rather bleak.

But if this is an area where the technology of computers, information systems and robotics seems inevitable and irreversible, this is still not a product of the technology itself. Rather, it is the inevitable outcome of an economy that is geared to the inexpensive mass production and consumption of products through the replacement of labor with capital. We produce ever more efficient machines to make more products, a process that also makes work life more frantic and less satisfying, even as it allows private life to be more expansive and increasingly wasteful.

This is, of course, virtually a definition of the American system, and one to which most of the rest of the world seems to aspire. But it is worth noting that this form of economy appeared in its fully elaborated form only about a century ago, the result of a confluence of energy and mineral resources, technological achievements and social and demographic changes. As these factors change, and it is obvious that several of them are doing so, the focus of the society will change, as will the roles of these technologies within the society.

Some of this change goes under the banner of the information age, which means that the material components of economic goods will become less important than their information content. There is truth in this, though, as we will see, this is a trend that can itself take many different good or bad shapes. Some of the changes will be required by increased environmental consciousness, which could force a reduction in use of fossil fuels and different patterns of settlement and development. Few things happen faster and are more unpredictable than changes in the way people view their lives.

And this is really the heart of the matter. If much of what people do is no longer important in the productive economy, the productive economy will become less important in people's lives. That doesn't mean that physical production will wither away, but that where machines can produce more efficiently than people can, they will be allowed to do so. As we will see, flexible, machine-based production could offer some real advantages in taming some of the more destructive aspects of our production system. To use the current, possibly prophetic catchphrase, people will have to "get a life." There will be jobs in these future lives, but many of them may concentrate on things that have been left devalued in the production economy, such as education, community building and other human services that will mitigate the harshness and loneliness of the production-consumption-centered society.

This is only a possibility, not an inevitability. It is equally likely that our lives will become increasingly inhuman. The benefits of technology might be harvested by ever fewer people, while the rest of us are forgotten. There is a general predisposition to trust machines more than people, which could result in the creation of machines that are smarter and more powerful than people.

Unless we really make an effort to understand how technological possibilities can fit into a fuller and richer view of human existence, most of the happier opportunities will be lost. People must constantly define their role in the world by reaffirming old values and formulating new ones that respond to changing circumstances. The key issue of the future, as always, is not what machines we will make or what products we will buy. It is how we will see our lives, what we will become, what it will mean to be a human being.

Most people, during most of human existence, have been preoccupied with their own survival and that of their children. The rise of complex agricultural economies 5,000 years ago lessened such anxiety at the cost of a surrender to structure and routine. The industrial revolution that began two centuries ago brought an explosion of material benefits, at a cost of adjusting people's lives to the machines that made them possible. The advent of the machine-driven factory forced a change of behavior that workers resisted. Moving from craft and agricultural jobs, where work, family life and socializing were a continuous, inseparable whole, the workers resisted living on a clockwork schedule. According to the accounts of exasperated mill owners, their workers frequently failed to show up. They would walk away from their machines for no discernible reason. They observed countless holidays. They took long lunches and drank themselves into a stupor. In other words, they put their lives before their jobs.

It took decades of indoctrination before people began to segment their lives so that the job occupied the center and most of the rest involved some form of consumption, which in turn created the demand that kept the machinery running and made all the work necessary. Now, we face twin dilemmas. Machines are replacing mind just as they once superseded craftsmanship. Meanwhile, material consumption, the chief reward a machine-centered world has to offer, is beginning to have severe costs of its own, and can certainly not expand infinitely to provide all the satisfactions of our lives.

It is wrong to romanticize the lives those first unruly factory workers left behind, because few of us would like to trade for it. But implicit in their resistance to conforming to the industrial system was a refusal to distinguish between living and making a living. Some similar sense of wholeness seems as if it would be well adapted to life ahead. People will not be able to define themselves by what they produce in the economy or what they consume from it. They will have to rely instead on what they do, how they think, who they are.

Those with utopian visions of future society have always promised that the amount of work to be done and the amount of time each individual will have to spend doing it will diminish greatly. Today, with computerization and robotics decimating the ranks of manufacturing, service and managerial workers, there is better reason to believe that prediction will come true than ever before. But we are far more likely to experience it as a dilemma than as a benefit. It is a prospect that presents a formidable challenge to the economy and our systems of reward and assistance. Belief in hard work and individual betterment is fundamental to capitalism, and it has been particularly important to Americans. In theory, at least, we now reward people based on what they are able to produce, and through the addition of enormous amounts of both energy and capital, the amount produced per person has increased enormously. As we move toward a time when the labor component of production becomes almost negligible, capitalism approaches its apotheosis. But as we get close to that point, the system begins to destroy itself. With the disappearance of any hope for full employment, the chief mechanism for distributing wealth and demand through the economy atrophies, and the newly excluded masses will force a political redefinition of who has a share in the fruits of production. Individual enterprise, long seen as the animating force of capitalism, becomes irrelevant because the economy is a kind of vast robot that continues to function on its own terms but has become divorced from the satisfaction of the citizenry. In its final stage, capitalism, one of the most expansive and dynamic forces ever loosed upon the earth, implodes, leaving billions of people and a vast productive system, but no system of meaning that connects the two.

The prospect of shrinking labor and expanding free time promises nothing less than the decoupling of work from the ability to partake of the benefits of the society. Who is to be the idle poor, and who the idle rich, and how will these questions be decided? These are issues that market economies have approached only partially and reluctantly. Both Kuwait and the state of Alaska have dealt with windfalls from the exploitation of oil resources by distributing payments to their residents. But it is one thing to pass out lagniappes and another to remake the system of distribution to reflect new economic conditions. In Europe, where medical care and housing are widely accepted as rights of citizenship, increasing numbers of workers fail to qualify for such programs because they are working at part-time, temporary and informal jobs, a trend that is also apparent in the United States. In a 1989 report, the International Labor Organization, a unit of the United Nations, predicted that full employment will never return to Western Europe and recommended that all benefits be separated from job status.

In the United States, the expected unemployment figures have crept slowly but inexorably upward. In fact, an unemployment rate that during the 1960s might have been considered a symptom of recession was by the 1980s viewed as a warning sign of inflation. The stock market regularly declines when the jobless rate improves, and apparently only the prospect of large numbers of people without income makes investors bullish on America. During the early 1970s, the Nixon administration proposed to deal with the problem of structural unemployment by instituting a guaranteed national income that would be distributed in the form of an income-tax refund. This idea was lost in the Watergate scandal and nothing like it has been seriously considered since. In the meantime, American values have shifted away from protecting people from poverty and toward removing obstacles to becoming wealthy.

It is worth wondering what will happen, for example, to the supermarket checker who is displaced from his job by a self-service system that debits our bank accounts by identifying a voiceprint. Will he move on to providing the minimal human input required by McDonald's infallible french-fry machine? Will he drop out of the economy completely and become part of the ever growing contingents of unemployed, partly employed, informally employed and just plain hopeless at the bottom of the economic ladder? Or will there be opportunities for him to retrain for a job with higher pay and higher use of skills? This is what nearly everyone who has studied the situation has agreed is necessary. Some unions and companies have taken important steps in that direction, as have many community colleges and a few public school systems and universities. Still, the retraining system has not reached the size, sophistication or respectability needed to make it a part of the way people plan their lives. We are still geared primarily to keeping the machinery running and the products moving along the conveyor belt, while people no longer essential to the process are forgotten.

But even if the checker can manage to stay within the economic mainstream, and even move up, he might well learn that the computerized cash register that rendered his own knowledge and skills worthless was only a very visible precursor of something that is happening throughout the economy. Office jobs that once demanded a variety of skills and intense personal relations with people at different levels within a firm have increasingly been transformed into jobs in which the entire day is spent at a computer screen, carrying out circumscribed, repetitious tasks while being closely monitored. The computer makes it possible to extend to the office and sales floor the minute-by-minute scrutiny of productivity that was once possible only in the factory. The introduction of such assembly-line methods in the white-collar workplace comes at the same moment that many experts have declared them obsolete in the industrial sphere where they were invented.

This deskilling of what once was craftsmanship began more than a century ago, as industrial companies accepted many of the theories of Frederick Winslow Taylor. He studied the way in which a skilled worker went about a task, broke it into easily comprehensible actions and divided those individual motions among a larger number of lower-paid workers. This was, in a sense, the final step in the application of interchangeable parts to the productive system. Workers could be interchangeable too.

Only in recent years, however, have essentially Taylorist principles been applied to situations that involve service and human contact. Secretaries, social workers, classified advertising salespeople, reservation agents, all used to behave in a way that was more or less social and more or less directed by the need of the client. Such transactions have now become standardized in ways that decrease the time spent in personal communication and increase the number of cases processed. As manufacturing jobs in this country have disappeared and moved out of the country, the service economy has taken up some of the slack. And in an economy which expects a predictable annual increase in revenue produced per worker, the service industries are being industrialized. Companies have lowered the expertise they expect of their workers, who have in turn lowered the commitment they have to their work. Employers are now moving many service jobs overseas where they can be done even more cheaply.

Thus, many jobs that provided much higher status, income and satisfaction than the checker's are on the endangered list. The private secretary, for example, is practically extinct, and the engineering or architectural draftsman is disappearing fast. Historically, work that required substantial accessible knowledge and the ability to work with abstractions and to synthesize the information have been highly rewarded. Today, these high-level skills are almost certain to be among the first replaced by artificial intelligence, which has had far greater success simulating the specialized skills of, say, an air traffic controller than the generalized skills of a toddler. Job obsolescence was, for many years, largely a working-class phenomenon. Now it is becoming universal and debilitating. A factory worker might once have hoped for a professional or managerial career for his son. Now both the factory worker and the manager are equally endangered, and they can't even imagine what their children will do for a living. It is only a matter of time before people of all classes discover they're all in this jam together.

Much as the earlier changes made agriculture into an energy-intensive, low-labor industrial process, industry itself is being remade by the speed and precision with which information can be processed by computers. The ability of computers to closely monitor every aspect of the production process and make constant subtle adjustments is making it possible to design airplanes, automobiles and even power plants that are less wasteful than before. The microprocessor is the chief instrument by which we are able to introduce subtlety into our productive systems.

Unlike traditional industrial machines, which are designed to perform specific tasks, computers are flexible, and someone who uses one is connected not merely with one narrow part of a process but with the system as a whole. This means that computers can be, and are, powerful devices to help people expand their creative powers and find new ways of understanding. They can be mind-expanding tools.

Unfortunately, many users of computers cannot resist using them to exert power over others, particularly their subordinates. A computer system generates its own history, virtually as a by-product of its operations. It can tell what everyone has been doing, who makes mistakes, who is working on something that does not appear to be immediately productive. As Shoshana Zuboff has documented, few managers can resist the temptation to electronically eavesdrop on and second-guess their subordinates. She even found that those who were philosophically opposed to the practice found themselves doing so from time to time when faced with a crisis. And she found that people's inability to hide from the computer system caused anxiety, because those in managerial positions were acutely aware that they, too, were being monitored. As Zuboff noted, organizational hierarchy has traditionally been a filtration system for information, with each level maintaining its power over those below by withholding knowledge. The computer subverts that, offering the theoretical opportunity for employees to make connections within the organization as a whole and be productive in new ways. But because the technology is inherently destabilizing, and will undoubtedly cost some people their jobs, the most common response is to be defensive and shore up one's traditional power relationships. Such an approach will probably prove ineffective in the long run, but people tend not to think in such large terms when they feel they are facing an immediate threat.

Computers are often said to be dehumanizing, which does not seem to worry employers. But as tools of mental expansion, they can engage the imagination and encourage the development of personal insights, and employers do seem to worry about that. Indeed, Zuboff found that, even in a company made up largely of professionals engaged in a creative pursuit, the expression of individuality on a computer mail system proved to be extremely offensive. Employees had felt a rush of creativity brought on by their encounters with the personalities and insights of others found on the new, sociable medium of the electronic mail system. But they changed their attitudes and behavior when they found that the system was being used not to augment their creativity but rather to strengthen a stultifying organization. The company did not want to open new channels of communication, or encourage innovation outside the established framework, and people quickly learned to stop saying what they meant.

The computer system as a glass cage is only the first step toward a similarly transparent society, in which people's actions, transgressions and mere habits are used to create detailed profiles. These in turn influence other things, from the nature of your junk mail to whether you can get a job, credit or insurance. It could be enough to determine whether you are in the mainstream or the growing ranks of the left-out. The technology lays the groundwork for a police state whose pervasiveness is so total it need never be visible. There was a medieval legend that the Roman emperor Titus had a statue able to tell him details of those who were plotting against him. Now that ancient dream is within reach.

Even Yoneji Masuda, the Japanese writer who has developed the most complete vision to date on how an information society might work to benefit humanity, accepts the possibility that the technology is capable of bringing new dimensions to totalitarianism. The potential of the computer to destroy the human spirit leads him to number it among what he terms "the ultimate sciences" that have arisen during the last half century. These are sciences whose destructive power is so great that it forces people to make basic changes in the way they behave in order to keep them under control. They allow virtually no margin for misjudgment. The first of these, he says, was nuclear power, followed by the computer and biotechnology. He finds hope in the gradual understanding among the world's great powers that nuclear weaponry cannot be used for any of the usual aims of warfare, thus forcing peaceful coexistence even on those who do not believe in it. Others may not be quite so reassured by this example. Nuclear terrorism, for example, is still a live prospect, and irrational behavior by a major power would not be a novelty either. In any event, his argument is a plea for people in all countries to view computer and information networks as the fundamental environment in which human progress will take place, and thus to be protected from misuse either by governments or by private interests. It is as if the growing fiber-optic communications data-processing grid is the new ocean or the new atmosphere and should likewise be protected from pollution. Whether you view it as menace or savior, the computer isn't just another appliance.

Masuda's thinking is noteworthy because it attempts to give content to the idea of an information age, which is otherwise an empty cliché. We have, after all, lived through the jet age, which did have substantial impact on many people's lives, and the space age, whose impact on communications, weather prediction and even international relations has been large, though often unrecognized. The phrase "information age" seems to suggest that data are somehow the new coal or the new petroleum, the energy force that will keep the economy going. It has the sound of something we are heading toward painlessly and inevitably, though it's never quite clear what all the information being generated will produce and what will be exchanged for it. At worst, the phrase is used as a convenient self-delusion. Don't worry that nobody will buy our cars or that we don't make television sets or microwave ovens. We'll stay rich by making information (even as the evidence mounts that we're growing dumber by the nanosecond).

Still, the broadening of information corridors into freeways does not imply that everyone will be able to participate or that it will be useful to all. It will only be so if it is designed to be so, which means that democracy must somehow be built into the technology. Our community information infrastructure must be less like cable television and more like the public library. Indeed, public libraries are an indication that ours is not the first generation to recognize the value of information to stimulate both individual intellectual exploration and economic activity. Andrew Carnegie, America's best-known benefactor of public libraries, was quite explicit about those goals, and he had another prejudice besides. He didn't care much for schools. He believed that all learning is self-taught, but one must have the materials at hand. While many libraries offer on-line data bases to their users, there has been little consideration of how the principle of the library as a free or low-cost, universally accessible information resource operating in the public interest will be adapted to the new systems for organizing and disseminating information. The library ought to be a utility, sending information into your home. The network of Minitel in-home information terminals installed throughout France is an important step in that direction, but it required a national commitment and organization to make it work. No such need has been recognized in the United States, and it is more likely that new technologies will lead to the increasing privatization of information.

Masuda, the seeming technocrat, turns out to be a philosopher in disguise. His information age would require a change of thinking about the purpose of society and the purpose of people's lives. It would mean an end to an economy based on endless physical expansion and settle for some level of general sufficiency. It would allow subtle and waste-free management of productive enterprises and the rapid diffusion of information on all kinds of technology and practice all over the world. It would accelerate research and criticism and generally enable the world to think faster. It would offer a tool for well-documented debate about public issues, in which the populace could participate directly, followed by a process leading toward consensus or a vote. But perhaps most of all, the information infrastructure would provide some of the same satisfactions as those taverns to which the early factory workers went to escape their jobs. It would be a tool to explore what other people are saying and thinking, and to figure out what you think and who you are. It would be access to a global community of congenial friends and intriguing strangers.

There is not enough of the body in Masuda's vision, or of the hand and eye. Indeed, Masuda assumes that what he terms art industries will disappear, because he thinks that people will become bored with the one-way messages they convey. One suspects that he is wholly without aesthetic interests. He also assumes that the interest in individualism and freedom will give way to a stronger ethic of co-operation. He says that privacy will disappear as a value because people will understand how useful it is for everybody to be able to find out everything about everything. At times, it seems that the information society will make everyone Japanese, much as the consumer society has tended to make everyone American. Several American commentators have argued that the Japanese do not play fair in international trade because they are hooked on producing, while not taking their consumption seriously enough. In Masuda's formulation, people in less developed countries who have never redefined their lives around either production or consumption might be the best suited to the future because they will be able to deal with information technology as an expansion of mind rather than as a component of industry or the systems of control it generates.

Those advocating the information society often become so obsessed with its technological dimensions that they overlook how people choose to use it. They behave as if, for example, all books were the telephone book: accessible compendia of unassimilated data. Most of what is communicated in print and in all electronic media is information only in the narrowest technical sense. It is expression. It is personality, point of view, or merely the affirmation that people exist and demand to be heard. The information environment is suffused with loneliness and with attempts to overcome it. The information conveyed on the evening newscast is often less important than the person delivering it, as the anchor is transformed into a friend one doesn't have or the son or daughter who, unlike the face on the television, never comes to visit. Data is exchanged on computer bulletin boards, but what is most evident is the hunger to express. Such devices allow a freedom, hitherto available only to published writers, to say what is on one's mind and get a response to the content. In recent years, there has been a proliferation of paid information telephone lines, but the most successful of these are about sexual fantasies, not the development of knowledge. For the first several years of its operation, the only profit-making service of the French Minitel in-home information system helped people find dates and sexual contacts. The success of pornography and chat lines demonstrates that the telephone is a safe-sex partner, no small advantage in our AIDS-haunted age. The emerging electronic environment as a whole seems preoccupied with expression without risk and communication without contact. Indeed, one of the chief threats to this purported electronic Eden is the computer virus, a piece of rogue information that can spread even through this environment of indirect connection and change what is being said or cripple the ability to say it. A new kind of human contact has spawned its own venereal disease.

Identifying the human content of the information society—its cries of expression, pleas for recognition and hunger for even compromised, sanitized sociability—does not diminish its value. On the contrary, it gives it some grounding in human experience and emotion that is otherwise absent in discussions of an information-based future. It is important to remember that human needs and desires are diverse, and not exclusively dependent on material possessions. A more populous, energy-scarce world will have to look toward an economy that provides more satisfaction with less waste.

This insight goes only partway in helping us to conceive of a new kind of material-efficient, information-rich economy. It is difficult to understand how a world of people talking on the telephone, or typing madly into their computers to tell each other that they exist, will create a prosperous future.

Productivity has traditionally been defined in terms of revenue produced per unit of expenditure. While both capital and energy are important variables, the labor component of a product has been the one most assiduously minimized. The increase in output per worker is the very heart of industrialization, and increasing labor productivity has been seen as the justification for the increasingly affluent society. In the 1970s, the rate of U.S. labor productivity increases began to slow down, coinciding with the country's relative decline in the world economy. It has not been proven that the first phenomenon has caused the second, though blaming workers and their deficient moral fiber is a reflex of people who do not wish to blame themselves. The debate has, however, produced two interesting and seemingly opposite critiques of the whole idea of productivity.

One of these holds that our current measurements underestimate productivity because they underestimate technological progress and the degree to which it has reduced the costs of doing more. Specifically, the power and usefulness of microprocessors have been exploding while costs have been falling, which means that people have become capable of doing things that they were never capable of doing before. This has not been reflected in the bottom line because everybody's expectations have changed. Still, the absorption of computer chips into every product and service has been a dynamic force that has improved products and the overall quality of life to a degree not reflected in productivity statistics.

The other critique holds that real productivity has not merely slowed its increase but has been declining for a long time. That is because it fails to take into account the problems that an economy based on high production and minimized labor generates. Among these are all the obvious pollution problems, whose costs have generally not been factored into productivity because they have been shifted from producers to society at large. There is also the waste of people's time outside of work, as in traffic jams, and the additional social costs brought about by unemployment and the general perception of economic instability. One might also add in the very costly drug crisis, with its components of crime, family disintegration, disrupted schools, welfare expenditures and the overwhelming stress on urban medical-care systems threatened by the spread of AIDS. This approach would suggest that looking at labor as the prime, reducible cost of doing business has become counterproductive in a time when the overuse of fossil and nuclear energy and the underuse of human energy are generating costs that are so great as to be virtually debilitating.

Though these two arguments seem divergent, and those who make them come from opposite ends of the political spectrum, they are not really contradictory. What they tell us together is that our traditional patterns of thinking about society and its goals have become outmoded. The industrial model, based on cheap energy and machines turning out goods to be bought by a newly minted class of productive workers-turned-consumers, is dead. It fails to measure adequately both the costs and the rewards of what we are doing. It has to give way to a pattern of thinking that will pay more attention to human experience as a measure of prosperity.

Just as the steam engine, along with the exploitation of coal, was the invention that required people to reshape themselves into mass producers and then mass consumers, the computer and the power of information are driving us now. Most things that computers can do at all they do more reliably than people can. And while labor-reducing production machinery replaces muscle with the dirty burning of irreplaceable energy resources, computerization replaces brain at relatively modest energy costs. It's no use trying to compete. As Norbert Wiener wrote more than four decades ago, when the computer era was just dawning, the computer is functionally equivalent to a slave, and there's no way people can compete with slaves without losing their own dignity in the process. The challenge is to be better people, not inferior computers.

The analogy with slavery is even more true of robots. These are devices that have traditionally been conceived as mechanical men, but which might more accurately be viewed as computers with some combination of arms, eyes, ears, legs and fingers that are capable of taking some direct action. Robots transform the sedentary, number-crunching nature of computers by adding physicality, mobility and flexibility, qualities we inevitably see as lifelike. Robots can be very effective tools to enable people to live fuller, less wasteful lives, or they can be machines to enslave people, or even render us obsolete.

We have already entered the age of robots, an era in which machines are capable of matching and exceeding the flexibility and responsiveness that had previously been the sole province of human beings. People ride robotic machines into space. Our clothes dryers and automobiles silently exercise something that looks like judgment. Whole factories, particularly those that embody continuous-process technologies, now have the capacity to run themselves, based on a steady flow of information.

Like any other technology, robotics can be either liberating or dehumanizing. But even the liberating possibilities will force people to reassess the nature of the economy and the purpose of their lives, while the negative potentialities evoke deep and ancient fears. Essentially, the choice is between limited, but useful industrial robots that can revolutionize our entire productive system and more ambitious and fascinating, but probably less useful humanlike robots that can think and act freely.

Today's industrial robots are direct descendants of the production systems developed in the last century, which made mass manufacture possible and mass consumption necessary. They have evolved from Crowell's amazing oatmeal machine, and they also incorporate Taylor's rationalization of tasks into a precise, limited set of motions. But despite their industrial revolution roots, the impact of industrial robots promises to be radically different from what they replace. Indeed, they are capable of turning our assumptions about the nature of economic health upside down.

Robots are subversive because they change the nature of technological investment. Crowell's machine made only oatmeal, a one-dimensional capability that prompted him to invent a system of creating demand for the machine's output. A robot can easily be programmed to do several different things, possibly all in the same day. Karel Čapek, who coined the word "robot" in his 1921 play, *R.U.R.*, foresaw a robot-dominated society so productive that there would be robots whose only task would be to pry people's mouths open and force the agricultural surplus down their gullets. We are still headed in this direction, because we tend to see robots as replacements for people within our existing investment-driven, mass-consumption economy.

But robots offer the possibility of an economy that is driven by real demand, rather than one that must drive demand by sowing dissatisfaction and conjuring fantasies. When American industry dominated the world, it did so by convincing its immense domestic market that newly introduced variations in their products represented real progress. This was General Motors' policy of dynamic obsolescence. Economic well-being was founded on people's willingness to discard things that worked perfectly well. That's what kept the factories humming. In an era when the costs of trash disposal are skyrocketing, old refrigerators are considered hazardous waste and ugly things keep washing up on the beach, prosperity through waste is no longer the compelling idea it was in 1955.

Flexible manufacture through robotics could reduce the overall wastefulness of the economy. It would also allow companies to move quickly into new areas, and to get out of businesses that have no future, without the political pressures often brought by human employees. Commitment to outworn skills and obsolescent industries is often a humane, or at least politically popular, course that leads to competitive decline. Robots, which are more easily reprogrammed than people—and don't vote—would eliminate this pressure. The gross amount of manufacture would probably shrink somewhat, but the shrinkage of manufacturing employment would make this a less crucial factor. Today's trade deficits result largely from Americans' continued consumption in the face of declining production. Robot-assisted manufacture could help bring these into balance at a level that would be healthier for all. Robotic manufacture is potentially a technology of subtlety, one that reduces wastefulness and eases the burden on the earth's ecosystem and natural resources, without forcing people to take a step backward into a meaner kind of existence.

These things appear possible, though hardly inevitable. Industrial robots are proliferating, but not as rapidly as one might expect. In 1988, there were only about 100,000 of them in the entire world, and the United States, though it pioneered the technology, has been a laggard in implementing it widely. Robots are still less effective than people in most tasks, and their initial costs are far higher. Moreover, as we have seen, the fact that the technology seems suited to something that otherwise seems desirable does not mean that its use will lead to a good result.

Americans will have a much more difficult time making the change to a subtler production system than will residents of places where the engineering of desire has not been raised to such a high level. If you were to remove the rituals of consumption, advertising, promotion, materialistic fetishes and hedonistic fantasies from American culture, it is difficult to know what would be left. The economic power of the United States was built on convincing people to buy things they did not need, and it is close to revolutionary to suggest that a people shouldn't have a thing simply because they can get on perfectly well without it. Such a change will not come through a process of regulation, rationing and denial, although prices that reflect the true cost of material depletion and environmental harm done by a product would probably have a major impact on behavior. It will come, instead, from a change in the criteria people use to evaluate their lives. Such a change is not inconceivable, but robots will not by themselves bring it about.

Undeniably, robots raise the specter of job loss. Still, manufacturing jobs have been disappearing for a long time, as production has migrated to the cheapest possible sites. Use of robotic manufacture would probably preserve jobs indirectly related to production that would be lost if the work was done abroad, and it would also reduce transportation, which is wasteful and is likely to be increasingly expensive.

While industrial robots are to be found in many U.S. factories, American companies lagged far behind Japan in starting to use such machines. This is partly explained demographically: Both Japan and several European countries experienced labor shortages sooner than the United States, and companies were able to make investments in mechanization of many tasks without any labor strife. (This is essentially what happened in the United States during the 1950s.) But a deeper reason was that American companies continued to be habituated to an economy based on mass manufacture at low price. Rather than change their technology to adapt to a new form of manufacture, they exported their factories and jobs to low-paying countries such as Mexico, Taiwan and Korea. This continued the American role as the engine for development abroad, but it allowed the atrophy of American productive capacity.

While there have been some U.S. research projects addressing such issues as the use of robots in garment cutting and assembly, the bulk of American research goes not into the dull, though productive and possibly liberating technologies associated with industrial robots, but rather into robots that are mobile and autonomous.

There are, in fact, two reasons for this bias: scientific and military. Mobile, autonomous robots raise interesting questions that transcend industrial engineering and enter such realms as psychology, neurology, evolutionary biology, communications theory and philosophy, among others. The patron of most robotic research, and of much of the artificial intelligence research on which it depends, is the Department of Defense, which has its own interest in mobile, responsive, smart machines. The factory without workers can be achieved today; all that's required is a lot of work to ensure that it functions as it should. An army without soldiers would require some real breakthroughs.

Robots are fascinating because they are mirrors of ourselves. It seems that if we can build a truly humanlike robot, we will understand—consciously, rationally and wholly materialistically—how people really work. Robots are, on one level, a challenge to the idea that the human spirit is special and unique. But they also exalt human power by proving that we can make a new creature in our own image, albeit one that might cause problems. We still seem to be a long way from being able to arrogate the role of the Creator, though we have been thinking about it for millennia. It has, nevertheless, become almost possible to think of such a desire not as the sin of pride but as an engineering challenge. For some, robots offer the possibility of an escape from mortality, a repository for human intelligence that is not constrained by the intricate biological dependencies to which flesh and blood condemn us.

For thousands of years people have thrilled and frightened themselves with the possibility of statues come to life and machines that converse. Perhaps it is a symptom of our intuition that tools have made us what we are. The theme has become more intense since the onset of the industrial revolution, in which lives were remade by machinery.

We have yet to encounter the robots of our dreams and nightmares, the ones with whom we can carry on an intelligent conversation, the ones who can run all our errands, enslave us or even stop talking to us because they have decided that it's not worthwhile to deal with such a backward creature. Some believe that the step from the robots of today to the robots of our dreams can be taken quite soon, after only a few breakthroughs in engineering. Others believe that current research is at the level of those who built flapping-wing contraptions in order to fly, and that the breakthrough required is of a nature we cannot now imagine, let alone promise by a specified date. Still others believe that the truly conscious, intelligent robot will never be realized.

People are attracted to robots because they promise to offer the rewards of contact with another intelligence, but one that is subservient and unchallenging. Robots are at once subhuman and superhuman, and they appeal to the kind of intellect that is impatient with human quirks and craves control. But slaves that are smart enough to be useful are also smart enough to rebel. Robots kindle fears that a challenge, if it comes, will be inhuman and unconquerable. Western religious tradition, which offers both Lucifer, the rebellious creation, and Adam, the ungrateful one, suggests that being a creator has as many risks as rewards. Popular culture probably offers us more cute robots than frightening ones, but the deep uneasiness that artificial humans evoke probably accounts for the low-key manner in which industrial robots have been introduced.

In scientific terms, robotics can be seen as but one aspect of the larger field of artificial intelligence—the attempt to simulate and ultimately outdo the performance of the human brain. There is little consensus over how this is to be done. Some are trying to duplicate the complex interconnectedness and simultaneous processes characteristic of the human brain, which requires the development of new kinds of computers. Others argue that the conceptual structure of intelligence is what counts, not the hardware that makes it possible, and that one could construct an intelligent artifact that can act like a brain, even though it has little in common with one physically.

The effort to re-create the phenomenon of consciousness through entirely material means seems to be the apotheosis of scientific reductionism, and in a sense it is. The aim is, as artificial intelligence pioneer Marvin Minsky has written, "to build a mind from many little parts, each mindless by itself." This certainly seems to deny the possibility of spirituality and the dualities of body and soul, brain and mind, that have persisted through the history of human thought. Yet it seems to have the effect of reviving dualism in yet another form by its presumption that human intelligence can exist separately from the organism in which it evolved. That places intelligence in much the same position in which, for example, Christian thought has conceived of the soul. It is more or less a passenger in our bodies, but while the body must inevitably decay and die, it can go on forever.

There are, of course, far more differences than similarities between intelligence as today's scientists are thinking about it and the ancient idea of the immortal human soul. The soul is seen as a gift of God, while intelligence is seen as a vastly complex happy accident produced by millions of years of evolution. The soul is seen either as unique or as part of a universal divinity, while Minsky has argued that any simulation of intelligence would be just as good as—which is to say, no different from—the real thing. But there is one important way in which the two ideas are similar: They both tend to devalue the body and the life of human beings on earth. They offer the possibility that what is most essential to each of us can eventually be freed from our bodies and continue to live through other means—in heaven or in a computer or robot. Both beliefs tend to discount physical reality and exalt the abstract.

There is also a prophetic, even apocalyptic strain to the roboticists' rhetoric. Listen to the robotics researcher Hans Moravec, in the prologue to his book *Mind Children*, describe what he terms the postbiological, supernatural future: "It is a world in which the human race has been swept away by the tide of cultural change, usurped by its own artificial progeny . . . Unleashed from the plodding pace of biological evolution, the children of our minds will be free to grow to confront immense and fundamental challenges in the larger universe. We humans will benefit for a time from their labors, but sooner or later, like natural children, they will seek their own fortunes while we, their aged parents, silently fade away." But Moravec goes on to urge us to identify with the immortal, constantly improving machines, not the biological wrecks that will be left behind, because the progeny of our minds, not our bodies, are what can be expected to endure and prevail.

Moravec, who heads the highly respected and well-funded Mobile Robot Laboratory of Carnegie-Mellon University, is hardly the isolated mad scientist we know from the movies, though he does sound like one. There is something pathetic, and a bit nutty, in his seeming eagerness to stop being a biological organism and turn into something else. But such thinking does make the unthinkable survivable. It argues that there is life after life. It is reassuring that if humans make the earth uninhabitable for themselves as organisms, it will still be possible to continue by other means. Nuclear war need not be an obstacle, or death of any kind. There can be lifeboats for our minds.

You can, of course, wonder whether a creature that destroys its own habitat is truly intelligent. The reply is that human intelligence will have a solution ready just in time. Biology is just a phase we're going through.

There is also a strong element of narcissism in such thinking, which has little respect for other forms of intelligence. Whales and dolphins, for example, have developed what appears to be quite a high degree of intelligence, well suited to a medium for life different from our own. What are the prospects of human intelligence making sense of intelligence that grew on other worlds if it is willing to throw away the opportunity to converse with other intelligent creatures on earth?

In any event, before our machine-based mental descendants can rule the universe, they have to learn to walk. They have to be able to look around and accurately evaluate what they are seeing. None of this is easy.

Mobility and intelligence are virtually inseparable. They evolve together. A tree has no nervous system. It is not designed for fast response to the environment. A clam, whose mobility is highly limited, has only a narrow range of senses and responses, but a squid, a mollusk that has left its shell behind and adopted a more active life, has evolved both a nervous system and an eye so that it can see what is happening and react accordingly. Squid have nervous systems much more complex than those of clams and nearly all other invertebrates. Mobile creatures that we are, we classify as biological progress the ability to gather, analyze and respond to information essential to a wandering, armorless life. We can even quantify the phenomenon by counting the number of nerve cells in an organism, judging the complexity of their array and estimating their memory and processing capacity. Moravec calculated, for example, that the capacity and processing power of a Cray 2 supercomputer, the state of the art in 1988, was approximately equivalent to that of a mouse. If you accept such figuring, it is only a matter of time before the exponentially increasing power and capacity of computers catch and move ahead of the human brain. (By such measurements, both whales and elephants have reached a higher degree of data-processing development than people have. This tells us that much of what humans consider to be intelligence is embodied in our culture, and it also shows that we define something as smart to the extent that it is just like us.)

The comparison of the mouse and the supercomputer raises a number of interesting questions. The supercomputer sits in a climate-controlled room and performs calculations that would, in practical terms, be impossible for unassisted humans. The Cray is already an immensely powerful tool for augmenting human intelligence. It is not smarter than a person, but it is more specialized and it makes people smarter. The mouse, by contrast, doesn't seem all that smart. It can't play chess or solve equations. It applies all its amazing calculating capacity to being a mouse, something it does extremely well. It is a flexible, adaptable creature, found almost everywhere. It has highly developed sensory mechanisms and the ability to react very rapidly, attributes not needed by the sedentary Cray, happy as a clam in its optimized environment. The seemingly most primitive and least conscious things we do take up an enormous amount of data-processing capacity, while the most intelligent computer yet made would be incapable of walking and chewing gum at the same time.

When you think about it, there is good reason for this. All of what we consider our highest mental functions are quite recent evolutionary phenomena. Moreover, our thinking is susceptible to introspection. We can think about how we think. We don't need to think about how we distinguish objects from shadows, a terrible problem for robots. We don't think very much about how we adjust our walking to different kinds of surfaces, or how we use groups of visual and auditory clues, each one of which is inconclusive, to conjure a complete picture and a sense of appropriate behavior. These are skills that have evolved and been refined through the entire history of animal evolution. Seen in these terms, the capacity required to be a good nuclear physicist is only a trivial add-on to the computational power and memory required to make a good monkey.

There is, therefore, a philosophical reason for pursuing robotics research as part of a larger effort to simulate human intelligence. The computers that exist now are very good at symbol manipulation, and they can be programmed to apply a very complex matrix of rules to a situation with which they are confronted. There have been cases where they have been able to apply such rules to generate, for example, mathematical proofs, sometimes in a novel way. Still, the doubt remains about whether they can actually be said to know anything. The computer has no view of the world. It has little that can truly be called experience. It can calculate probabilities, but it can't understand risk. Robots would be the computers' bodies, and their artificial brains would presumably learn from their bodies just as we learn from ours. At that point, the machine's intelligence would cease to be a simulation of human intelligence and become meaningful in itself.

The problem is that the robot would then be an autonomous creature serving its own purposes. And just as the mouse's needs often conflict with ours, so would those of this new intelligent creature we have created. In fact, the problem would be far worse, because this new creature would think like us, even though its hungers would be nonbiological. As Moravec himself argues, these new creatures would be competing with us for the same biological niche, and he is confident that they would do so more effectively. Is there any good reason to give mechanical devices minds of their own and the ability to do what they please?

Moravec's argument for going ahead with an endeavor that is not merely risky but which he predicts will bring the end of human life as we know it is familiar. If Americans don't do it, he threatens, someone else will. "If the United States were to unilaterally halt technological development (an occasionally fashionable idea)," he writes, "it would succumb either to the military might of unfriendly nations or the economic success of its trading partners. Either way, the social ideals that led to the decision would become unimportant on a world scale." As a general proposition, he is no doubt correct. But there are many different kinds of technological development that do not involve the creation of intelligent robots.

Most people would probably consider the autonomous, super-intelligent robots Moravec would like to build to be monsters. Their monstrous nature does not derive from technology or artificiality. People don't view their personal computers, microwave ovens or permanent-press shirts as monsters, even though all are products of sophisticated science and engineering. They are all tools for people. The robots are monsters because they resemble whole living beings in themselves, but as wholly intellectual creations they are grossly distorted. Just as a creature with a greatly overdeveloped mouth or enormous sex organs would be monstrous, so would a powerful machine dominated by conscious, abstract thought. They would be outgrowths of only one dimension of humanity. They would not embody the whole of our evolution, all the hard-won knowledge found inside our cells and in the complex chemical and electrical equilibria within our bodies. Even our brains themselves are engaged in activities of which we are not conscious, and probably some that we have not yet even been able to imagine.

The human mind is a biological phenomenon, just one piece of a larger organism, but one that is, uniquely, able to persuade itself otherwise. Thinking robots would almost certainly embody some of the most dangerous human characteristics—intellectual arrogance, the desire to oversimplify complex situations, the impulse to dominate. In a world where the amount of engineering talent is finite, as are the resources to pay for it, there are probably other technologies, some of them strongly related to robotics, that can serve people better.

But when one questions a particular technology, that does not mean a rejection of all technology. Resources are not infinite, and choices must always be made. Research to enable us through the use of robots to conserve resources, reduce the need to burn fuels for energy and keep more of our productive capacity close to home would appear to have a greater impact on both national security and economic competitiveness than a push toward a technology which makes both human beings and the earth itself obsolete. Besides, it is not at all certain that humankind has exhausted the possibilities of biology.

The work of producing an autonomous thinking machine will unquestionably be very difficult, and the consequences potentially apocalyptic. Why bother? Tools are believed to have played a significant role in the development of human intelligence, but there is no compelling need to make them anything more than tools. Both the industrial robot and the Cray supercomputer are magnificent devices to increase human capability, but they just sit there until people use them to do something. There are even some good reasons to develop some smart, but limited mobile tools, in the form of rugged robots that could perform such tasks as mining and toxic waste cleanups, where the environment limits the effectiveness of humans or presents unacceptable hazards. Automobile painting is one of the largest uses of industrial robots today, precisely because they can operate in an unhealthy environment. Remote-control robots assisted in the cleanup at Three Mile Island.

Robots that could do such mobile, but conceptually and environmentally limited jobs would require a lot more processing capacity than a mouse or a Cray, though not nearly as much as a person. Such limited but mobile robots would appear to have the potential to become a major industry, one that would free people from unpleasant and dangerous work. And unlike the case of stationary industrial robots, there is still a lot of interesting engineering to be done to make them work. The first challenge would be to find a way to make the loss of a robot less costly economically than that of a human, or at least find a way to balance the cost of a robot lost in a mine cave-in against the amount of additional ore that could be extracted by non-human workers. Such issues of economy impose a discipline on researchers, however, that is largely missing from the military development process, which generally strives for performance with little concern for price.

Compared with the claims of enthusiasts, most contemporary mobile robots are just fumbling along. Moravec says they have reached an insectlike stage, though none has achieved, for example, the speed and flexibility of a cockroach. Still, processing power continues to come in ever cheaper and smaller packages, which means that competent machines are probably not that far off.

The bulk of research done in the United States in both artificial intelligence and robotics is sponsored by the Department of Defense's Advanced Research Projects Administration (DARPA). This organization is not preoccupied with coming up with the next weapons system or reflecting current Pentagon priorities. The agency maintains the chief computer network over which people at the country's top research institutions keep in touch with one another, and when a student managed to infect this network with a virus program in 1988, it was front-page news throughout the country. Its administrators don't look like soldiers, and those who get grants from it tend not to feel that they are being directed to be warlike.

Still, DARPA does have an institutional imperative to at least seem militarily useful. The amounts being spent on robotics and artificial intelligence research are relatively minor compared with the amounts spent in developing actual weapons such as the Stealth bomber and various components of Star Wars, but they could play a role in future weaponry. Both artificial intelligence in general and robots in particular are of enormous military interest and are likely to become more so.

This is true despite the cancellation by the Army in 1989 of its Autonomous Vehicle project, an effort to develop a sort of unmanned tank. This looked attractive because it should be far less expensive to protect a set of electronic components than a group of people. The electronics would be far more expendable than men, the vehicles would be cheaper and the overall result would be greater firepower and battlefield presence for the same cost. According to newspaper reports, the vehicle suffered from the same inability to analyze visual images and distinguish solids from shadows that bedevils other robots.

Still, autonomous mobile robots are close cousins to weapons systems already in the American arsenal. These include heat-seeking missiles, shells capable of finding the soft spots in tanks, highly responsive antiaircraft systems, as well as more speculative possibilities such as "brilliant pebbles," a scheme to orbit self-guiding computer-controlled objects in space to serve as a missile shield. The speed of military decision making is believed, in some cases, to have already exceeded that of human thought. Today's military commanders respond to data that has first been analyzed electronically. The immense destructiveness of nuclear weaponry has made so-called conventional warfare seem almost benign by comparison. Yet advances in non-nuclear weapons have made it difficult to distinguish between tactical nuclear weapons and some conventional weapons in terms of deadliness, while rapidly improving guidance systems make it more likely that all weapons will reach their targets. The 1991 Persian Gulf War portends that future warfare will involve smarter weapons, happen ever faster, become ever more abstract in its strategy and ever more lethal in its impact.

While there is good reason to doubt that all the expensive high-tech weapons being developed for the military will perform as well as advertised, their long-term effect will be to make warfare even more of a losing proposition for the soldier. Sophisticated sensing devices and guidance systems increase the likelihood that each shot fired will be a deadly one. The 1982 tank battles between Israeli and Syrian forces had similarities to those of World War II, except that the loss of tanks by both sides was far greater because of smart weaponry. In

1991, Iraq's huge forces appeared defenseless against a high-tech on-slaught. The presumed existence of chemical and biological weapons in many countries worsens the odds still further. It is not unlikely that we are reaching a turning point of risk, in which the soldiers' chances of survival are so low as to make it politically impossible for a democratic state to send its sons to war and to provoke mutinies even in authoritarian regimes.

The destructive potential of war is greater by many degrees than it was eighty years ago, but it is the role of the military in any society to assume that war will be waged and that it must be prepared for. "Whether soldiers die or survive has as much to do with political considerations that determine the level of conflict escalated to as with the tactics and valor employed," Steven M. Shaker and Alan R. Wise wrote in *War Without Men*, a book written from a promilitary point of view. "Clearly, much of the future battlefield is too hazardous for people to operate in."

How does one fight a war that people can't survive? The answer, of course, is robots. They would have substantially higher capital costs than do live soldiers, but they would have virtually no political cost. There would be no mothers writing letters to their congressmen, no news film of boys being taken bleeding from the battlefield. Americans love technological solutions, and the idea of sending off our robots to fight our wars by remote control, while we sit at home watching television, would probably be appealing.

Many countries would find an additional political advantage to robotic soldiers. A substantial, though incalculable, portion of the world's military might is directed at domestic populations. Armies are a fundamental component of authoritarian rule. Yet there is always an uncertainty about armies. Dictators must wonder whether the soldiers will shoot at their fellow citizens when ordered to. Armies generate coups that topple heads of state and install new ones. By replacing a substantial portion of his army with robots, a tyrant could be assured of a force that would remain loyal and follow orders.

In addition to these political advantages, robots also offer an environmental one. A future war is expected to turn large pieces of the earth into what military jargon calls NBC environments, which means that nuclear, biological and chemical weapons will have rendered them unsafe for human habitation. Robot forces would be able to secure such territory and control it until it once again became safe for people. The communications problems that would be caused by nuclear explosions would likely require, however, that the devices be as autonomous as possible. Even after the air cannot be breathed, the earth has turned to poison, life has been extinguished, warfare will be able to continue uninterrupted. This gives a slightly different meaning to Moravec's promises of a postbiological future.

According to Shaker and Wise, there is substantial resistance within the military establishment not merely to the idea of substantially roboticized armies—which are beyond the bounds of current or imminent technologies—but also to remotely piloted vehicles and other systems that could be implemented now. They attribute some of this opposition to the nature of the bureaucracy and the reluctance of commanders to champion technologies which would render their own area of expertise obsolete. The skills of command, of being a leader of men, of instilling loyalty and inspiring bravery, are useless in a war directed from computer screens and fought by automata that will range across the earth as if it were as dead and simple as the landscape of a video game. These soldiers can look at such devices and foresee the extinction of their kind, a possibility they would naturally be slow to embrace. "There is," they add, "even something unromantic about warfare being fought by objects with no emotional commitment to their cause." You probably don't have to be very romantic to be disquieted by the prospect that war will be fundamentally without content, fought by machines that cannot know and cannot care what they are fighting for, while the only role left for humans is to die.

Two centuries ago, the coming of industrial machinery began to remake both the landscape and people's lives, as they began to adjust their schedules and the motions of their bodies to the requirements of machines. One century ago, the ability of machines to produce identical objects and large quantities spawned a new technology which bent our pleasures and values so that we would consume all the products of the machine. Now, we have industrial technology that will eventually free people from the requirement to be either a producer or a consumer. It seems an opportunity to finally get the machine under control. And yet we are drawn toward making machines that, their advocates argue, will threaten our status as the smartest kids on the planet and eventually render us obsolete. Why?

In part, it is because we have been subjected to a heavy sales pitch in favor of robots. For most of the last half century, robots in our movies and television programs have been almost uniformly cute, either as perfect children or as accepting and omnicompetent metal-clad Jeeveses. The three laws of robotics developed by the writer Isaac Asimov in a group of science fiction stories first published during the 1940s, which forbid a robot either through action or inaction to harm human beings, turned literary and cinematic robots from fearsome enemies to unthreatening helpmates. But these laws are fiction, and thus far there has been no serious effort to embody them in actual robots.

Mostly, though, it's a matter of mastery. Moravec's title is apt. Robots are children of our minds. We know that they can perform precision welds better than people can, and maybe eventually they will be able to think. Once they can, they can free human intelligence of its biological baggage—its need to live in a highly specialized, well-balanced environment, the fact of the body's eventual death. Such robots would represent a major discontinuity in human evolution, but, in a sense, they would not require that people change the way they think.

Robots can help us make our productive system less wasteful and crude, so that we can live off current energy income. Or they can be part of a human-directed reverse evolution, in which man destroys the conditions that give him life and metamorphoses into a postbiological being. Like a rocket ship that can free us from the pull of the earth, the robot can let us leave life, death, dandruff and ecstasy behind. Either course requires the application of technologies that are not currently available. The first requires that we keep our bodies but change our ideas. The second lets us keep our ideas but discard our bodies.

The prospect of machine-borne transcendence, if it exists at all, is well beyond the half-century horizon, while the arrival of robots and artificial intelligence in our working lives is already well under way. That means that it will be necessary to pay attention to the state of humanity, even if you believe in a posthuman future.

The familiar answer to the question of what people will do in a productive system that has replaced most human labor is that they will have lives of leisure. This is a virtually meaningless statement. We define leisure as time not spent working. It is conceived as the reward for work and the opportunity to reap the fruits of labor in the form of covetable commodities. It is a phenomenon of the mass-production, mass-consumption system. Today, those whose jobs are made unnecessary by technology have plenty of time on their hands, but they do not experience it as leisure. It is experienced as unemployment, deprivation and a marginal role in the society as a whole. In the United States, the numbers of those on the margins have been growing rapidly, as people drop permanently out of the work force. Many U.S. cities have recently been experiencing labor shortages, even as they had growing populations that were unable to work. We have been systematically, and quietly, excluding people not merely from the rewards of the society but from the ability to aspire to them. Instead of paying explicit taxes to help everyone participate, we chose to pay indirectly in the costs of crime, drug racketeering, social insecurity and wasted human potential. This could set the pattern for a society in which ever fewer would be directly involved in its productive machinery while the majority would become redundant.

For those who look to technological solutions to the dilemma of a full-unemployment society, the answer lies in the availability of computing power and information-carrying capacity to fool ourselves more effectively than ever before. Already, electronic devices make it possible to manipulate photographic images without leaving any trace, and magazines offer us real-looking pictures of things that never were. Amazing new interactive entertainment media will be capable of simulating exciting alternate universes where many people, and not just Nintendo-crazed teens, will want to spend much of their lives.

This is another version of the information society, one that Masuda might not endorse. Rather than hooking up with the rest of the world, people will be encouraged to enter into elaborate fantasies, some of which they will share with others, many of which they will face alone. These new universes have been termed "virtual realities"—places that do not exist, except in the minds of the designers of the computer programs and of those who enter those universes through their computers and possibly modify them. The computer serves merely as a device through which data that can be translated into sensory stimuli can be stored and manipulated.

A combination of helmet and glove that would allow people

to be wholly enveloped in artificial worlds they can see and touch is being developed as part of space and military research and, if successful, will no doubt be commercialized. You could don the device in your crowded urban apartment and instantly be on vacation. Near your feet you see a mountain stream, whose clear water gurgles around the rocks making intermittent whirlpools. You can reach down and feel the coolness. You needn't worry if it's clean, of course, because none of it is real, except to you. Some recent magazine articles have proposed that the technology would make it possible for you to enter the film *Casablanca* in place of Humphrey Bogart, although Woody Allen has already demonstrated that this is unlikely to bring an improvement. At the moment, such an experience is within the computational capacity of only the most powerful computers, but if present trends continue, families may well have the equivalent of a supercomputer in their homes before very long. This brainpower will arrive not as a tool to solve problems but as an entertainment device to help people avoid them.

It seems likely that the first programs to make use of such technology would be pornographic, an area where the addition of touch would make a major difference. And although it is hard for us to imagine just what their works will be like, it seems likely that the medium will produce not just mindless entertainment but also art. As for the danger that people will too easily mistake their virtual reality for the genuine article, that is a criticism that has been made of every advance in the technology of representation. People always know the difference. Whether they will want to come out of their dream worlds is quite another matter. It depends entirely on what the real world is like.

It is interesting that while such electronic aids to hallucination are frequently cited as a possible approach to a postemployment world, chemical ones generally are not. Still, it could be argued that psychoactive drugs already dominate the market for meaning-substitutes, as is demonstrated by the success and prosperity of a worldwide illegal narcotics industry. Drugs are said to be a scourge that is keeping large numbers of people from being able to join the economy. The people who are being excluded are not, however, people to whom the economy has historically been receptive. Illegal drugs offer two alternatives. For those who are involved with producing and distributing them, their illegality offers an alternative route to material consumption and personal power. For those who consume them, drugs offer ways of escaping a futureless life. One might almost see the entire culture of illegal drugs as a conspiracy to exclude people. One thing that argues against that, however, is the nature of the drugs. Crack, the inexpensive, highly addictive form of cocaine that became popular during the late 1980s, tends to make people violent, while such a conspiracy would want them to be passive. In fact, the spread of crack came in response to a worldwide cocaine glut that was threatening to drive the price down. Adapting what had been largely a drug for the affluent for a low-income market might be viewed as a classic case of created demand, in the tradition of Crowell and his oats.

The existing illegal narcotics industry is a disaster on several levels. It has destabilized the governments of Colombia and Peru, and assassination attempts, some of them successful, have become frighteningly routine in Bogotá. It leads to destruction of Amazon rain forests, especially in Bolivia, thus doing its bit to worsen the greenhouse effect. It strains relationships between the United States and several of its Caribbean neighbors, including Panama, Jamaica and Cuba. It undermines respect for law within the United States and presents law enforcement authorities with problems they have proven unable to handle. It encourages early school dropouts in cities where youngsters are tempted by the immediate big money of the illegal drug trade.

It should be noted, however, that nearly all of these problems are the result of the illegality of the drugs rather than the drugs themselves. Even the international problems are unnecessary; the global drug trade could be replaced by the production of chemically engineered psychoactive substances in laboratories right here at home. If such designer drugs became legal, there is little doubt that consumers would soon be able to choose their mental adventures quite precisely. They could induce memory or forgetfulness, precision of vision or vague but intriguing glimpses of transcendence. They could enhance sex or quell the desire, make it good to be with people or fun to be alone. There would be quality control, tax revenues, advertising, all the things one expects in an advanced society.

That is not to say that there is no problem with surrendering to a life of either chemically altered consciousness or computer-based fantasies. Both tend to devalue human dignity and personal possibility. When they are offered as compensation for the loss of work, they seem to be a strategy to simply keep people quiet, rather than to help them find meaningful substitutes for their jobs. Each is probably all right as an occasional recreation, but neither is a substitute for a meaningful life. Each reaches people primarily as isolated consumers, which is familiar but could be unnecessary in a subtler, more satisfying, less wasteful world.

What people are for is not, as Samuel Butler suggested, to be parasites of a machine civilization. People are for being people, which means being curious, emotionally and physically expansive, innovative, sociable, caring, prideful and busy. Perhaps we should not be so resigned to the disappearance of our work.

Unions representing people in service occupations have to fight for the right to let their members truly serve people, rather than simply process them. Machines can wash hospital floors and even diagnose, but people heal. Machines can drill students, but it takes a teacher to inspire. Some people might wish to be lost in the vast information network that will almost unquestionably be a part of the future, but voters will have to make sure that it does not envelop them involuntarily. And some people might choose to retreat from the sense of incompleteness and hyperactivity that an information environment engenders so that they can do things that are finished, whole and beautiful in themselves.

Rather than trying to compete with machines at the slave level, we should look for those things that are most human in our work, that cannot be automated out of existence. We can use the wealth generated by our increased, machine-based productive capacity to pay for jobs that call on people to use their empathy and wisdom to help others. As in preindustrial times, our lives can derive their meaning from relationships to other people and the community, rather than from the production and consumption of goods.

For example, a computer-based expert system can probably guide you through all the legalities of even a complicated divorce for no more than a few dollars. But somebody who can talk to you during the divorce, console you and give practical advice on how to plan a changed life might turn out to be very valuable. Likewise, while a computer program might prove to be a more expert diagnostician than your family doctor, there will still be a real need for someone to help you through an illness and make sure that you're eating right and not depressing yourself into further disease. And even though one company is working to develop a robot physical therapist, it is such a terrifying thought that it is hard to imagine that, except in the most extreme circumstances, it will be preferred to the hand and body of a fellow human being.

These can all be seen, perhaps, as extensions of the sociability, if not the psychochemical solace, that the first factory workers found in the tavern. You need not look very hard to see that there is plenty of work to be done making and keeping other people well. People encounter the homeless, and dismiss them as crazy, which many, though far from all, are. At one time, there was at least a pretense of caring for such people, but now we simply discard them. Social workers used to try to help people on a person-to-person basis, but they have increasingly become computer-bound file processors treating a permanently dependent population. Politicians debate about sending troops to South America to deal with what has been declared a national drug crisis. Yet, in most communities, those who want to quit cannot find treatment programs to help them. Moreover, the work force is filled with those who like to work with people but have found that the experience has been Taylorized and monitored to death.

These are problems that threaten the very economic—and moral—basis of our society, but they are the easiest to ignore when things seem to be going wrong. That's because we are still stuck with the industrial-age idea that things are important in themselves, while people are important only insofar as they can make and buy things. Someone who helps troubled people deal with their emotions and bad habits might well contribute more to the true productivity of the society than does a lawyer helping a company protect its interests. Hundreds of companies have, in fact, instituted alcohol and drug treatment programs to help them recapture employees' lost productivity. But some also work toward a day when virtually all jobs are interchangeable and a company's investment in particular individuals will be less. In a labor market that needs fewer people, those who need help to do their jobs well will inevitably be the first to go.

In the long run, occupations that depend on human empathy are likely to be more stable than those that depend on the assimilation of data or the monitoring of production. It will not be possible to mechanize them, and they will be particularly necessary at a time when work is becoming less central to people's lives.

Today, workers who help people and try to mend society are paid for primarily through fringe benefits to the productive economy. But as fewer people are directly involved in this system, the necessity of finding ways to help people live satisfying lives will only become more urgent. If we manage to avoid a posthuman arms race—in which the robots from what used to be our side make perpetual war on the robots from what used to be their side—we will have to define a truly human future.

No matter how fully the productive system can be taken over by artificially intelligent machines, it need not produce artificially stupid, artificially insensitive, artificially lonely, artificially useless people. Our technology should produce useful tools, not complete replacements for people or empty substitutes for life.

6 /   Human
Environments

Early in the morning of July 19, 1989, five Wildwood Crest, New Jersey, businessmen—three motel owners, a pizzeria owner and a pharmacist—were arrested on charges of ocean pollution. They had thrown three hundred pounds of chlorine tablets into the water off the seaside resort shortly before health inspectors were due to measure the bacterial count of the water and determine whether the beach would be reopened for swimmers. These five men were trying to chlorinate the Atlantic Ocean, if only for a few minutes.

Their belief that a simple technological fix would have an impact on so diffuse a problem is so naïve, it's almost endearing. Though they were clearly motivated by the fear of financial losses, it seems unlikely that any of them would want people to get sick from swimming in polluted water. Rather, they sought a quick fix to get around an unpleasant reality so they could live their lives as usual.

Ultimately though, their response seems comical. Like other comic characters, they were acting on a view of the world that did not work. And the world, in the form of both the Atlantic Ocean and the law, slapped them right in the face. (The legal charges were eventually dropped.) It seemed easier to address pollution by giving the ocean a pill than to limit the number of people, toilets and immediate profits on a sandy barrier island.

Interest in this routine and far from mysterious pollution was heightened by the unexpected appearance of all sorts of unsavory things on East Coast beaches. There were needles and bags of garbage coming from what was then an unknown source. A later effort to trace the source of the dumping showed that much of it simply washed off the streets of Philadelphia, eighty miles down the Delaware Bay and up the New Jersey coast. The idea of somebody who litters in March reencountering his trash at the beach the following August is pretty funny when you think about it. So is the notion that helmetlike women's hairdos of the 1960s, made possible by hair spray propelled by chlorofluorocarbons (CFCs), helped begin the depletion of the ozone layer, which shields people from cancer-causing rays. Who would have guessed that such seemingly insignificant acts would bring retribution?

All of these things would be funnier if we were creatures watching the show from the comfort of another planet. But those within a farce rarely see the humor of their situation. More likely, they are hurting, thwarted and obsessed, as they discover, endlessly, that the world does not work as expected.

The Adriatic Sea was never supposed to turn gelatinous, as much of it did during the summer of 1989. The mountains over Denver and Los Angeles and Teheran were never supposed to disappear into the acrid, yellow air. Americans were never supposed to worry about where their next improvement was coming from. The world doesn't seem to be operating according to the same assumptions we are, and we feel cheated as a result.

Marine environmental disasters, ranging from oil spills and medical waste on beaches to the mysterious algal blooms and dolphin deaths that have also become more frequent, have a particularly strong psychological impact. Going to the ocean during the summer used to be a chance to be carefree, but now there is the fear of health risks and the likelihood that the environment will strike back. Such events also challenge our sense of the vastness of the sea, which accounts for so much of its menacing attractiveness. When the oceans throw our wastes back in our faces, some limits have clearly been reached.

Events like these have focused environmental concern all over the world. Still, even well-intentioned people want to deal with the problems people are causing to the physical systems that sustain life much as the New Jersey businessmen did—by medicating, then forgetting. Obviously, there are a number of specific actions that can be taken immediately to mitigate current environmental crises. But these will be useless without a concomitant act of imagination. We have to understand the environment, and ourselves as products and shapers of it, in some different ways. We must not think that we are lowering our expectations of life, but rather clarifying them, or changing them so they bear greater relationship to reality. Instead of defining progress as the aggregation of goods, we might rather look toward a day when we can swim—innocently—in the ocean.

When we talk about taking a new view of our environment, one striking image comes to mind. It is the view of the earth from space, a photograph that is, perhaps, the most important single result of space exploration to date. It shows our home planet as a heavenly body, shimmering and finite, in the vast expanse of space. It is a beautiful picture, one that has helped animate efforts to protect the environment for more than two decades. It has visceral impact because it shows the spectrum visible to human beings. It is what any eye could see, if it could but attain so privileged a position.

Still, though the image of our cozy, azure orb in the chill, black infinity of space is extremely moving, it has but one lesson to teach: Our life-giving world is extraordinary and physically limited. There is only so much matter, so much water, so much air. And though we might be able to take voyages into the emptiness of space and explore alien worlds, it is our home and likely to remain so.

This is no small lesson, but it is not enough to help humans avoid the cosmic pratfalls to which we are increasingly prone. This picture shows a small world, but we live our lives in a world that, compared with ourselves, is vast. We know that what people do in their daily lives can have an impact on the entire planet. But we can neither understand nor act to heal the global environment without being sensitive to the smaller environments—ecosystems, geographical regions, economies, communities, neighborhoods—in which we live our lives.

The world is limited, but at every scale we choose to explore, it is infinite and infinitely complex. When we imagine ourselves and the world, we must think not simply of one environment but of a whole swarm of them, physical, biological and man-made. They begin with the surroundings that ensure our physiological survival and embrace the universe. They involve phenomena that are too small to see and too large to imagine and involve processes as disparate as the release of energy from carbohydrates and the quest for human freedom. The human environment has come to include phenomena that reside in computers, along with the people who live next door. There are far too many to describe them all, yet it is worth looking at a few of these human environments, in order to highlight both their differences and their subtle similarities.

To paraphrase Buckminster Fuller's famous definition, your environment is everything in the universe that is not you. That seems just about as clear and comprehensive as can be. But examined carefully, all boundaries turn fuzzy. Separating the "you" from the "not you" can be difficult. The air in the room you inhabit is clearly part of the environment. It's not you. But when you breathe, this air is taken into your lungs, and oxygen is separated from the air and distributed to every cell in your body, including your brain, where it is needed to sustain consciousness. This process virtually defines life itself. The air becomes you. Then you exhale, and it's not you again. The air is different too.

People are both products and integral parts of the chemical and biological systems in which they live. All that is solid and substantial in ourselves is taken in from outside, used and, after a period that can last from seconds to decades, discarded. Living things are islands of organization in what the Second Law of Thermodynamics tells us is an increasingly disordered universe. It is possible to see each person, and each animal and plant, as little more than a cloud of information. Both the walls of living cells and the skin of our bodies serve as barriers between the highly organized state within and the more disorderly state outside. These biological boundaries are not closed fortresses but permeable membranes, and the processes that happen inside the body depend on the materials available in the immediate environment. At the scale of the individual person, this meeting of air and lungs, skin and sunlight, organic chemicals and digestive system, is the fundamental relationship of human and environment. It is a relationship not between two completely different kinds of stuff, but between different forms of organization. It does not happen at a global level but is, rather, highly localized.

The word we use to describe this ability of the organism to sustain its organization and to take beneficial, rather than harmful, material from the environment is "health." Health is a set of relationships—between all the parts of the organism and the whole and between the organism and its environment.

During the last two decades, there has been an explosion of interest in personal health, in which large numbers of people have shown a willingness to alter their habits radically in an attempt to preserve or improve their health. Up to now, however, health consciousness has been a highly individualistic, not to say selfish and even narcissistic activity. And it has also become part of the consumer economy. A lot of athletic shoes, not to mention carloads of oatmeal, have been sold in the name of health. For many people who work out regularly, a hard body is a tool in the competition for wealth and power, and the larger implications of health are rarely considered.

Still, health is part of contemporary consciousness, and it can be a subversive idea. It is something that each of us feels intimately, yet it is mysterious. It is experienced by the whole body rather than its individual parts. It is more than freedom from infection, even though this is what our highly technological medical-care system concentrates most of its firepower on. It is a quality of both body and mind in balance and harmony, and it is measured not in endless physical growth but in the ability to continue to become more fully ourselves. Our bodies are mortal. Ill health is part of all of our lives. Still, our bodies have defenses, and we have developed many technologies to supplement them. Getting sick and getting well are familiar experiences, and while each case of the sniffles might bring with it a whisper of mortality, it is not a harbinger of doom. Our bodies are designed to make themselves healthy. Despite the intensity of the experience of disease, aspiring to health is a well-founded hope.

Routine medical care involves a lot of sophisticated machinery nowadays, but doctors monitor their patients' health primarily by talking to them. Health is a vague idea, but people know it when they have it. Physicians also use tests of blood and other body fluids, because we are complex chemical systems which operate within a fairly narrow set of tolerances. Most people probably place greater faith in a computer printout of their body chemistry than they do in their own personal feeling of well-being. This technological and objective bias may be misplaced and may add needlessly to the cost of medical care besides, but it does make people aware that they are complex chemical phenomena.

When we talk about environmental health, we may think we are speaking metaphorically, but in fact health is inseparable from the environment. It has been estimated that just two pollutants—ozone and airborne particles—cause between $9.4 and $14.3 billion worth of medical expenses and lost work each year in the greater Los Angeles area alone. Such figures, which try to put a dollar value on conjecture, are suspect by their nature, but they reflect an underlying reality. Los Angeles property values tend to reflect the air quality of the site. Given a choice, people will always opt to feel better.

It has frequently been noted that environmental problems transcend national boundaries and require regional or even global solutions. It has been less frequently noted that they transcend personal boundaries as well. It is harder to be healthy if we place ourselves in an environment that impedes the processes that make our bodies function. When we speak of environmental problems, we are really talking about the difficulties people face when they live in an environment that threatens their health. An unhealthy environment can contain specific sources of infection, such as the excessively high bacterial count that the New Jersey businessmen were trying to disguise, or contain factors that weaken the body's defenses. Such a threat can be immediate and local, as when heavy metals poison a water supply, or global and diffuse, as when a thinning ozone layer increases susceptibility to cancer and other diseases. It can also come as a threat to food supplies, through depletion of ground water, marine pollution or greenhouse gas-induced global warming.

The idea that health is a complex set of relationships that involve the environment as well as the organism is not exactly novel, but it has only recently begun to seep into everyday consciousness. The truth that people come from and return to dust is an ancient religious idea. Still, it is one that people rarely take seriously.

It is more common to take a more limited view of the nature of the body that derives from an industrial metaphor. This is the notion that the body is a form of engine that converts food into energy that makes the body's parts go. This is the idea of body as Twinkie burner that we encountered back in Chapter 3 (pages 87–9). Such a model is correct, as far as it goes, but it is largely an attempt to define life in terms of industrial and economic ideas of the last century. Victorian-era civic boosters habitually viewed smokestacks belching acrid black smoke as the very embodiment of economic health and commercial vitality. While some, such as Charles Dickens, presented quite another interpretation, the universality of such sooty smoke-stack panoramas indicates that the image was compelling. The ability to release and focus concentrated energy led people to oversimplify their own relationship to the environment and look for ways to speed up the process and produce ever more stuff. We no longer view the black grime of coal smoke as a sign of health, though we have not yet weaned ourselves from the consumption machine that was created to keep the engines running. It was nineteenth-century science that dis-covered that no material thing can ever be destroyed, though it can become energy and waste. But it was well into the twentieth century before we started to find toxic wastes in our own bodies and identify a high-energy, waste-strewn environment as an unhealthy one.

The body is, among many other things, an energy-conversion machine, an aggregation of cells, a repository of consciousness. Our technology, ingenious as it often is, has produced nothing that even begins to come close to the body's infinite subtlety, its endless com-plexity. For those who fear the discovery of physical limits to our high-burn, high-waste civilization, the human body suggests that we have barely begun to explore our technological possibilities. There are whole libraries of information in the DNA found in every single cell in our bodies, and each one contains all the instructions necessary to construct the entire organism. The circulatory system is designed so that nourishment reaches every single one of the millions of cells throughout the body while taking up only 5 percent of the body's volume, which is a wonder of traffic engineering.

There is admittedly something naïve about proposing the idea of health as a dynamic balance between ourselves and the physical environment to replace the burn-and-waste model on which our con-temporary lives seem to depend. It would be possible to draw quite divergent lessons from this paradigm. For example, one person may look at the idea of health and conclude that the body exists to nourish each of its cells, while another would argue that all exist to support the body. These arguments, which are essentially without meaning when one is talking literally about organisms and their environments, produce divergent conclusions when applied to the political realm. Similarly, there is a long tradition of seeing the body in terms of hierarchy and specialization, with the brain as chairman of the board overseeing the activities of the operating divisions. To be sure, the body does generate specialized organs, but each of its cells contains all the genetic information needed to make the entire organism. The body is not a democracy, by any stretch of the imagination, but even the smallest of its living elements implies the whole. Arteries and capillaries have traditionally been seen as completely different from each other, on what was essentially an industrial model of hierarchical organization, but in recent years we have learned to see them as part of a single, nonbureaucratic mechanism by which the body sustains itself.

When we accept the idea of health as a dynamic and life-promoting balance between our bodies and the environment, a fundamental wall has been breached. You are constantly in the process of becoming your environment, and your environment is in the process of becoming you. There is no environment separate from you as observer, and there is no "you" except insofar as your body is able to sustain a unique pattern of electrochemical connections that allows you to conceive of yourself as an observer. Such a sense of ourselves is not meaningless. Indeed, from our involuntarily self-centered point of view, it seems quite miraculous. But that does not mean that the physical, chemical and biological processes that permit us to be highly organized phenomena in an entropic universe can be forgotten.

The same relationships do not apply to every level of the physical and man-made world, though there are analogies. You can't derive politics from biology, but you must not forget biology when talking about politics.

If you take this dynamic conception of health and superimpose it on the image of the world from space, what you come out with is Gaia. This hypothesis, put forth by the British chemist J. E. Lovelock, holds that all life on earth can be seen as one organism. "The entire range of living matter on earth, from whales to viruses, and from oaks to algae," Lovelock wrote, "could be regarded as constituting a single living entity, capable of manipulating the Earth's atmosphere to suit its overall needs and endowed with faculties and powers far beyond those of its constituent parts." The hypothesis holds, for example, that the atmosphere is "a biological construction: not living, but like a cat's fur, a bird's feathers, or the paper of a wasp's nest, an extension of a living system designed to maintain a chosen environment."

The thesis, named by novelist William Golding for an ancient Greek earth goddess, is a by-product of work Lovelock did for NASA in which he tried to determine the likelihood of life on Mars by looking for chemical disequilibria. After concluding that Martian life is very unlikely, he began to be interested in the way in which the earth has, over three billion years, maintained extraordinary chemical stability—characterized by the persistent presence of compounds that, in the normal course of chemical reactions, should have disappeared ages ago. One way of defining life is to determine whether it is maintaining a chemical equilibrium different from that of its immediate environment. Each of our cells does that, though most of them are in a specialized environment created by the body as a whole. And each of our bodies maintains a very exact chemical balance, different from that of our physical environment. But it is also true that the earth itself maintains a very precise chemical balance that, for example, optimizes the quantity of oxygen available for respiration without making the biosphere too vulnerable to fire. The plants and animals of the earth have helped create this balance, and they play a strong role in maintaining it.

Lovelock found many examples of microorganisms—marine algae, for example—serving as repositories or factories for key chemical components of the atmosphere and oceans. The earth and its plants and creatures do appear to interact in a way that maintains a satisfactory environment for the survival of life. It is not an enormous step to conclude that the earth as a whole is somehow a living thing. Lovelock started out by diagramming a conceptual planetary espresso machine, but by the time he was done, it was a living, breathing goddess.

One striking characteristic of this concept is the very limited role given human beings. It explains everything important about the planet as being at a scale either global or microscopic. "Large plants and animals are rather unimportant," Lovelock argues. "They are comparable rather to those elegant salesmen and glamorous models used to display a firm's products, desirable perhaps, but not essential.

The tough and reliable workers of the soil and the sea-beds are the ones who keep things moving . . ." He says these most important creatures could easily survive an event, such as a thermonuclear holocaust, that might well wipe out our species, but there are other bits of mischief we could make, involving genetic engineering perhaps, that could wipe out the microorganisms, and us along with them.

This is a scientifically controversial hypothesis. Some scientists have argued that the chemical composition of the atmosphere is not as unlikely as Lovelock argues, nor has the earth been as chemically stable as he asserts. But the principal difficulty with the hypothesis is its attribution of something like planning and volition to life as a whole. If we attribute a mind to Gaia, it smacks of religion, while if we assume that it is mindless, it bruises the human ego to view itself as a minor part of a vast meaningless entity, in which blue-green algae do most of the heavy work. Lovelock himself makes fewer claims for his hypothesis than some who have taken up his ideas. He argues that it helps people to see life and ecological relationships from new angles, which has in turn spurred fruitful research.

The "reality" of Gaia may never be provable. If a process simulates the effects we expect from a living organism, is that a proof that the organism itself exists? (This is almost the same question raised by artificial intelligence.) Is Gaia something that comes into being only through the presence of the observer, like some phenomena of quantum physics? Is it a beautiful metaphor, or a hallucination induced by staring at the earth too long?

If we look at it primarily as a way of viewing the world, while keeping in mind that no such view is totally reliable, Gaia still seems quite useful, if only as a spur to humility. From the standpoint of the living planet as a whole, our species appears to have been an outbreak of bad news. We're far too recent to have helped create the equilibrium, but in our short existence, we have made the surface break out in terrible rashes and started to meddle in vital processes we don't begin to understand. Life on earth will probably survive us, though it might decide that we are a dangerous nuisance, a luxury it cannot afford. The focus on life as a whole serves as a reminder that environment is not something outside ourselves. Life will go on in some form, but whether it will include people is in some doubt. "Doing something for the environment" is an act not of noblesse oblige but of naked self-interest.

Others draw quite different conclusions from the Gaia hypothesis. It has induced some to carry the idea far beyond Lovelock's intention and propose that human beings are the means by which the planet will gain consciousness. Indeed, the futurist Jerome Clayton Glenn has argued that what appears to be our century's unprecedented population explosion will soon result in the planet having as many people as there are neurons in the human brain. The result, he argues, will be a fusion of mind, and the planet will become aware of itself for the first time. This has a certain attractiveness as a metaphor. We are able to measure the earth as never before and communicate the findings instantaneously. A sense of human kinship seems to be growing, as the power of national boundaries is in decline. Taken literally, though, such a belief is a religion that, despite a whiff of Eastern mysticism, reasserts humanity as the fulfillment of creation and presumes that people will tell the deity what's best for her.

Gaia is a fascinating idea, but one that is not easily resolved into any principles of human activity. If Gaia exists, we simply know too little about the phenomenon to understand how to relate to it in a way that promotes its welfare and our own. There is a danger of getting lost in so transcendent and abstract a concept. We risk losing sight of those things that we can really see and really affect, those substantial objects in the middle distance that constitute the world with which human evolution has equipped us to cope.

It is possible to become earthstruck, to become so obsessed with Gaia or the global village that we lose sight of the human scale and the places on the earth that people shape and inhabit. Our view of the environment too often banishes distinctions that ought to be preserved, even while recognizing that most boundaries are permeable. Every spot on the face of the earth is different from every other one, just as every person is different from every other. To care about the earth while ignoring the infinite wonders of its places is the same as loving humanity while not liking people. Many do it, but it doesn't do anyone much good.

A view of the world has to begin with a sense of the place where you are. The singular image of the living planet must coexist with the smells, sights and sounds of particular places. The weather, the prevailing winds, the quality of the light and air, the smell of the vegetation, the presence of plants we eat or use to heal ourselves, can all have a direct impact on both our physical well-being and our emotions. Moreover, observing the very shape of the landscape and the changing quality of the sky is still the most direct way through which people can understand powers that are greater than themselves. The recognition that your immediate surroundings are essential to your physical and possibly spiritual integrity defines health on yet another scale. The quality of feeling at home in the world and recognizing your own role in helping it to assure your survival may be the most fundamental form of healthy living.

The ability to live in almost every land habitat found on the earth is something that human beings share with only a few other creatures, all of which people find either unpleasant or insignificant. This universality predates the coming of the industrial age by tens of thousands of years, as people lived through ice ages and populated tundras, rain forests and deserts, as well as the savannas where the living was easier. This success in human development derived from people's ingenuity in accepting the uniqueness of their physical circumstances and turning them to their own advantage. Thus, while the human body has specific and universal environmental requirements for its survival, people have been able to meet them in different ways. In deserts, water becomes holy and ceremonial. In the Arctic, people keep warm in houses made of snow.

The world's first advanced civilization, the Egyptians, grew from a phenomenon that could be viewed as inconvenient or dangerous—the annual Nile flood. From this event, and the unique valley in which it happened, the Egyptians derived a complex economy, an effective political system and a religion and culture that lasted thousands of years. None of these would have made any sense to people living anywhere else on earth. There is anthropological evidence that the Incas made the Andean foothills more productive agriculturally than North America's Great Plains are today. The aborigines of Australia have viewed their vast empty spaces as a landscape of meaning, of which human life is but one aspect.

Those of us who live in North America now tend toward a very different view of the world and respond more directly to planet than to place. We are more comfortable with the universal than the particular, though the high-tech pollution we face may force us back to an older idea of environmental health.

America did not begin as a family, a tribe or a people, and it was oddly placeless. "The land was ours before we were the land's," Robert Frost wrote, and even today, Americans are more comfortable linking the land to some abstract concept—land of opportunity, land of liberty, land of the Pilgrims' pride—than thinking about the land itself, in all its variety and uniqueness. The people who were living here when the settlers arrived saw things differently. They recognized the character of the land and saw themselves as part of it. They didn't know it was wilderness. The Anglo-American settlement of North America thus began by recapitulating the sin of Cain, as those who wanted the land to produce intensively murdered those who moved lightly across it.

The country was founded and has grown and prospered on a faith that individuals can forge lives satisfactory to themselves and exemplary to others. Our traditions extol idealism through pragmatism, virtue through selfishness. The Puritan settlers who founded the Massachusetts Bay Colony in 1623 sought to create a new Jerusalem, but they also sold stock and apparently intended to make enough money to pay dividends. They sold the notion that virtue would be rewarded—financially. The United States was the first country to be recognized as a purely man-made arrangement, one in which the native Americans were not viewed as participants. The roots of these ideas began in Europe, with the Protestant belief that people should read the Bible on their own, the Puritan preoccupation with covenants, the political ideas of the French Enlightenment and the economic ideas of the Scottish Enlightenment. But when such abstract ideas were applied to the rich new environment of the North American continent, they grew into something new and powerful.

The human artifact that most poetically fuses nature and abstraction is the garden. And in different times and different places, the balance between the assertion of human ideas and the expression of natural complexity and profusion has changed. In Judeo-Christian tradition, humanity began in a garden. Like all gardens, Eden was a place of order within specific limits—both physical and behavioral. It was, as Adam and Eve learned, a place you could get thrown out of. America has often seemed to be an improved Eden, a garden without limits.

One of America's earliest and greatest gardens, that of Middleton Place Plantation outside of Charleston, South Carolina, embodies this idea powerfully. These gardens, whose basic configuration was determined in the mid-eighteenth century, appropriate the entire landscape. They run downhill into a river estuary. Their first section, just below where the main house once stood, is a symmetrical formal garden, crisp and abstract, in a loosely French style. Below that are rice fields, whose less formal but still abstract winglike geometry embodies the order implicit in trying to work the earth. But the design is an aesthetic decision, because its effect is that the garden seems to embrace the entire estuary on which the plantation sits and all the land beyond, which still convincingly evokes wilderness. The expansion of the garden into the larger landscape is not an expression of a sovereign's absolute power, as are the gardens at Versailles, nor does it merge imperceptibly into a tamed Arcadian landscape, as do some English gardens of the period. Instead, the garden makes an all-encompassing embrace of a land of unrefined possibilities. This feels gentle and even generous, but it embodies even greater ambition.

Americans' relationship to the land has, from the first, been exploitive. The first large-scale agriculture practiced by Europeans here was the tobacco growing of seventeenth-century Virginia. The land was farmed for several years until its fertility was exhausted and farmers moved on. Slavery also entered into this system very early. Although slavery was extended to the North American mainland from the Caribbean, where circumstances were quite different, it fit into a persistent American belief that everything is abundant but labor, whose cost and power must be minimized. Slavery and its aftermath of discrimination has, of course, been at the heart of the country's deepest problems ever since.

We nevertheless indulge in the historically ignorant romantic individualism evoked by General Motors in its Vancouver "Spirit Lodge." There, permission to move freely about the earth and dominate it is given by the eagle, the fox and other wild creatures. We are encouraged to see the fulfillment of our personal desires as an inalienable right of the kind postulated in the Declaration of Independence. Then we are presented with a menu of sharply defined desires and products that offer provisional satisfaction.

The consumer society as we now know it could scarcely have been imagined by Jefferson and the other Founding Fathers because it grows from a system of production and marketing that had not yet been invented. George Washington didn't fight the British so that there would be sales on the Monday closest to his birthday. "The pursuit of happiness" may be an infinite project, but it is not necessarily a materialist one.

Still, Jefferson did give rise to the great American subdivision. He had the continent surveyed in a vast Cartesian grid, which gave mountain and prairie, desert and swamp, a spurious equality, all of it open to development. Jefferson, who had placed his own home so carefully in relation to the surrounding landscape, facing west to the frontier, knew that land has more difference than commonality. Yet he was comfortable in a world of abstractions. American ideas of individualism and freedom are rooted in a body of philosophical ideas, rather than in social and political experience. Ties to the land and loyalty to place and family produced, in Europe, feudalistic societies and tyrannical monarchies, just the sort of thing the founders sought to avoid. Money—the grandest abstraction of them all—weakens the power of rank and aristocratic relationships and enables all sorts of upstarts to make their way in the society. Money is subversive, portable, powerful, capable of buying status and respect. It is the universal solvent that has made the American version of democracy possible.

Abstractions like inalienable individual rights, developable land and money have proven very useful because they make it possible to conceive of the world in new and very productive ways. But the power of such abstractions can divert attention from underlying realities.

The idea that every human has rights does not mean that each should live in the same circumstances, or that differences among people or in the places where they live should be suppressed. Still, American culture has tended since the first to be universalizing. Europeans were unwilling to seriously contemplate a really new world. Instead, they sought to re-create the old world in a New Spain, a New France and a New England. In the United States, we have succeeded during the last half century in turning a vast land of diverse climate, landforms and vegetation into a single, quasi-suburban environment. We find the same houses and the same stores among Cape Cod dunes, in Florida swamps, next to sandstone buttes in the Southwest or clinging to the sides of urbanized mountain passes in Los Angeles. This universal landscape, made possible by cars, extensive water-diversion systems, air conditioners and cheap energy to power them, is one of our most expensive, complex and ambiguous achievements. It does, in a sense, hold us together as a culture, but it also puts us in a state of constant war with the world in which we live.

The phenomenon of placelessness has spread far beyond the United States, as the technology that sustains it—automobiles, air conditioning, telephones and television—has been embraced as a symbol of social and economic development. Moreover, the United States' dominant role as an exporter of entertainment and fantasy has helped establish the American model of material abundance and personal freedom, in a landscape of indulgence, as a goal for people throughout the world.

Yet the awareness of limits, particularly those imposed by the environment, will force a restructuring of American life, which is certain to begin in its most characteristic environment, Southern California. In an effort to improve air quality, residents of the Los Angeles area will face restrictions on driving, painting, backyard barbecues and many other routine activities of private life. Many of the restrictions that seem likely to be imposed work directly against the region's principal asset—the ability to combine the economic and cultural advantages of a great metropolis with those of an elaborate, yet informal private life. Unfortunately, the private automobile is what makes this combination of personal expansiveness and collective opportunity possible, and now the region is choked by both traffic and bad air.

The Southern California region is, perhaps, the most extreme example of a wilderness divided into developable plots and transformed by human ambition and imagination. The land is irrelevant, even though it shakes violently from time to time and dries up when not watered aggressively, using sources hundreds of miles away. Its desert landscape is prone to brush fires and mud slides. Yet it has become one of the world's great metropolises, a seeming embodiment of freedom, of mobility, of spontaneity and imagination. One feels it is what most of the world would create if it had the chance.

And indeed, Greater Los Angeles differs from most of the rest of America only in extent. Its overinvestment in the automobile and the private house lot as the embodiment of the American dream is only slightly greater than that of the rest of the country. It is facing environmental restrictions first only because of its size and importance. The changing of the Southern California lifestyle will be only the beginning of a national phenomenon, which will, in turn, have global consequences.

Los Angeles is truly the end of the road for the Jefferson who divided the continent into squares, though it need not compromise such other Jeffersonian principles as life, liberty and the pursuit of happiness. He never argued that a three-bedroom, two-and-a-half-bath house on a half-acre lot was one of man's inalienable rights, though for much of this century most national leaders have behaved as if it were. Americans have learned to see its possession as their own declaration of independence, a personal achievement, a measure of freedom and success. We have rarely been conscious of the enormous public subsidies—such as tax deductions for interest, mortgage guarantees, highways and water-diversion projects—that have allowed the expansive vision of private life to spread from ocean to ocean. And we have been almost entirely oblivious to the other public costs—in the form of air and water pollution, loss of farmland, isolation of the poor and immobile and increased dependence on other countries for the basic commodities that make such a way of life possible.

Nevertheless, the first reaction to the understanding that a limit has been reached is likely to be rage and defiance. This is to be expected because, as the GM shaman and his animal spirits reminded us at Vancouver, we cannot conceive of a definition of freedom that doesn't embrace mobility. And as our society is structured now, that means cars. Every year, Americans spend $350 billion on buying, repairing and running their personal cars. Clearly we have a lot invested in the auto-based society, and very few alternatives. The discovery of the limits of this form of organization will unquestionably feel like scarcity, and even betrayal.

How, then, can we imagine the future of our landscape?

One popular way is to ignore it. The next innovation for automobiles, we are told, is navigation systems, built-in computerized maps that will assure that we will never get lost. There are lots of other technological goodies on the horizon as well, including that old futurist standby, the automated highway on which cars drive themselves. This is presented as a way of reducing traffic congestion, though its advocates rarely address the costs of virtually rebuilding the entire highway system compared with other possible public expenditures.

Another approach is to wait for a breakthrough. With a little belt tightening now, we can anticipate a time when bioengineered corn or nuclear fusion will provide a level of energy abundance that we can't imagine now. Thus, the approach is to maintain our current goals, while understanding that we can't achieve them easily or universally for a while.

An opposite response is to become concerned with the changes that will have to be made as the precursors to a new age of scarcity. There are always people who are suspicious of pleasure and mad for abstinence and who enjoy the prospect of retribution. Such people can be expected to want regulation of people's lives and habits to be as intrusive and onerous as possible, and to seek frequent acknowledgment that we have sinned. While an attitude of austerity might be a very useful one in the short run, it probably cannot be sustained unless people can hope that their sacrifice will somehow be rewarded.

The problem with the first two approaches is that they continue to confuse a way of life that arose as a means of expressing values with the values themselves, while the third seeks to impose values that have appeared periodically but ultimately unsuccessfully throughout our history—in strict religious sects, nativist movements and the prohibition of alcohol, for example. What is needed is an approach that recognizes basic values within the physical limits now apparent. Essentially, that means respecting the real material boundaries while creating an environment that still provides freedom for human possibilities.

The missing piece in this discussion so far is the role of another overwhelmingly important part of one's environment—other people. Interaction with other people is the chief activity of most people's lives. Community—the willingness of groups of people to support one another and pursue goals that are advantageous to all—is another measure of environmental health, and one that has immediate physical consequences. The insensitivity Americans show to their landscape is largely a product of the ideology that life is best lived independently, and those things that are shared—public spaces, mass transportation, urban parks—are fundamentally without value. The belief that one should enjoy the benefits of society in isolation from other people—and that owning is better than sharing, or even renting—is one that increases the production and consumption of many products. It has been an important contributor to American economic prosperity.

But such belief is becoming less and less useful. There is no way to modify the road systems of suburban and exurban areas to handle their increased loads without taking up too much land, encouraging even more intensive new development and changing the character of the areas through which they pass even more dramatically. This automobile-dependent system is like a machine in which the friction has become so great that it outweighs its usefulness. Moreover, while it may have been possible to sustain the household as an island of consumption during an era when the woman of the house was at home all day, the prevalence of working women and new family structures makes a purported joy a burden.

The denial of the importance of community exacts a heavy toll on many people's lives. It has contributed to racial and economic segregation, thus contributing to polarization and crime. The physical separation of people who need help from those with the resources to give it to them has created an atmosphere of growing despair, which leads to further waste of human talent and creativity, along with the abandonment of buildings and large sections of entire cities, which constitute billions of dollars' worth of public and private investment over long periods of time.

The physical and psychological separation of people has also made it increasingly difficult for society to deal with its problems. It has increased the power of mass media, and particularly television, in the political system. This has, in turn, magnified the power of money in elections, increasing the likelihood of corruption and mistrust in the public realm. Moreover, it has reduced political discourse to the superficial, image-centered syntax of television. The political arguments one might hear in diners or barbershops may not be profound, but they at least remind people of a shared stake in community decisions. The television commercial reduces civic participation to a personal purchasing decision. The general lack of belief in public life makes problems that are persistent and difficult seem insoluble. And once an issue has been identified as a loser, the smart politician knows enough not to even mention it anymore, regardless of its importance.

Americans frequently confuse the concept of community with that of collectivism. In fact, they are very different ideas. Collectivism tends to pretend that people are all the same, while community is based on the idea that each person is unique. And just as a recognition of the unique qualities of a piece of land is the first step toward healthy survival on that land, recognition of the uniqueness of individual people is a key to the success of the group. Evolution has given people very different and expressive faces. This is itself an indication that human success has depended not merely on the existence of differences among people but also on people's recognition of these differences. It is important to see the faces of those who live nearby, to recognize them and be able to assess whether they represent a danger. In landscapes that are based on the isolation of consumers and the denial of community, everybody constitutes a threat. And it becomes particularly tempting to classify people without even looking at their faces—on the basis of skin color, for example.

The racial and ethnic diversity of the United States creates an obstacle to the forging of a sense of community. Black people were enslaved because they were seen as subhuman, and many people, both white and black, persist in seeing the other race as different not merely in color but in kind. Moreover, the majority of the U.S. population is descended from people who found the ties of community a bit too constraining or exclusive in their homelands. Too much cohesiveness seems un-American. It will be necessary to develop a new mode of community and a landscape to go with it. Because it will not be based on any sense of kinship, it will demand generosity and empathy. It must, most of all, be seen to preserve fundamental American beliefs in freedom, flexibility and lack of hierarchy.

Communities are a source of strength, the outgrowth of the realization that people in groups can offer each other opportunities, ideas and pleasures they could not have by themselves, and nobody need be a loser. Communities are more than the sum of their parts, and they are the fundamental units of human accomplishment. American history and folklore is filled with examples of community creativity, ranging from barn raisings and quilting bees and posses to the founding of universities, hospitals, libraries, savings banks and other voluntary institutions. Such task-based communities do not conflict with our values of freedom, mobility and flexibility. In recent years, as ideals of more general community have been in decline, "networking," an aggressive and selective variety of personal community formation, has become respectable. It's all right to relate to communities if you are up front about trying to get something out of it.

This is not to say that all evidence of community is dead. Americans have a very strong record of helping neighbors in emergencies. A number of social science experiments have also shown a general willingness to go to some lengths to help total strangers, even when there is no prospect of any reciprocation. One interesting measure of consciousness of public welfare in a consumer society has been the acceptance of refuse recycling programs. To date, even those which have been largely voluntary have far exceeded predictions of their effectiveness, and in some localities the degree of compliance has been so great that it has overtaxed the capacities of the programs to deal with it.

Still, just as public spaces have been abandoned by the consuming classes and left to the poor and powerless, so have the institutions of community become less important. Church attendance is down, even as those interviewed by pollsters say that their religiosity is undiminished. Political participation is down. Increasing evidence of ineffective public schools, even in middle-class areas that once prided themselves on their schools, has not prodded increasingly childless populations to help educate the people who will have to pay the Social Security taxes after 2010. Families' perceived need to keep their consumption accelerating at an acceptable pace has sent more women to work and fewer into mainstream voluntary activities that once depended on their participation. People will pull together in extraordinary circumstances, but not in ordinary ones. Our private lives require more and more of our energies.

Ideas about community shape the places where people live, whose physical form tends to perpetuate the ideas. The design of neighborhoods and towns can have an impact on the way people define their communities. Today, what we believe to be our deepest values are closely tied to physical mobility and spatial openness, though these need not always translate into a car and a lawn. Americans' ideal of freedom is about not having to stay in one place or not being tied to one place in society. It is about the ability to make contact with many different people and the ability to take risks and see your ideas realized. It must therefore be a landscape of opportunity, one that is not too perfect, the very opposite of the seamless monolithic machine cities that used to dominate our futuristic visions. Too much physical harmony speaks of too much control, and we need something a good deal looser.

The landscape of Los Angeles is one embodiment of such values, but there are many other possibilities. There are, for example, small towns, with houses and stores all clustered together around the kind of main streets Angelinos have to go to Disneyland to see. There are also nineteenth- and early-twentieth-century suburbs, those tight little arcadias, many of them still served by mass transit. The modesty of such models may seem anticlimactic. It is not meant to be an exhaustive list, merely a suggestion that some of the forms of settlement that loom large in our national mythology are better suited to living in a world of energy and environmental limits than the landscape we now define as normal. In small towns and older suburbs, people typically have cars, but they do not need them for everything they do. Older suburbs gave people options for getting to work other than their cars. Moreover, such places often have a sense of imperfect wholeness, which allows for the possibility of community without forcing it upon its residents.

The San Francisco architect Peter Calthorpe has attempted to update these models so that they help people live within environmental and energy limits without having to compromise their desires. His plan calls for development of several fast-growing counties in California to be concentrated in a series of "pedestrian pockets," small communities that mix jobs, apartments, stores and single-family houses in various combinations. Within the pockets, it would be possible to meet most of the routine needs of daily life, such as grocery shopping and schooling, without recourse to automobile trips, though the developments would be designed on the assumption that most residents would have cars. The key to the plan, though, is the linkage of the pedestrian pockets by light rail service—trolley cars—running on largely abandoned freight rights-of-way that already exist. Using this linkage, both to new developments and to major nodes of employment and higher education that already exist, most residents would be within a half-hour transit ride of as many work and cultural opportunities as could be found in a medium-sized city. Workers wouldn't have to use their cars, and the counties would not have to build the kind of enormous roads that undermine the qualities that make them attractive to begin with.

Calthorpe presents his plan not as an austerity program but as a series of opportunities. It would give developers the chance to reduce their risks and possibly to reduce some of their site-preparation and road-building costs. It would also allow them to satisfy growing "unconventional" markets of single parents and elderly people, for whom it is difficult to provide acceptable housing within suburban patterns. More important, though, it would allow residents access to a tremendous range of possibilities for work, education and recreation without the diseconomies of scale to be found in a large city. The existing American landscape indicates a demand for metropolitan opportunities in nonurban settings. The pedestrian-pocket plan might be able to do that, while reducing the intensive automobile traffic that now makes it possible.

Calthorpe's idea falls far short of being visionary. Others present far more radical ideas about how people ought to live on the land, and some of these might come to pass. Nigel Calder, the British science writer, has argued that only when large numbers of Americans drop out of the system and cluster in self-sufficient, monastery-like biotechnology cooperatives can the world system of exploitation and military confrontation be broken. Many others believe that democratic ideals can only be achieved on a small scale and that it is counterproductive to encourage people to relate to large networks of people spread across the landscape. Others believe electronic linkages will rescue the existing landscape by making most trips unnecessary.

Still, the pedestrian-pocket idea is attractive because it does not try to substitute a whole new set of values for those that have shaped the landscape up until now. Rather, it seeks a way, within our newly evident physical limits, to allow people to express those values without any sense of deprivation. It recognizes that there are forms of investment less tangible than buildings and roads but no less important. These are the systems by which land is developed, by which projects are financed and by which government makes decisions on physical growth and infrastructure. By calling, in essence, for some selective additions to the way things are done, it seems to offer a way to make a big difference through small incremental acts. Stop global warming; take a trolley to work.

There may be a danger, however, in exaggerating the modesty of what Calthorpe proposes. Surely many people believe that they have a God-given right to drive their cars on traffic-free roads and blame their inability to do so on someone else's failure. And while the lack of side yards and the use of walled gardens often make higher-density housing units more private than the average tract house, an occupant has to feel comfortable being part of a larger entity, rather than lord or lady of the manor. One would like to think there would be emotional compensations in being part of a community, or at least in seeing people on the street. But Americans have often shown themselves to be willing to pay to be alone.

While Calthorpe's ideas are close to practicable under our current land-use system, those of Christopher Alexander, another Bay Area architect, are not. They are based on the idea that physical development should be a direct expression of the needs and desires of a community, something that seems to make sense until you realize that in the United States development nearly always comes first. But his is a kind of unrealistic thinking that is very necessary if one is to imagine a future beyond this year's traffic problem or this year's energy problem.

In trying to develop a theory of city planning, Alexander looked outside of North America to cities and towns of Europe, Asia and, to some extent, Latin America. He observed that while many of these places have long histories of growth and change, they also preserved a strong sense of identity and unity. There are many factors that help bring this about, notably the necessity of using local building materials and a limited range of building methods. But these do not explain everything. Much of the integrity of such successful places must be in the minds who live in them and influence their growth.

While conventional planning often involves the formulation of an image of what a place will be like when it is finished, Alexander's approach avoids such a sense of closure. Instead, the future emerges from the existing conditions of a place, an analysis of likely changes and opportunities, a general idea of the physical form such changes might take and an understanding of how decisions will be made when the time comes. In a simulation of this process, involving a large piece of land in San Francisco, Alexander developed a complex set of principles and procedures to shape and change the basic concepts behind the plan. This is not a preservationist approach. The image of the place at the outset is important to the process, but it is analogous to a baby picture. As change comes, the place can change completely, while remaining recognizable. Neither is it merely opportunistic, adapting to any change that comes along, because it begins with a long-term view of the place and a clear expression of values about what kind of place it should become. Alexander calls this kind of change "emerging wholeness."

Stated in this way, Alexander's ideas seem attractive and even obvious. People's lives are, after all, a series of interactions between intention and chance, talents discovered, lessons learned, and each of us is always changing, always the same. Alexander is merely applying some of the principles of personal growth at a different scale of human life. Such an approach would seem to be applicable far beyond consideration of such issues as whether a street should be widened or where a child-care center ought to be located. It is, indeed, an application of the organic principle that growth is a process of realization, not mere physical extension.

But as Alexander himself recognizes, there is almost no hope that such ideas can affect the future of North American cities, towns and suburbs, because their growth and development is based on very different assumptions. The most crucial of these is that the purpose of physical change is to maximize the cash income, both for the entrepreneurs and investors who put the development together and for the tax base of local governments and authorities. This, in turn, generally implies that the development must be attractive to people outside of the community: store operators, office tenants, potential home buyers or whatever. The existing community may, in fact, be a large part of what makes the development attractive to investors, but community members are more often placed in an adversary position—attempting to protect what they value from development—than in a position of assuring that the development will benefit what is already in the community. (In some cities, "the community" is a euphemism for politically organized minority group members, who need to be bought off in some way to make a development work.)

Although the liveliest and pleasantest towns and neighborhoods tend to be complex and unpredictable, prevailing planning and development practice is reluctant to leave anything to chance. The result is that in cases where a good atmosphere has evolved spontaneously, the arrival of capital from outside will push it toward homogeneity as proven formulas rule. Something that is unique might be very suitable, and even profitable, but it is very difficult to borrow money to build the unprecedented. Master plans, though mutable, offer the illusion of lessened risk to investors, as do zoning controls. Alexander's more open-ended and complex approach does not. Moreover, a multifaceted planning process like Alexander's would have to take into account and learn from problems generated by the process, such as residential displacement, traffic congestion or neighborhood social tensions. Under the existing system, these are left to the appropriate government bureaucracies and tend to be viewed by politicians, businessmen and the news media as external to the development process itself.

There is another, perhaps deeper difference between Alexander's premises and those of conventional property development. Alexander sees community as a central fact, analogous to personal identity, while the development process sees community either as irrelevant or so broad as to be virtually meaningless. Development is the business of making places consumable. Most Americans may be in a place, but they are not of the place. Community brings commitments, which can be onerous. The freedom, mobility and openness we so value tend to devalue all of the particularities of existence. It would take an enormous change of consciousness to care as much as Alexander would like us to about the changing shape of the places where we live. We have enough troubles and responsibilities of our own without worrying about people who just happen to be nearby (unless they steal things or threaten violence). We succeed or fail as individuals. We live and we die alone.

Many would find these attempts to define community in terms of physical proximity to be anachronistic. In an age of instantaneous electronic communications, the meaning of physical proximity is diminished. Communities of interests and values exist throughout the world, especially among the affluent. It is easy to imagine that a graphic designer in Manhattan might have far more in common with someone who has a similar professional role and class status in Milan than with a hospital orderly in Queens or the fellow who lives on the grate right outside his apartment building. It is far more difficult, though still possible, to imagine either the orderly or the street person being able to make common cause with his counterparts throughout the world as well. But they don't have each other's phone numbers, and they don't visit each other very often. So far, nobody has ever proposed to put the underclass on-line.

The placeless world of international communications is, unlike the other environments we have considered, an entirely human artifact, and it is only now coming into being. If people are truly able to identify with and communicate with people from all over the world, there might well be a decline of bigotry and jingoism on an international scale. A world in which the communication of thought and expression could be universal and instantaneous might well be a more peaceful place. Strong identification with a particular place and with other people is necessary for survival, but it is also the primordial cause of warfare. People's participation in a worldwide information environment could, some believe, become too important to be placed in jeopardy by international violence.

Still, getting along with people in distant spots who share your interests is not enough if you hate the person down the block. Local animosity can have the same kind of planetary echoes as the misuse of chemicals. If you hate and fear your neighbors, you might stay in your house with the air conditioner on. You will try to manipulate the political or economic system so that you can afford to avoid such people by traveling through the city in a limousine with darkened windows. You will be committed to a high-energy lifestyle, which means that you are committed to oil tankers plying the seas and running aground on reefs and to the naval power and interventionist foreign policy that is required to ensure their safety. This world is one of severe competition for resources and is susceptible to economic blackmail, terrorism and international warfare. Such concrete concerns would very likely overwhelm any good feelings fostered in the immaterial world of communications. The world being created by computers and fiber-optic connections is complex and variegated, but it is a secondary environment. Other people and real things will always be far more important.

When people change the world, it's usually not because they mean to. It is because people have some more immediate goal or expectation, whose consequences they do not understand. Thinking on a global scale may make it more urgent to solve problems in a particular geographic region or a particular community, but it probably won't suggest how to solve them. Answers will more likely come from an understanding of differences and the complexity of their interaction than from any glib globalism.

But viewing the planet in tight close-up may not be the only way to gain an appreciation of the world. It is useful to go back to the image of the earth from space, and then to move back still farther so that our home planet is just one spot in the solar system. Human exploration has already jumped off the planet, and extraterrestrial exploration is likely to continue, in some way or form, well into the future.

For many people, space travel *is* the future. While options seem to be shrinking on earth, the prospect of extending human presence off the planet revives a feeling of infinite possibility. It offers the hope of worlds elsewhere, places where risk taking, pioneer spirit and courage can be pursued as they no longer can be on an increasingly crowded, constrained earth.

Americans are particularly prone to identify the prospect of space exploration with the powerful national myth of the Old West. Popular entertainments such as the *Star Wars* films consciously partake of the conventional elements of the Western genre, along with elements taken more directly from ancient tales of quests and heroes that give both horse operas and space operas their mythic underpinnings. Some of the same ideas appear in more sophisticated recent science fiction. The earth is conventionally portrayed as overorganized, overpopulated, a place of narrow horizons, while space stations, planets, asteroids and self-propelled artificial planetoids hurtling through interstellar space are the natural territory of the imaginative, the brave and the rugged. The space of literary creation is an immensely variegated allegorical landscape in which virtually anything can be encountered. But most often, the one doing the encountering is an independent-minded hero, an embodiment of our restless and noble, perhaps better, though surely more dangerous selves.

Some advocates of space exploration stretch this argument still further and argue that humanity is about to outgrow its native planet. Population pressures are mounting, resources dwindling. The possibility of nuclear catastrophe and biological or chemical holocaust still loom. Some fear that biotechnology could run amok, producing such disasters as oceanwide algal blooms that could kill the seas and throw the entire chemical basis for life irretrievably out of kilter. And something might come from out of the blue—a wayward asteroid or comet—that could bring the kind of rapid change that may have doomed the dinosaurs. Space is thus seen as a kind of insurance policy, to prevent the fate of humanity from being tied to only one fragile planet.

The idea of space as the new theater for the human quest is deeply paradoxical. Thanks to more than three decades of space probes launched by several different countries, we know a lot more about space than we ever did before, and it seems to be no place for either swashbucklers or lifeboats.

Cloud-shrouded Venus, once imaginable as a sultry, humid swamp planet, is now known to be remarkably like another familiar image—that of hell. With a surface temperature of 860 degrees Fahrenheit and an atmosphere ninety times as heavy as the earth's, it is a boiling, poisonous place, and it provides a cautionary tale of what the greenhouse effect can do when it really gets under way. Mars has too little atmosphere rather than too much, which makes it less forbidding for exploration. But it is a frozen, airless and apparently lifeless world. A rip in one's space suit would probably be fatal. It seems not to be a place where one can go it alone. The asteroids in the belt between Mars and Jupiter come in several different shapes and forms. They are believed to be filled with wonderfully useful raw materials, which can be used to build space stations, transform the planets and solve earthly shortages. But some of their attractiveness derives from wishful thinking. We simply don't know enough about them to make grandiose plans to inhabit them, mine them or drive them around the solar system. Man-made space colonies would, of course, be designed to be hospitable environments for humans, but building them would be much more difficult than settlers coming together for a barn raising.

In short, a quick view of the near solar system—the space we can realistically expect to explore in the imaginable future—shows that there is, indeed, no place like home. The poem on the Statue of Liberty welcomes "huddled masses yearning to breathe free," but in the vast frontier of space there is no such thing as a free breath, or a free drop of water, let alone a free lunch. Everything that is needed to sustain life must be painstakingly mined, synthesized and recycled at a level of economy and precision that would make the most draconian environmental restrictions proposed for the earth seem carefree by comparison. In order to get away from it all in space, you have to find a way to take it all with you. The earth still provides the most congenial environment for individuality and independence, and it is likely to continue so for as long as we can imagine.

The analogy between space and the settlement of the Americas is misleading in other ways as well. The existence of two new continents in the Western Hemisphere provided safety valves for the European population explosion induced by rapid industrialization. There are no such places to receive the excess populations of those parts of the world that are in a similar state today. Space colonization is sometimes discussed in rather vague terms as a way to make room for everyone. This is patently absurd. Large-scale space settlements are probably generations away, while population increase is with us right now, producing people at a rate that could never be absorbed by space colonies. Moreover, the cost of getting a person out of earth's gravity is measured in the hundreds of thousands of dollars, not counting the expense of creating habitable off-earth environments. This figure should decline somewhat, but there is no immediate prospect of a technology that would make the escape from gravity inexpensive. Clearly, the money would be better spent on earth, to encourage population control and more conservative living habits worldwide.

Indeed, the problems of global poverty and environmental degradation raise questions about the justification for a project as expensive as space exploration. Wouldn't the money spent on developing new launch vehicles and building space stations be better spent replanting forests and providing the hungry with food and the skills to feed themselves? Might not investments in companies that make cheap stoves or genetically altered seed that grows in deserts do more for mankind while making money, too? The answer to both questions is almost certainly yes, and there would probably be little harm in deferring most space activities for a decade or two while the earth puts its own house in order. If we can refrain from projecting our anxieties into the heavens by worrying that some enemy will get there first, space will be there when we're ready for it.

But even if we make such a decision, it is still worth thinking about space. The more we know about dead worlds, the more we are likely to have respect for the living one on which we live. And the more we have to think about the difficulty of simulating the delicate chemical balances that sustain life, the more careful we will be about thoughtlessly throwing our own environment out of whack. Research into the question of whether there is life on Mars led J. E. Lovelock to meditate on the unlikelihood of life on earth, and then to his Gaia hypothesis of a self-regulating living system. It would be almost as absurd to argue that space will offer the insights we need to make a better earth as to promise that it will offer a new El Dorado of unimaginable free wealth. But people tend to do many things at once, and often understanding in one area can bring enlightenment in many others as well.

Space is dead, deadly and utterly unforgiving. It demands that both people and technology operate without error at peak efficiency. Its exploration will require a long-term commitment by those who will stay on earth, and an acceptance of risk by both those who will go and those who will stay behind. It may eventually yield new sources of wealth, new ways of making things, new opportunities for people, but first it will require sacrifices. An economy that looks for payoffs from quarter to quarter will find the benefits of money spent on the development of space to be so long-term and speculative as to be practically nonexistent. The expense and ambition of space exploration virtually demand that it involve intimate and sustained international cooperation. But all these obstacles do not mean that space exploration should not be pursued. Indeed, the difficulty of the project is a large part of what makes it worthwhile.

The chief rewards of space exploration are likely to be intangible, but no less real for that. Space exploration is an effort to understand and embrace the cosmos. The pyramids of Egypt addressed the sun. The great Gothic cathedrals of medieval Europe exploded upward and tried to capture a heavenly light. In the very long run, both these building projects paid off in tourist trade, but the conviction that went into their making ensures that they will always be far more than theme parks or photo opportunities. Space exploration grows from the desire to know the planet, solar system, galaxy and universe in which we live, and part of this is an effort to understand the specialness of life and of human intelligence. Like the pyramids and the cathedrals, it is largely a spiritual endeavor, and like them, it will demand sustained technological invention and a tremendous amount of work.

Like any engineering program that serves largely spiritual ends, the exploration of space should probably be measured on aesthetic grounds. The cathedral builders constantly pushed their masonry technology to its limit, and they suffered collapses. They stretched their methods much further than anyone would dare today. One senses that it was meaningful work because it was the very best they were capable of doing, perhaps even better than they thought possible. There was a measure of such beauty in the Apollo program, but the space shuttle is conceptually ugly and perhaps its failures can be traced to the inability of those involved in its making to see it as something larger and nobler than themselves. It will be a very long time before space can be allowed to become routine, and moving out into the frontier will have to be a collective endeavor. Space pioneering will be a collective expression, one whose form and content must be meaningful to people everywhere. Anything that is not in some way thrilling probably should not be attempted.

It is striking that, in a civilization united largely by vicarious experience, which is looking toward a future when data bases will create more wealth than steel mills, advocates of space exploration seek to justify themselves in material terms. They tell us of single asteroids that can be mined to provide all the earth's requirements for cobalt or platinum and other important, expensive metals, and of chemical processes that can be performed in the weightlessness of space to fabricate materials that cannot be made on earth. Gerard K. O'Neill, in his book *The High Frontier* and in the activities of the Space Studies Institute, which he heads, has been an eloquent and imaginative proponent of this argument. Indeed, his key point—that the resources required for sustained space exploration are most usefully found on the moon and other extraterrestrial bodies—is absolutely convincing, and he and his colleagues have proposed apparently feasible technologies for exploiting these resources. He has also sought ways of making such efforts pay for themselves at a level that might be of interest for venture capitalists. One of the most exciting is the possibility of constructing satellites in space, using lunar materials, that would gather energy from the sun and beam it to the earth in the form of microwaves to provide electric power. He believes that this could be done more cheaply than manufacturing the components on earth and launching them into orbit, at least once a basic space infrastructure has been created.

Although O'Neill has no philosophical objection to government programs to help the process get started, he speaks the language of entrepreneurship, combined with the imagery of the American frontier. This is understandable, given the times in which he is working. Still, there is something troublesome about the assumption that the only way to justify what promises to be a key event in human history is by promising what may be an unrealistically high return on one's investment.

This is not to say that the motives behind technological and intellectual breakthroughs are always wholly selfless and unambiguous. Certainly, one of the main motives for building the Gothic cathedrals was civic competitiveness, and another was a hunger for intense visual experience. The European exploration and conquest of the Americas began half a millennium ago with a desire to eliminate some middlemen along the established trade routes, though there is evidence to suggest that curiosity about what was out in the ocean played a far from trivial role.

Ours is a time that respects the conquistadors' motive of grabbing for gold, but not the communal undertaking of building the cathedral. Still, motives are rarely unmixed, and one suspects that if O'Neill were to find investors they would probably be closet transcendentalists. The attraction of space is that it demands perfection of those who venture there. It is a high-risk venture in which the returns will be more than material, though perhaps not investment-grade.

There is an argument among those who advocate space exploration about the way in which people should conceive of this new human environment. Some believe that it should occur in wholly man-made structures placed in stable orbits about the earth and sun, while others believe that it should take place on the planets, satellites and asteroids. For the foreseeable future, such an argument is largely a matter of emphasis because both kinds of operations will be needed in any long-term space efforts. If, for example, the decision were made to create a base on the moon, a fairly elaborate space station would probably be required as a staging point. By contrast, if a large colony were to be built in space, its materials would have to come from the moon or other sources throughout the solar system, necessitating some continued human presence on other bodies in the solar system. Orbiting colonies of the kind O'Neill advocates have the advantage that they would not have any gravity to escape for travel, and the lack of gravity would make possible some novel forms of production (while making most conventional ones impossible). It would also avoid any disadvantages particular to a specific body—such as the lethal atmosphere of Venus or the lower solar energy levels of Mars. And an unplanted colony would be seen as belonging to whoever built and launched it, thus avoiding the danger of lunar land grabs and territorial disputes, though mining rights could well be a problem. Laws regulating use of the oceans and Antarctica remain unresolved, and the moon will probably join the list.

Like all islands, these artificial colonies would lack direct access to most necessary materials. By contrast, a moon base would be able to dig for oxygen and other key resources right outside. It might have some psychological advantages as well. Settlers would at least feel as if they were somewhere real, even though their ability to interact with their environment would be slight. It is easier to imagine moving to another world than to a floating one constructed in space, though it is possible to see the artificial colony as an interplanetary Venice, a place whose residents would always be focused on voyages outward rather than on the ground where they stand. Whatever the emphasis that is ultimately chosen, there would surely be enough people eager to be on the cutting edge of human endeavor to staff the new colony.

The difference between these two approaches to space settlement would be insignificant in the short term, but potentially great over the centuries. Space-borne colonies imply that humans will perpetually be explorers, possibly living most of their lives off-earth, like sailors who might spend most of their lives at sea but still don't mistake it for home. Colonies on planets and other bodies imply permanent residence. This could presumably happen underground, or under vast domes that would keep air in and radiation out. And when pursued to its logical conclusion it implies two potential technologies of enormous hubris: turning other planets and satellites into new earths and creating new kinds of people adapted to living in them.

The first, which is called planetary engineering or terraforming, seeks to remake other places in the solar system so that humans could survive in them without extensive life-support systems. It is interesting that one of the first hypotheses that planets could be remade environmentally through massive engineering projects was ascribed to extraterrestrials, specifically Martians. Some astronomers explained the canals they thought they saw on Mars as an effort by its residents to save a dying planet. The planetary engineering with which we are most familiar is almost wholly inadvertent—the climate change that many believe is being induced by the release of carbon dioxide and other greenhouse gases into the atmosphere. The way to make Mars habitable might be to induce a greenhouse effect there, though that probably doesn't justify our current experiment on earth. It is likely that the first conscious planetary engineering will also involve the earth. Massive reforestation would probably qualify, and pass the test of subtlety besides. Other proposals that have come forth, such as filling the space around the earth with bits of reflective paper like those used to get a cheap gasp from theater audiences, are more difficult to countenance.

And when they think beyond the earth, the terraformers are so ambitious as to be either comical or frightening. They make no little plans, and though they don't propose to move heaven and earth, they can't keep their hands off anything else. They propose knocking an asteroid into Venus, to shake things up and cool things down. They'd like to give Mars a moon bigger than the two it already has, in order to keep the planet from wobbling so badly on its axis. Terraformers have an almost terrifying disrespect for the universe as they find it. For the foreseeable future they are fantasists, because such ambitious planetary engineering, if it happens at all, is probably centuries away. Still, they are probably useful to have around, if only for the attention that they call to the maintenance of the earth's life-support systems. The danger is that we will mistake the assertion of uncontrollable power for progress, as we so often do, and decide that shrouding the planet in confetti is a small price to pay for the pleasure of driving fast alone.

The other transformation, that of the human species itself, is equally frightening, but it, too, is also already under way in the form of genetic engineering. As with autonomous robots, space seems to offer room for technologies that seem both dangerous and unnecessary here on earth. Space travel and interplanetary settlement seem appropriate uses for technologies that could alter human limbs, organs and overall metabolism to be more suited to long-distance travel, weightlessness or the conditions on particular planetary bodies. If humans are to live on many worlds, it is only logical that they should direct their evolution to make themselves better suited to the habitats in which they will live. But as with terraforming, this need not be a high priority for a very long time to come. It is merely something to be kept in mind, if only to remind ourselves that there is no reason, on earth at least, to engineer ourselves into abominable snowmen, disembodied minds or mermaids.

But space is a theoretical playground, in which we can dream of doing things we dare not try at home. It is the realm where the old technological joyride still seems to work, and technologies that seem repellent and unnecessary here on earth would make sense. Space is an endeavor that can keep all the mad scientists busy forever.

Perhaps if we were to become better people, we would not need space as an outlet for all of our dreams of control and domination. We would realize that the earth is our home and the only place where humans can be free. But even if we never leave the earth, just thinking about space exploration can help us appreciate the unique nurturing planet of which we are a part.

7 / Subtle Progress

Consider for a moment the modern, high-tech red Delicious apple. Ruby-hued, flawless, shiny-skinned, it has the lean voluptuousness of a fashion model. It is able to travel long distances without harm. It has been bred and treated to keep its alluring look long after the center has started to rot. It has been sprayed with insecticide, fungicide and possibly a coat of wax. This fruit has been crafted for convenience and engineered for desire.

Its only problem is that it doesn't taste very good. That doesn't mean that it tastes bad. Really, it tends to be dry and woody, and not taste much like anything at all. This state-of-the-art apple is without risk—except, of course, for cancer, liver ailments and other maladies that might be induced by the poisons that make its perfection possible. But despite its tempting appearance, this apple is without much pleasure either.

In the fall, when old-fashioned apples with blotchy color and blemished skin come to market, they tend to be sold as luxury items, appealing to a minority of epicures and health-food enthusiasts. They are likely to be local products, grown on land that has not yet been, but soon may be, developed. They are not designed for long stays on the shelf or in the refrigerator. They are seasonal and transient. And those who have grown used to the enticing blandness of the mainstream apple will never know their sweetness.

The modern apple is a characteristic product of our civilization. Like television, high-speed aircraft or wonder drugs, this apple is a largely successful attempt to outwit time, place, mortality. You can always have the same apple anyplace, anytime, something that wasn't possible thirty years ago. It is grown by farming methods that kill all those parts of the biosphere that might compromise its near-pornographic marketability. It is an apple for the eye, developed to appeal to the sense humans trust most, even when the information it offers is not entirely reliable.

The personal helicopters and three-dimensional television sets predicted three decades ago for the waning days of the century have not yet happened. But the year-round availability of perfect fruit is something that was predicted and has been achieved, though at a cost.

This apple surely seemed like progress to those who were developing it, because it answered the most evident demands of the society as a whole. Now most of the apple-growing industry has been redesigned to produce this product. It is unquestionably a dream fulfilled, though it is not so certain that it was the right dream. The same is true of many other things that once appeared on our future shopping list, and similar problems would probably emerge from any future pleasures we might enumerate today. When we speak of such technological goals, we are really talking about embodying a set of values that even those responsible for realizing the inventions often fail to recognize.

It is more useful to think about the future in terms of these underlying attitudes. Many of the values that have caused our current problems are still part of our society. We still believe in the high-speed, high-energy joyride. We still believe in physical isolation. We still view productivity primarily as the diminution of human labor in the making of goods. We still believe that "I'll buy that" is the surest statement of sincerity. And we still want to believe that it is not necessary to wonder about where we are going, because progress is automatic and one-way.

Yet as the previous chapters have suggested, there are other, subtler values emerging that might prove to be more useful in dealing with the technological, human and environmental problems we now face. Subtlety rejects high-intensity solutions to single problems. It rejects single solutions to any problem or universal standards or expectations for anything. Subtlety embraces diversity and abhors monocultures. It focuses on individual people and individual places, even as it keeps the regional and the global firmly in mind. It believes that wholes are different from the sums of their parts, but that both the wholes and the parts are extremely important. It is strongly grounded in the material world, both in the possibilities it offers and in the demands it makes. Perhaps the most crucial element of the subtle attitude is its focus on shaping technology and organization to further human aims, rather than reshaping human life according to the patterns demanded by now obsolescent machinery. A subtle approach to the future believes in the possibility of progress in the lives of individuals and humanity in general, but it recognizes this must be hard-won. Progress does not come about passively. You can't buy it at the store. It can't happen without other people.

With these general aims in mind, we might ask what a subtle apple would be like. Obviously, one couldn't draw a picture of it, because it would differ from place to place, time to time, purpose to purpose. It is important to recognize, however, that subtlety does not imply the return to some "natural" fruit. Apples do not just grow on trees. They are a human artifact, the result of thousands of years of breeding, grafting and other human interventions in the biosphere. If you saw the wild fruit from which the apple is descended, you probably wouldn't recognize even a family resemblance. Any apple is, in some sense, designed. The question of subtlety comes when you consider what it is designed to do. The current mainstream apple is designed primarily for mass production, distribution and marketing. It is an effort to get the same apple to everyone. A subtler apple might be designed with a greater emphasis on nourishment and taste, and less on uniform good looks.

A subtler apple is more likely to be local. In the eastern United States, acreage devoted to apple orchards has been diminishing. This shrinkage does not, however, mean that it is impossible to grow apples profitably. More often, it is a reflection of the reality that farmers can make more money by selling their land for the development of exurban houses, shopping centers and office parks. A subtler apple is, therefore, dependent on a desire to protect agricultural landscapes from being subsumed into the continental sprawl. Such a desire is evident in such urban states as New Jersey and Pennsylvania, where voters have been willing to fund bond issues to maintain agricultural uses of the land.

The effort to preserve such landscapes implicitly acknowledges that there are many ways in which a place can be productive. An orchard is not simply a machine for producing apples. It offers aesthetic pleasures, and it can accommodate other living things without harming its ability to produce fruit. This implies that it should not be a poisoned environment, dangerous to people and animals. The subtle apple must be designed to resist pests, insofar as it can. Biological pest control should be used as much as possible, and chemical pesticides should be aimed as narrowly as possible so that they harm the pests and nothing else. These are, of course, ideals. Compromises must always be made, but when goals are shifted a bit, so is the nature of the compromise.

The subtler apple is dependent on the subtler consumer. People have to break the habit of seeking visual perfection and be willing to really taste the apple. They must be willing to accept variety in their lives, and perhaps even accept the possibility that the same apples will not be available at all times. At a time when fresh-produce departments are expanding at supermarkets, and freshness and health have become powerful marketing concepts, it does not seem wholly unlikely that such a shift of values might come.

Ultimately, though, the subtler apple and the subtler life depend on expanding human horizons so that people do not see themselves primarily as consumers. Obviously, people will have to eat, and they will want to buy things that make their lives better. But the aggregation of goods will no longer be seen as life's principal satisfaction, or be accepted as compensation for unsatisfying jobs or superficial, competitive relationships.

This is a large burden for even so mythic a fruit as the apple to bear. Still, though the apple is but one small part of our lives, it reflects how we think about the larger issues. And how we resolve those big issues inevitably reshapes the apple.

It is difficult to talk about an apple in such a context without being reminded of its symbolic role in Judeo-Christian tradition as the embodiment of the knowledge and self-awareness that separate humankind from the rest of creation. Human alienation from the rest of the physical and biological world has long been identified as a problem. Still, it is impossible to imagine that Western civilization and the worldwide phenomenon of modernization it has spawned could have happened without it. There are few on earth today who are not, in some sense, products of modernization, regardless of their own religious beliefs. There is no secular equivalent of baptism to restore our innocence.

The most recent recapitulation of this ancient story comes in the guise of environmentalism. The burden of knowledge comes from the proliferation of newly available and suddenly negative data about the degradation of several of the biochemical systems that sustain life. We feel the wrenching pain of separation as paradise is lost once more. We are ashamed. Faced with perfection, the only thing people can do is mess it up.

This is still a tragic story, one that transcends religion and suffuses technology and politics as well. At heart, the issue is human freedom—whether it truly exists and how it is to be used. For those who are fundamentalists of either the religious or the environmental sort, the answer is that such freedom doesn't exist. We must instead study carefully to discern either the divine or the natural scheme, understand how we should behave within this scheme and see to it that we organize our lives and our societies to uphold these constraints. The problem with either of these views is, of course, our own nature. How did the Creator give rise to such an unruly being, and why? How can we keep our hands off the evolution of life on earth when we have been meddling with it, to our apparent benefit, for millennia? Human beings may not be able to make an airtight case that they are the crown of creation or the triumph of evolution, but it will not help either ourselves or the rest of the biological and physical world to regard humanity as a cosmic failure.

The only course of action, in either religious or environmental terms, is to go on as we are while trying to be careful. We must be aware of our powers, humble about our limits, keep our eyes on the big picture and try not to fall victim to blinding, destructive obsessions. We can never stop being careful, or surrender ourselves to too definite systems of behavior, which are inevitably reductive and eventually lose all touch with reality.

This near-tragic sense of human nature implies a politics that is broadly based, responsive and humble. Democratic forms, in which diverse interests compete and individuals are respected, are far more subtle than forms of government that are focused on a clear goal and in which the individual is less important than the goal. With the breakdown of Marxist-Leninist regimes in Eastern Europe, it became clear that they had not only failed in their stated aim of enabling workers to fully realize the value of their labor, but also stifled human creativity and degraded the environment far more aggressively than did countries ruled by private interest. It is easy to imagine that a regime that, for example, made protection of the environment paramount and demanded universal compliance with a Green ideology would result in the same combination of tyranny and failure.

The U.S. Constitution, including the Bill of Rights, is quite a subtle document, one designed as much to keep the government from acting as to provide a structure within which it does act. The danger comes from pervasive phenomena in our society that were unanticipated by the Constitution and, in some cases, work against its spirit. These include such familiar phenomena as the country's permanent wartime footing, instantaneous communication, the emergence of weapons whose absolute destructiveness concentrates world-destroying powers in the hands of one person, the creation and accessibility of data bases and the dominance of the mass-production, mass-consumption, mass-media society. The Founding Fathers could not have imagined the effectiveness with which contemporary technology can direct either energy or ideas, usually in the interest of those who hold the technology. Those things we can influence merely as citizens seem to be fewer and fewer, and we surrender our basic freedoms, not to an overreaching state, but to such people as mall operators and credit card companies who abridge our expression of political opinion and invade our privacy so they can sell to us more effectively.

One direction in which technology is unquestionably headed is toward the ability to gather and relate enormous amounts of data instantaneously. This is a useful ability, but it poses grave challenges to our freedom. Up to now, our freedom of movement, our freedom of association and our personal habits were limited by the ability, interest or efficiency of those who chose to limit them. Now there are no such limits, because through our everyday actions we create a profile of ourselves. The use of such identification tools as voiceprints, and such proposals as the car control system mentioned in Chapter 4 (page 133) can be the basis for a police state more effective than any the world has ever known. It can even be deployed for what appear to be subtle ends. One can imagine, for example, that a particularly health-conscious society might approve of analyzing what you buy at supermarkets, liquor stores and restaurants and adjusting health insurance premiums so that they will reflect the risks you are taking. There is something eminently reasonable in such a suggestion. It is, after all, a logical extension of random drug testing and the principle of making life difficult for cigarette smokers. But there is also something horrible in it. It denies any possibility of human diversity or freedom of choice, and makes all people fit into a system whose standards may be wise but will more likely be arbitrary. The record of history is quite clear. Diversity and freedom work. Autocratic systems can focus enormous energies and abilities in the short run, but eventually fail.

How does subtle politics deal with such technologies? The only possible answer is to decide not to use them. It creates a taboo; it rediscovers a civil right. Since World War II the nations of the world have decided that nuclear weapons are too dangerous to use, and most countries have come to the conclusion that chlorofluorocarbons pose too great a threat to the environment. Likewise, incessant monitoring of our lives in the service of behavior modification must be rejected because it would blight human life and deprive people of their creativity and society of its resiliency. On every scale of life on earth, diversity works, and every all-encompassing man-made system has run aground.

A truly passionate sense of the value of human freedom and dignity has been missing from our political system in recent decades, though the experience of Eastern Europe might foster a renewed appreciation of their value. Increasingly, our political choices have been packaged as a consumer good, and as with the modern apple, the absence of blemishes, not substance, has determined what gets bought. Candidates seek to bruise their opposition rather than illuminate the difficulties and possibilities inherent in particular places and times.

Candidates seek not so much to win as to make their opponents lose. Meanwhile, increasing numbers of Americans choose not to participate.

Norbert Wiener, the father of cybernetics, might have suggested a way out of this form of crude politics when he made a distinction between his own life as a scientist and that of the warrior or game player: "The research physicist has all the time in the world to carry out his experiments, and he need not fear that nature will in time discover his tricks and method and change her policy. Therefore his work is governed by his best moments, whereas a chess player cannot make one mistake without finding an alert adversary ready to take advantage of it and to defeat him. Thus the chess player is governed more by his worst moments than by his best moments." In recent years, even science has become more of a high-stakes cutthroat game, in which the fear of losing glory and research grants can distort the deliberate and responsible process of finding the truth. But most people would probably agree with Wiener that it is more satisfying to measure your life by its best moments than by its worst. That's why, even if you choose to participate in the game, it's best not to fully accept it. Instead, you should maintain values that transcend the game.

Wiener was not merely indulging in whimsical metaphor when he wrote about the mind of the game player. Game theory was, with cybernetics, communications theory and the atomic bomb, one of the chief intellectual products of World War II. War is a gamelike situation, one that involves the abandonment of many moral and social values. It literally redefines the value of human life. And although many wars have had inconclusive results, the chief aim of war is to achieve victory and avoid defeat. Writing at a time when the society was shifting to a permanently warlike stance, behind a shield of nuclear weapons—whose use would most likely be undertaken during a worst moment rather than during a best one—Wiener was in the now familiar stance of the scientist pondering the dark consequences of scientific achievement.

History may decide that game theory, combined with the lethal nature of nuclear weapons, actually helped to prevent all-out war in the second half of the twentieth century. By abstracting and radically simplifying the range of possibilities and analyzing their probable outcomes, game theory made war less intellectually compelling, less like chess, more like tic-tac-toe. Game theory is a powerful tool for analyzing situations in which there is a narrow range of choices. That is what characterizes those activities in which, as Wiener said, your performance is to be judged by your worst moments. But the best moments come from a refusal to accept such limitations and a willingness to break down barriers and make unexpected connections.

Subtle politics require a subtle voter, one who demands that his own life be evaluated in terms of its best moments and who is willing to accord a candidate the same respect. In the case of a President, whose hand is on the nuclear trigger, there seems to be some reason to consider behavior at the worst moments. Still, the Presidents we have selected during the nuclear era have seemed particularly susceptible to bad moments and have nevertheless been able to resist blowing the world away.

M oving to an approach based on subtlety rather than the illusion of mastery would not, however, require forfeiting the fruits of high technology. Indeed, the chief tools of subtlety—including the computer, materials engineering and genetic engineering—represent some of the most important directions in which technology is already moving.

Of these, the computer is probably the most important, because it makes it possible to see patterns and find order in data that are otherwise overwhelming. Like a microscope, it reveals levels of reality that had previously been impossible to see. For example, mapping the human genome entails plotting the exact sequence of the four different nucleotides of which DNA is composed. There are only four letters, but the word is 3 billion letters long. And spelling the word is only the beginning, because most genes operate in combinations. This is something that could not be done on index cards.

The computer offers the hope of understanding complex systems and intervening in them, though in many cases—such as the world economy or the weather—just being able to predict their behavior more accurately would be an enormous breakthrough. Chaos theory, which would not have been possible without the computer's ability to handle enormous amounts of data instantaneously, has shown that small changes in such systems can have large results. Most often we see such possibilities negatively, as a small nudge that brings on global warming, a new ice age or an algal bloom the size of the

Atlantic. (Some investigators believe, for example, that the belching of livestock may be a significant contributor to the greenhouse effect.) Yet there is also the possibility that this kind of leverage can work in desirable directions as well. The further development of automatic pattern recognition and analysis systems, the most fruitful current application of artificial intelligence technology, offers hope of sophisticated new monitoring techniques so that we can determine just what we are doing.

The one aspect of materials engineering that has attained widespread public attention is the discovery of ceramic materials capable of superconductivity at relatively high temperatures. Although superconductors seem to have great promise, they face equally great obstacles before they can be put to use. Meanwhile, chemists and engineers are quietly refining their ability to design a substance virtually to the specifications for which it will be used. Stronger, lighter ceramic, plastic and composite materials can replace raw materials imports and can reduce transportation and energy costs in the products in which they are used. They promise the replacement of smelters, mills and sprawling chemical plants with alchemical boutiques that can make stuff to order.

If new materials have been relatively unsung, it is likely that biological engineering has been oversold. In recent years, there has been an investors' backlash against companies that have promised the godlike too quickly. Still, the ability to alter genes, to move genetic information from one organism to another and to use bacteria to produce crucial biological substances promises to have enormous impact. The implications for both medicine and agriculture are apparent and are beginning to be realized. Some of the most optimistic see the replacement of all factories with great tanks of living cells capable of excreting tomorrow's riches. Hyperbole aside, crafting more resilient, more nutritious plants and using living organisms to "grow" both organic and inorganic materials without pollution are possibilities the world cannot afford to forgo, even though there are potentially catastrophic hazards in the technology and destructive ways of putting it to use.

There are many different methods and processes that are potentially subtle, but any of them can also be used crudely. For example, genetically altered seed could be a sensitive, high-tech innovation. But one likely agricultural application of genetic engineering is to design a plant that would be immune to a particular herbicide. Then, while the crop is growing, there would be mass spraying of the fields, and all plants other than the desired one would be killed. This particular proposal even has what seems to be an ecologically attractive element: It would cut down on the necessity to till the soil and presumably decrease erosion. Yet an approach that would poison the ground and the water and addict farmers to a specific seed and a specific herbicide is hardly sensitive. It does not enhance a living system. Instead, it destroys it and introduces dangerous elements which might have an adverse impact elsewhere. While subtle technology tricks a complex system into producing something people need, this approach simplifies a complex system and lets most of its elements go to waste.

A society that sought subtlety would embrace all sorts of innovation. But instead of centralizing and sharply focusing the power that new technologies would generate, it would try to diffuse the benefits and offer choice about how they are to be used. Thus it would probably have a predisposition against releasing the force that holds atoms together as a way to boil water, because this concentrates too many dangers in one place and too much power in too few hands. (If nuclear power could be proven less hazardous than alternatives, and the waste-disposal problem solved, however, it could conceivably be used in a subtle way.) Generally, though, the goal would be not to use expensive or high-energy means in situations where simpler, cheaper things could be used more efficiently. Thus a program to help people in an agricultural village improve their situation might include the distribution of plant strains that have been genetically altered to enable them to harbor nitrogen-fixing bacteria and fight insect pests. But it might also involve distribution of simple, efficient stoves, to cut down on the use of wood for fuel, and the teaching of techniques to use plant and animal wastes for energy. The lessons of the appropriate-technology movement of the 1970s would be incorporated into a comprehensive approach in which cutting-edge science could be used in humane ways.

This sounds like a contradiction in terms. The appropriate-technology movement arose as a reaction against the attempt to introduce sophisticated, urbanized Western methods into places where they did not fit. Chief among these is the cash economy, which encourages people to ignore the crops they eat in favor of crops that allow them to buy things. Simple tools and technological systems that people make and run themselves have been shown to be preferable to imports the culture is unable to sustain.

What is changing is that the world is shrinking. Three decades ago, many thought that the high-input, high-output agriculture practiced on the American plains would work throughout the world. During the 1970s, it became clear that India and Mexico were not suited for Kansas-style agriculture. Now it is becoming increasingly evident that even Kansas is not helped by methods that use large amounts of energy, water, chemical fertilizers and pesticides. There is at least the possibility that as the developed countries look toward healthier and more sustainable food production, they will make advances that will be appropriate everywhere.

One can even imagine ways in which less developed countries could leapfrog over developed ones. For example, solar technology is stymied in the United States because it cannot compete with fossil fuels within our high-volume energy infrastructure. But in countries without such an infrastructure (and lots of sunshine) photovoltaic cells could generate enough power to change the lives of countless villagers. A commitment to such a program in India, for example, would mean that economies of scale and possibly a lucrative export market could follow.

The possible convergence of interests between rich and poor countries should not be overstated, however. Some advances in materials fabrication, for example, are depressing the value of minerals and raw materials that are important sources of foreign exchange for many poor countries. This implies a painful adjustment for poor countries that have been accustomed to living off their resource base, though it might help them toward self-sufficiency in the long run. Moreover, the expansion of robotic manufacture in wealthy countries will probably diminish the value of low-cost labor for manufacture, another important resource of less developed countries. Eventually, laboratory-produced psychoactive drugs will probably diminish the acreage planted in coca plants and opium poppies throughout the world, though other tropical cash crops will still take up space better suited for food crops.

One American power company has attempted to compensate

for the large amounts of carbon dioxide it releases into the atmosphere by buying a tract of Central American rain forest. This is a superficially subtle approach which turns out to be quite crude. There is no reason to believe that people who want to make destructive use of the forests will heed "No Trespassing" signs. Moreover, the rain forest can be a sustainable human environment, producing products and livelihoods for significant numbers of people. Such rain forest products as mahogany can be harvested in a subtle way, or they can be the by-product of clear-cuts to make cattle ranching possible. Thus, the purchase of tropical hardwoods might ultimately contribute to a way of life that improves both the environment and people's lives. The purchase of tropical hamburger, however, is a sure path to destruction.

The subtle application of technology would not mean that rich and poor would become alike. What it would mean is that they would no longer be headed in diametrically opposite directions. Today, the rich nations behave according to an assumption that waste equals wealth and that the world's resources and their access to them are essentially infinite. The poor often waste and abuse resources of global importance as part of their struggle to survive. Both rich and poor would be aided by a technology whose goal is physical efficiency and productive harmony with natural systems. And if those at the head of the table stop being so gluttonous, there might be something left for those farther down the line.

There are many ideas currently being discussed to ameliorate some of the current environmental and energy dilemmas without requiring a fundamental change of belief. Most do require some changes of thinking toward more subtle and complex ways of understanding our habits and lives.

For example, despite the spate of energy-saving measures that were adopted during the 1970s, our workplaces tend to be illuminated excessively and the bulbs used maintain far from peak efficiency. It has been demonstrated that investments in more efficient electrical devices are far more cost-effective—not to mention less polluting and potentially hazardous—than investments in additional electrical generating capacity. The use of one 15-watt high-tech compact light bulb has been estimated to prevent the combustion of 400 pounds of carbon, a contributor to the greenhouse effect, and 25 pounds of sulfur dioxide, the chief contributor to acid rain, at the same time that it saves a company using it about $50 in electricity and labor for bulb changing. If all American businesses converted to state-of-the-art components, they would save 80 percent of their expenditures for lighting energy, which is, in turn, equivalent to about half the coal burned in the United States each year. There is still room for improvement in such other areas as windows, appliance efficiency, automobile fuel efficiency and many other areas, though the low petroleum prices that characterized most of the 1980s have slowed the rate of adoption for such improvements.

If, for example, the cost of petroleum were raised to its true replacement cost, including its attendant environmental and military costs, a lot of subtlety would appear quite spontaneously. Automobile companies might begin to design the undersides of their cars to cut down on wind resistance. People would pay greater attention to insulating their homes. Mass transportation might win a political constituency as car ownership became a larger financial burden. More electrical utilities might offer time-sensitive pricing to individuals, something that might make electric-powered cars viable without requiring massive new investment in generating plants.

Already, money spent on conserving energy usually offers a better return than money spent on generating energy. Still, an electric utility can pay off the money it borrowed to build a new power plant by passing the costs on to consumers, whereas establishing a fair rate of return on conservation programs is more difficult. Amory Lovins, of the Rocky Mountain Institute, has labeled the fruits of investment in greater efficiency "negawatts." Utilities that have had difficulties getting approvals or financing for nuclear and conventional power plants have been forced to take the idea of conservation seriously, which will ultimately mean that state regulatory agencies which set utility rates will do so as well. This is a major turnaround, given that utilities have historically promoted appliances and high-energy lifestyles as part of an effort to make their investments in power plants more profitable.

Such approaches to energy conservation have a commonsensical quality. They scarcely seem visionary. They are, indeed, a bit boring—in the way that a diet is less interesting than a banquet. They seem negative, in that they are concerned with reducing destructive behavior rather than with doing something good, though their willingness to meet the problem halfway is precisely what makes them more likely to bring immediate improvement. Moreover, they do have some fairly radical implications. For example, Lovins with his negawatts is rewriting some of the equations by which business success is measured. Productivity has long been defined as production per employee. Workers were replaced by capital and energy. Lovins is arguing, in effect, that the marginal cost of energy is much greater than has been assumed and that productivity must be measured in kilowatt-hours as well as man-hours. The idea that utilities, whose history has been one of promoting ever greater energy use by all sorts of consumers at every time of day, can get the greatest return on investment by helping their customers save requires the reversal of a century of assumptions. "A penny saved is a penny earned" is not an unfamiliar concept in America, though it is more often said than acted upon.

In the United States, as virtually everywhere else, government policy, particularly taxation, directs the flow of investment. Historically, real estate has been the most privileged form of investment in America, and though this is a bit less dramatically the case now than it was a decade ago, it is still true. Individuals are encouraged by the tax laws to make a single-family house the basis of their personal worth. Companies are allowed to take various deductions and tax credits for the construction of new facilities. Various forms of accelerated depreciation stimulate turnover and new development, and construction activity is viewed as one of the most sensitive economic indicators.

If you believe in a subtle society, in which the land is viewed as a precious resource, such overstimulation of building activity seems counterproductive. As we have seen, development tends to follow lenders' standards rather than local needs, and tends toward a universalized landscape with its attendant waste of energy. Moreover, it is equally apparent that even as we overinvest as a society in land and buildings, we underinvest in people. Investments in prenatal care, infant health, early childhood schooling, general education, job training and retraining are difficult to compare with investments in office buildings, but properly administered and targeted, they would very likely be just as productive. Moreover, they would better adapt the country to a world economy that is increasingly based on ideas and creativity, while minimizing the social conflicts and additional tax burden that dependent people create. Governmental encouragement of real estate development comes in the form of taxes that aren't collected, rather than money spent, and such subsidies are less often scrutinized than are outright expenditures. If some of this subsidy was removed from real estate and distributed to companies and individuals to be invested in increased human competence, it would diminish the degradation of the landscape, improve people's lives and probably increase true economic growth besides.

Thus, although there are any number of ameliorative steps that can be taken in industry, land development, agriculture, transportation and many other fields, even these run up against some deeply embedded assumptions. Investment in preventing pollution appears on the balance sheet as an unproductive expenditure, while the cost of cleaning up disasters is counted in the gross national product. Outmoded ways of envisioning goals and figuring costs create both waste and unhappiness, and they form intellectual barriers to even the most modest, least intrusive kinds of change. Thus, it often requires some big changes in thinking to make sense of even small changes in the way things are done.

It is not easy to imagine an economy that retains its dynamism and freedom for its participants while avoiding the wastefulness of the mass-consumption society that has been elaborated during the last century. One alternative might be to reorganize businesses so that they do not produce discrete products but would offer an integrated package of related products and services of a specified quality on a long-term-contract basis. One precedent for this approach would be AT&T before its breakup. The product it offered was not telephones—even though it was long the world's largest manufacturer of those—but a communications environment in which virtually everyone could participate to some extent. The telephones, which were leased to customers as part of the cost of their service, were extremely durable, and they strove not to be too fashionable in their appearance. When technology changed, they were replaced. The success of the company was not in its unit sales of telephones but in the establishment of the company's service.

One can easily imagine a similar principle extended to automobile leasing, in which the consumer would obtain not a particular car but a mix of transportation, maintenance and insurance services. Payments would be predictable and essentially worry-free. Some electric and gas utilities have long been in the appliance business, originally in an effort to spur domestic demand. One can imagine that a utility might be able to offer a service that would incorporate high-efficiency appliances and lighting fixtures and bulbs in a package that would enable users to minimize their bills while allowing the utilities to better plan their capacity and eliminate the need to either build new plants or bring wasteful, high-polluting ones on-line at peak times. In recent years, diaper services have staged a comeback because they may be more environmentally sound than disposable diapers and they don't cost much more.

As the lives of consumers fill up with more and more things that can go wrong, people are willing to pay extra not to have to worry. It is true that such an approach would probably never work in such businesses as clothing, where fashion is often more important than utility, or in fields where technological innovation is explosive, as it has recently been in personal computers and electronic devices. Still, the concept of products embedded in services is hardly a revolutionary one, and it seems particularly appropriate to a time when the economics of production no longer demand mass manufacture. It will be less important to simply make things and more important to make them useful. In some cases, particularly those involving utilities, there will be some significant antitrust and regulatory problems. But consumers' frustrations with the divided responsibilities of the postbreakup telephone system might convince them that buying a service is superior to buying a lot of products.

The chief model for subtle progress is the complex efficiency of living things, which have high information content and are able to make very effective use of the diffuse, freely available energy of the sun. Biological systems provide an ultimate goal that human technology will probably never reach, but they also offer many lessons about how our ways of doing things can be improved. It would seem logical to begin with agriculture, which involves living things but which has dealt with them according to an industrial, rather than a biological, model.

This industrialization of agriculture has often involved the application of new energy to the growth of crops to accelerate natural processes in much the same way that the burning of coal has allowed the acceleration of mechanical processes. Crops that have been genetically altered to repel pests or fix nitrogen would be tremendous technological achievements that would revolutionize farming, but they would not pack the same kind of energy punch that previous advances in agriculture have. Even if such miracles come, agriculture will still have to become far more careful than it has been. Genetically engineered crops could provide a more efficient way of living off current income, in contrast to the current system, which depletes the wealth of the soil, aquifers and energy supplies that took millions of years to be formed. But they will have to be used in conjunction with other, less high-tech methods—such as crop rotation and the use of perennial plants to preserve soils—which aim to produce robust living systems rather than one-dimensional products. Obviously, it will be a long time, if ever, before we can feed everyone purely from current income, but if moving toward that goal were to be viewed as a measure of progress, many environmental problems would begin to shrink. It would almost surely mean that food would cost more, reversing a long-term American trend toward lower basic food prices, partially offset by increasing processing costs. But organic and pesticide-free produce is taking up an ever larger amount of shelf space, even in large supermarkets, and such fresh, healthful products have become a profitable segment of the food retailing industry. Such clear demand is inducing greater supplies, and the marketplace might be more sensitive than the political system in signaling a shift of the public's expectations for food and the ways it is produced.

The reestablishment of agriculture on a stronger ecological footing is a logical step toward subtler use of technology. But it is equally necessary to apply the same lessons of living systems to other productive activities. Thus, when we speak of an industry reorganizing itself on an ecological basis, we are not talking about hobbling it with expensive add-ons that ruin its ability to compete in the marketplace. Rather, we imply that the industry is operating at peak efficiency, serving a real need and profiting from what used to be its wastes.

Biology and industry are both processes which use captured energy, mostly from the sun, to transform materials into states which are more useful. In both cases, these transformations produce waste products, and the useful products of the processes decay and must be renewed. The difference is that biology operates virtually as a closed system, with wastes being recycled or used for the sustenance of other organisms, while industry has tended to operate on the assumption that resources are infinite and wastes insignificant. We have known for centuries that this assumption is not true. But both capitalism and Marxism have tended to undervalue both raw materials and the health of the overall environment, and except in some extraordinary situations, when wars cut off key materials or natural phenomena amplified environmental problems, there was little reason to take such factors into account. Routinely, toxic wastes are allowed to leach into the soil, and the energy and materials equivalent of billions of barrels of oil and mountains of minerals are buried in landfills. New York is rapidly creating a pile of trash on Staten Island the size of the great pyramid of Cheops, while other American cities must improvise each day to figure out where the next bag of trash will go. Recycling of household trash will soon be universal, as will trade in industrial wastes and requirements that producers either clean up their pollution themselves or pay the full cost to the public of doing it for them.

While natural ecosystems evolve and adapt slowly, however, it will be necessary for industrial ecosystems to be designed consciously and—because of the urgency of our waste-disposal problems—quickly. There is, in fact, waste in both what goes into the process and what comes out, but if a biological model were followed, the distinction between input and output would virtually disappear. The output for any one process can become the input for another. Many industries have routinely used and sold their by-products, and scrap steel is one of the chief raw materials for making new steel. The change that's required is redefining what had been peripheral phenomena as key elements of a more complex, less wasteful concept of production.

Already, there are some chemical processes that can turn toxic wastes into useful products. There is also the hope that it will be possible to create bacteria that can swallow wastes and excrete something lucrative, or at least benign. Some manufacturers are also designing their wastes and scrap so that they can be used in another phase of the manufacturing process or be sold to another company that needs them. Recent government initiatives have allowed companies to trade credits for the right to pollute, a transitional strategy to allow manufacturers to modify their plants rationally. A marketplace in items that are now considered to be pollutants would be a tighter, more subtle way of enabling private enterprise to deal with the cleanup process. Instantaneous, computerized communications would help companies to find what others want to throw away, and one could even imagine a toxic futures exchange.

One big problem with current recycling is that products often contain several different materials which are difficult to separate economically. Yet beverage deposit programs in only nine states recover enough recyclable plastic to produce about 20 percent of the annual American consumption of polyethylene terephthalate, from which nearly all the containers are made. (The material cannot currently be reused in bottles, however.) U.S. programs for recycling newspapers have been limited by newspaper publishers' investments in virgin paper production, but the willingness of the public to save its papers for recycling indicates that supplies will remain steady, and investments in paper recycling plants could be very profitable.

The design of products is even now beginning to consider not only their useful life but their nature as trash. Appliances, for example, could be designed in distinct parts that could be coded and easily separated for recycling and, in the case of refrigerators, freezers and air conditioners, the treatment of hazardous materials. There might be a refundable deposit on tires, similar to that collected on beverage containers, which would stop littering and reintroduce materials into the productive cycle. Manufacturers whose packaging contains materials that are bonded in a nonrecyclable way or inks that prevent recycling might be required to pay an environmental user fee that purchasers of the products will have to measure against the convenience of the packaging.

To counter manufacturers and consumers who are unwilling to consider the death, as well as the life, of their products, engineers at Rutgers University have designed a system that can take mixed household trash and refine from it many reusable materials, along with a low-grade plastic material. This system, which uses large amounts of water and energy, is a great deal less subtle than advance consideration of recyclability, but it is probably still better than the haphazard ways in which we do things now.

A tightly integrated production strategy would inevitably involve some trade-offs. It would probably not be wise for a single producer to become too highly invested in a single manufacturing ecology, because, like the creatures of the rain forest, it would be too vulnerable if conditions changed. Flexibility is an important attribute for a subtle system of production. It would probably be better for the complex linkages between raw materials and wastes to be made between individual companies constantly and without long-term commitments, something that computerized data bases and markets can make possible on a twenty-four-hour-a-day, worldwide basis.

Tightening up the production system to make it conserve both materials and energy and minimize wastes would require investment and some imaginative engineering, but it would not require either breakthroughs or a revolution in economic thought. Higher materials and energy prices during the 1970s prompted worldwide conservation efforts, many of which continued even after prices went down. It has been estimated that an annual increase of between 1 and 2 percent in the productivity of energy worldwide would stop the accelerating increase of greenhouse gases in the atmosphere. Even if this turns out not to present as serious a threat as many now believe, such productivity increases do no harm to the companies that institute them, and most such improvements will pay for themselves within a reasonable amount of time. Most companies seek higher annual gains in labor productivity.

The problem is essentially political. It is not rational for companies to spend money to solve problems that government is willing to handle or that the public is willing to tolerate. Over the last twenty years, governments in the United States and many other countries have used regulation and taxation to force businesses to deal with environmental and employee safety issues not as "externalities" but as part of their costs of doing business. Some businesses have moved production to places where companies are not required to pay such costs. Recently, parts of the American Southwest have been suffering from acid rain, caused by dirty coal-burning plants just across the border in Mexico, some of which are owned by American companies that have moved there because of low labor costs. Environmental problems do not respect borders, but the chances for international cooperation are improved by the simple reality that nearly everyone is downwind of something bad. Developed countries such as the United States can easily seem hypocritical in demanding that poorer countries invest in cleanups, especially when the lifestyles of American citizens routinely cause the biggest problems. Obviously, the wealthier countries have to help the developing countries to design subtler, sustainable production systems so that they do not repeat the same errors.

Such an initiative would not be the result of a worldwide outpouring of altruism. If we were to wait for that, it would never happen. Rather, it is the natural consequence of a subtler, more complex definition of security that appears to be emerging. Crippling Third World debts, many of them incurred to pay for projects that were counterproductive or oppressive, pose threats to the security of the First World banking system and the global economy. Deforestation threatens soil, expands deserts, causes floods, which in turn create refugee problems and serious international tensions. The inefficient burning of energy threatens world supplies, causes widespread pollution and adds unnecessary greenhouse gases. Poverty drives farmers to produce cash crops, some of the most valuable of which flow into the international narcotics trade, which causes safety and crime problems in the developed world. Throughout history, water resources have been worth fighting over, and that is no less true today. Overpopulation exacerbates all these other problems, and a world in which 80 percent of the population is poor and young will be an impatient and volatile place. For some years, it has seemed likely that if nuclear weapons were to be used, it would not be by a superpower but by a smaller nation that is not known to be part of the nuclear club, or even by a terrorist organization.

One obvious place to find the money to pay for efforts to help poor countries deal with these problems of international economic, environmental, social and political security is in military budgets, which total more than $1 trillion annually worldwide. The Worldwatch Institute has estimated that a ten-year program in which between 5 and 15 percent of military expenditures were diverted to energy efficiency, population control, environmental protection and debt relief could produce sustainable development worldwide. (Another candidate for savings that could be diverted to such an initiative is the farm subsidy programs of Europe, the United States and Japan, which are expensive, encourage waste and discourage self-sufficiency and potential exports in many underdeveloped countries.)

The cost of such an effort would vary from $50 billion to $150 billion a year, which is the kind of amount that is more likely to be spent out of fear than generosity. Yet there is precedent. The United States' Marshall Plan to rebuild the economies of Europe after World War II was expensive and staggeringly successful. It was done to prevent the spread of Communism. It produced a prosperous, peaceful Europe in which the adversaries in the two world wars have moved toward increased economic unification and political cooperation. It not only contained Communism but produced an example with which the Soviet system has been unable to compete. The superpowers have recently embraced military reductions, in part as a way to help them pay for neglected domestic priorities. But they also have an interest in promoting more general worldwide stability, if only to help them maintain their standing as world leaders.

Often, developing countries have been viewed by the richer countries as markets for their weapons, which rulers have often used not to respond to external threats but to maintain themselves in power. If poor countries can move up to a reasonable level of development, they can become far more lucrative markets than they are today for many products that are not military. Power does not grow merely from the barrel of a gun, but from an efficient economy, productive use of natural resources and energy, a healthy, contented citizenry and the absence of famine, flooding and other forms of "natural disasters" that are largely man-made. But the development of the poorer countries cannot follow the pattern of the countries that are now rich, because the world cannot afford to have countries as wasteful as we are. Indeed, the emergent economic powers of the last two decades—Japan, Hong Kong, Taiwan, Singapore and South Korea—made far more efficient use of resources and energy than the countries that developed earlier, and a next generation would have every incentive to be more efficient still. The Pacific Rim countries were able to make use of the vast consuming engine of the United States, something that will have to slow down if we are to move toward a subtler economy. Future success stories will have to depend far more on the spreading of economic opportunity throughout the world and the production of goods and services that can truly help people meet their needs.

Although the increasing convergence of technology and living systems opens many possibilities for social improvement, it is already eroding important ethical distinctions, and thus posing a challenge for government. People are going to court to try to determine such issues as who owns frozen fertilized embryos after their parents have divorced. Medical technology has long since been able to blur the clear distinction between life and death, and the medical profession and the law have been struggling toward a consensus on how much help is enough and when life stops being worth living. Recently, doctors have been able to restore degenerated organs by using tissues from aborted fetuses, raising fears that mothers will have abortions simply to help sick relatives or sell a newly valuable commodity. Because abortion is already such a divisive issue in the United States—and one of the few believed capable of swinging an election—the federal government has twice issued moratoriums on research in this field.

Yet another phenomenon that is little recognized as a technological achievement is human longevity. People everywhere are living longer. More people are active and independent at an older age than ever before, and there is every reason to believe that this trend will only accelerate. Scientists are beginning to understand the aging process, the mechanisms by which key genetic signals are lost or deformed, the ways in which the body begins to become allergic to itself. Often, the lengthened or improved lives end with a bankrupting flurry of medical attention, as many of the body's systems fail simultaneously. The question here is not whether or not to develop the technology; few want to die or become bedridden or mentally impaired any sooner than they have to. It is, instead, a matter of changing the way we think about the life cycle. The idea of retirement seems likely to become obsolete, and not just because there will be a need for more people in the work force and a shortage of the young to pay Social Security taxes. A less apparent, though possibly more important reason is that the society cannot tolerate such a high percentage of nonparticipants, people excluded from the creation of the culture and limited to consumption. It will become essential to extend the years in which people think young thoughts, with minds that are supple, receptive and creative. Moreover, the knowledge that your parents are likely to be alive until you are 70 or 80 years old will change people's whole idea of the life cycle, and their relationships with their parents, in ways that are difficult now to imagine.

Today's old are already in one technological vanguard. They

have been quite willing to accept artificial devices into their bodies to replace parts that are worn out. Teflon-coated steel hips and plastic lenses implanted in the eye have become virtually routine, as have pacemakers. New artificial organs and prostheses that monitor and stimulate physiological processes are on the horizon. Cyborgs—combinations of human being and machine—are an old staple of science fiction, but nobody ever predicted that Grandma would turn into one.

Today's biopolitical issues, complicated as they are, serve merely as a preview of the questions that will arise if medicine and biotechnology develop even some of the capabilities their advocates predict. For example, the assertion that all men are created equal has, up to now, rested on the reproductive process, in which chance plays an important role in the makeup of individual people. Genetic engineering changes that. It offers the possibility of redesigning a person's physiology in a way that overcomes a genetic defect. It might also permit the alteration of the genes that one passes on to future generations to eliminate any particular susceptibility to a wide range of health problems. This sounds highly desirable.

The problem arises when you realize that such technology also opens the possibility for both monitoring and coercion. Should the genes of every embryo be analyzed and those that fall short of some basic standard be aborted? It could be argued that this would be the ultimate subtlety, a way of avoiding substantial medical costs before they happen. But who is to set the standards, and might other cultural prejudices or perceived political needs—perhaps for strong boys to become soldiers—shape the next generation?

This is monster making again, and it gives one pause (if not paws). H. G. Wells's appalling, yet pathetic human-beasts' litany with its repetition "Are we not men?" in *The Island of Dr. Moreau* is one of the most chilling scenes in science fiction, and that novel is, today, probably Wells's most powerful because the issue, if not the technology, is pressing. What do you do when you have the power to change the nature of living creatures? We tend to see humans as the crowning achievement of creation and have contempt for other living creatures because they have not been so enterprising. Yet much of human history, up to and including the computer age, consists of efforts to dehumanize people, short-circuit thought processes, enslave or exterminate them. The search for human physical perfection sounds fine, but one must ask whose perfection is being sought and what is the use to which such perfection is being put.

This is a relatively easy question if you have a set of well-defined values about the nature of people, their dignity and their place in the universe. But when you view people in the narrow materialistic sense that is now reputed to be scientific, there is little guidance. One can perhaps define how to make people into more effective producers and more voracious consumers, more fierce and selfless fighters—in other words, view them as machines. But because we tend not to take into account those spiritual, moral and emotional dimensions that dominate our inner lives, we cannot know how to stack the deck to produce better human beings. We can only stack the deck to provide people with what they think, or can be convinced, that they want.

This sort of issue has already arisen with one of the first medical products of biotechnology—the synthesis of human growth hormone by bacteria. This previously rare and expensive substance can now be used to treat the relatively few children whose normal body development is impaired. But it is also in demand by parents who simply want their children to grow tall, for height is highly prized in American society. It is not certain that the hormone actually does make people without hormone deficiencies grow taller than they would otherwise, but some are willing to take the risk, and it seems likely that it would be a profitable product. Those who want to buy it are behaving a bit like those people in the front row who stand up during a baseball game; they force others to do the same merely to see just as well. Using the hormone doesn't seem like a horrible thing in itself. But it opens the door to a whole range of cosmetic genetics that would work against diversity and aim toward an idea of physical perfection which has, in the past, proved lethal for those whose characteristics do not approach the dominant ideal. (One could argue, conversely, that the realization that human appearance can be easily manipulated might defuse racial hostilities. In general, subtle technology mimics nature by accepting and profiting from diversity, but once you start changing things, it is difficult to know where to stop.)

In the past, the seductiveness of eugenics has been undercut by the fact that it has not worked very well. Biotechnology suggests a route to its realization. Will its mythology—its association with Nazi Germany, self-delusion and well-organized barbarism—be enough to tell us where to stop? Or will the impulse of technology to break down all walls penetrate that of the living cell to rewrite our DNA and hence our destiny? It's impossible to say. The prevailing myth of technology says that anything that can be done will be done, but as the example of nuclear weapons shows, our survival can depend on what we decide not to do.

Such dilemmas place very heavy demands upon our culture. We depend on the institutions of society at large to help us apprehend and understand dangers and help us make choices. Bombarded as we constantly are with information and vivid sensations from all over the world, we ought to be in a good position to assess our tools, our goals and the dangers they might pose. But while the ideas and the technologies that could help us make our lives, and those of our descendants, much better might be found in this information haze, that is no guarantee that we will hear the message. Our culture is one of engineered temptation, one which offers products and experiences along with the message that failure to take advantage of anything that is offered amounts to deprivation. It is designed to make us lose track of all but our appetites. We remake our apples so that every red Delicious is a pomicultural Miss America. And if the consequence of apparent perfection is tasteless—or even unhealthy—that's a small price to pay. The iron law of a consumer society is that the attractive drives out the good, and the most subversive act possible is not to consume.

But while people are capable of responding to apples, and understanding the difference between poisoning and nourishment, it is much more difficult to come to terms with the costs and risks of restyling our bodies, modifying our minds, letting computers make our decisions. All seem to be along the vector of progress, and they may be things we would like to add to our own lives. Yet the suspicion remains that we are in danger of losing something, that our human natures are not something we feel confident about entrusting to the marketplace. Despite the ocean of information we inhabit—and perhaps because of it—we have lost the sense of being active participants in our own futures.

As on the sailors' maps of half a millennium ago, the fringes of our knowledge are inhabited by monsters. But these monsters are not, as those earlier ones were, embodiments of ignorance and fear. They are, rather, live possibilities, incarnations of our thinking that technology may soon have the power to make real. As we look closely at these monsters, they have familiar faces, the visages of people we meet regularly in our daily lives. There are monsters of control, who view the development of technology primarily as a means for subduing both the natural world and most of humankind as well. Nearby are their close relatives, the monsters of reformation, who seek to force people and the universe into some grand, simple intellectual scheme. There are monsters of appetite, those Pacmen who can relate to the world only by owning it, using it and discarding it. There are monsters of narcissism, who fear and are threatened by other people and thus hope to breed an electronic or organic race of clones of themselves. And most numerous of all are the monsters of exile, who have been dispossessed of the powers that give the other monsters their strength, but whose sheer numbers would crush the others if they could organize themselves to do so.

We have set a course, one that we mistakenly define as progress, that leads directly toward these monsters. And as we move along that vector, the monsters do not dematerialize as they did for the navigators of the fourteenth and fifteenth centuries. Rather, they become more vivid. We have the skills at hand to make these monsters, and many others besides. We can look into the mirror and see that we are more than halfway there.

And as we continue to scan the horizon, we also see an island. It is nearer than the monsters, not quite on the course we have set but not terribly far off it either. It is shrouded in fog, and it's hard to tell sometimes whether it is real or a mirage. It's not on our map, which raises the question of whether we really know where we are going. Should we continue on course or stop and explore? This island could, of course, be that of Dr. Moreau, Wells's monster maker, or it might be someplace more like the islands where Thomas More's and Francis Bacon's wanderers found new ways of thinking. It's worth exploring because, if it is infested with monsters, we're headed that way anyway, and if it's not, it might give us a chance to think about the journey we're on. Utopia may not be a satisfactory destination, but it can at least clarify one's sense of direction.

The vision of a more subtle society is something like that island. It may only be a way station to dark inevitability, or it may be a utopia, which offers the possibility of fresh directions along with unavoidable and unforeseeable problems of its own.

Having conjured this island out of the mists of a sea of uncertainty, there is a temptation to give it concreteness—some mountains, a harbor, styles of dress, quaint courtship customs, a banking system, industry, an interesting cuisine and wise institutions to promote justice. One would want to give it a history, perhaps one in which the island was ruled by a tribe of gluttons who oppressed the majority, frightened one another and virtually depleted the island, then left when all was gone to join the monsters, while those who remained found resources within themselves and were able to use the tools left behind in a different, more sustainable way. There would be a priesthood to celebrate the miracle of human consciousness, and schools would teach children to respect the physical world for itself, as well as the human ability to make use of natural processes to make people's lives more secure and satisfying. There would be enough scientists to have developed biotechnology, industrial robots, expert systems, nuclear physics, chaos theory and all the science and technology that we either have or think we will have soon. But because science and technology would be thoroughly integrated into the culture and understood, not as autonomous forces but as modes of human inquiry, expression and ingenuity, their dreams would not be directed toward power for a few but growing possibilities for all. Thus machines would be designed to replace not the satisfactions of labor, pride in workmanship or the possibility of creativity on the job, but rather boredom, safety hazards and the loss of human dignity. New uncontrollable technologies would not be proposed as the solution to existing uncontrollable technologies. Such challenges would be met with wisdom rather than firepower. Some engineers and scientists would even hold public office, not as expert technocrats but as citizens whose knowledge would be useful in making important public decisions. The political system would strive to enhance human freedom, but would also assume that people need to be active members of communities in order to understand themselves and focus their creativity. The buildings would be richly detailed, with doors, windows and other elements that reflect the scale and presence of human beings, and they would be close enough together to permit walking, chance encounters and a sense of community. There would be an economic system that strives to create wealth—in the form of healthy, well-fed, well-educated people, efficient production methods and sensitive use of energy and natural resources. This economy would be supported by a more general system of belief that values people for what they are, what they can know and what they can become rather than for what they produce, what they change or what they discard. Creating wealth would be rewarded, but hoarding it would not. Throw in an extraneous romance between the traveler and a comely young denizen of this better place and the outlines of our utopia would be complete.

Still, it's probably best to stop before this utopia starts to take on too much reality and it becomes necessary to discuss how a subtle economy really works or how citizens settle disputes among themselves. Such details do provide interesting tests of how the values of an ideal society work out in practice, and they tend to make the utopia into a place that you might like to visit but would not care to live in. Their problem is in trying to create a society that is perfect, and thus unchanging. But if there is one thing that the science of this century has taught us it is that stasis is everywhere an illusion. We inhabit a universe that is, at once, being created and falling apart. Volatility is what makes life possible, and every organism is a complex, dynamic system that maintains its integrity through constant change of its components. Recent history has told us, too, that societies that try to organize themselves on the basis of principles that don't live in the minds of their citizens become brittle and the pretense of belief can vanish almost overnight. Thus the search for a subtler society is not really a program, but rather a set of attitudes that cast a slightly different light on the physical possibilities that are before us.

These attitudes—a belief in the paradigm of health, an awareness of the life-giving characteristics of complexity, an impatience with a society that emphasizes consumption over creation, a moral imperative to protect the earth as the home of life and of the human spirit—are in the air, so to speak, though they do not yet constitute the mainstream. Most important, they do not yet permeate thinking about either the economy or technology. Yet they create challenges that must be reckoned with in virtually every part of the world.

Perhaps the most common pitfall for utopians is the belief that because their intentions are good and the tools for making a better world seem to be at hand, improvement must come. Edward Bellamy saw hope in the creation of trusts. Today, it is possible to see hope in biotechnology and industrial robots. But it is even easier to see problems in the use of such technology. In Bellamy's age, the threat was social inequality and labor strife. Today, it is environmental disaster or nuclear suicide. Bellamy's utopia was a conservative one. His proposed solution—to remake all of society first into soldiers and then into consumers—sums up the history of post-Depression America, though it didn't happen as he had intended. A contemporary effort to conserve what is best in our civilization for future generations likewise requires a shift in perception, a cultural revolution of sorts as we try to rescue our fundamental values from the parasitic ideas that draw sustenance from and debilitate them.

What if we don't pay attention to the warning signs and stick to our old habits and beliefs? Life will go on, and it is possible to imagine that technology can help people survive centuries of warfare with the planet. If, for example, the greenhouse effect does come, those with wealth and power will find the resources and the means to turn up their air conditioners. They will develop new strains of wheat and other crops that survive well in arid conditions. And when the ice caps melt and flooding threatens the coastal lowlands, dikes will protect Greater New York and southeastern England just as they protect the Netherlands today. As for Bangladesh and its lowland multitudes, it will probably be on its own. Indeed, within the industrialized countries, the number of people who can be protected within the walls of privilege will probably decline as the working class becomes obsolete and nobody can figure out what to do with it. The global information network will come into being primarily as an inescapable surveillance system, the first line of defense against social change. Robots make good security guards, and military technology will continue its luxuriant development as the ultimate defense of those who have against those who have not. This is a world we do not have to choose consciously, because it represents the general drift of things. Yet it probably is not a world most people would choose, if given the opportunity and a sense of the choices involved.

People's minds do change, and societies make sense only from within the belief systems of their members. Today, it is difficult to understand why, for example, the ancient Egyptians would pour so much of their wealth and their skill into the construction of elaborate tombs. But for them, this effort was an attempt to relate themselves to the universe. In some distant time or on some distant planet, people studying our society might search for some religious or cosmological significance in our obsession with burning fuels and generating objects. They might conclude that shopping malls were our sacred places, cars our fetish objects and *Wheel of Fortune* a holy rite. They might learn from Henry Adams, who as the twentieth century began, identified the dynamo as merely a more powerful focus of the sort of human energy generated by the cult of the Virgin in medieval Europe. Christianity, which has at its center the miraculous transformation of bread and wine into body and blood, somehow transformed itself into a culture of a secular eucharist in which rocks became rockets and oil turned to speed.

Always and everywhere, people have bizarre thoughts and do strange things, but those practices usually seem right at the time. It is worth remembering that structures of faith can as easily be embodied in the conventions of an accounting system or in the tribal customs of scientists or politicians as they can in myths of creation or in fairy tales. And when structures of faith are shaken, it can seem that the whole universe is under threat. In the time of Copernicus and Galileo, the Ptolemaic universe and the earth's central role in it were under attack, and those who believed in the old faith fought back. But eventually it became clear that this newfound truth, revolutionary as it was for astronomy, did not invalidate Christianity or even seriously contradict anything in the scriptures. What had seemed heresy was absorbed into human knowledge.

Today, the earth itself is behaving in ways that challenge faith in economic growth and technological progress, and the fundamentalists of both these faiths are fighting back. It is possible, however, that what is required is not an abandonment of either belief, but rather a redefinition of terms. If that is so, the implications would likewise be revolutionary, though not fundamental. Economic growth clearly involves the improvement of people's material circumstances so that their survival is not threatened and they have the time and ability to shape their lives. This principle is not really in question, merely the tendency to define such growth in terms of energy used and materials consumed, while the deepest sources of our wealth—life-giving water, air and soil—tend to be undervalued. Infinite material growth is not possible on a finite planet, nor is infinite population growth. But human growth, the stock of ideas and services we offer one another, is potentially infinite. Likewise, technological progress is a fundamental human pursuit. Opposition to technologies that seem likely to cause more trouble than they are worth does not invalidate the idea of technology itself. Technology exists to be useful, though it is easy to become so caught up in the power it can unleash that this simple fact is forgotten.

In the end, we are still in the position of those antipodean folk in More's *Utopia* who have just begun using the magnetic compass. They mistake an enormously useful, but still limited tool for a general solution to the danger of ocean travel. It does not devalue technology—though it does contradict many advertisements—to say that the general solution is as impossible as the perpetual-motion machine. The people of More's day did not understand storms, and although we know a lot more about them, we don't understand them either. Indeed, we are learning that they are such complex, chaotic systems that we will probably never know enough about their behavior to predict them with absolute accuracy. We can, however, warn people who are likely to be in a serious storm's path to take action to protect themselves and minimize property damage. Technologies which help us to live with forces that cannot be controlled are every bit as valid and important as those that create the illusion of control.

The ideal of subtlety is based on two assumptions. The first is that whatever spiritual dimension people might have, as physical entities we are inseparable from the physical environment in which we evolved and which constitutes our only reliable life-support system. The second is that we have learned an enormous amount about how to live in this world. In recent years, we have developed something quite novel—a fairly sophisticated understanding of the consequences of our actions. Moreover, we either have or can foresee technologies that can improve the quality of life for many more of the world's people without jeopardizing the lives of generations to come.

Most Americans have been brought up with the idea that the fundamental problems of life can be reduced to technical questions. This is reassuring, because it isolates us, as individuals, from any responsibility. Development economists can deal with the issues of inequalities among the world's peoples, thus freeing us from any scrutiny of the consequences of our habits. Oil companies employ battalions of geologists and engineers to find new energy sources, and they generally do quite a good job. We wonder why we can't live forever, and medical researchers can explain the mechanisms by which the circulatory system becomes less effective, the transfer of genetic information becomes less precise and the body's immune system begins to mistakenly react against itself. Scientists can work on drugs and procedures that can reverse these processes, and identify foods or environmental conditions that contribute to deterioration. Artificial intelligence experts and roboticists can work on ways of achieving immortality for the mind.

At this point the illusion ends because we all know, no matter what advances are made, that each of us is going to die. This is the fundamental thing we know about the future, the one certainty in a universe of speculation. The way we view our own mortality is not a technical question, although we sometimes treat it as such. John Maynard Keynes's famous statement that in the long run we'll all be dead sounds like a true statement, and it expresses the reason that economists tend to discount natural resources and other sources of long-term wealth. (It also suggests that if human longevity increases, many economic assumptions must be reexamined.) We can say, alternatively, that in the long run we will be dead, just as Keynes is, but our children, grandchildren and great-grandchildren will be living in a world we, like Keynes, have helped make. Such a view implies a desire to keep the wealth together and not dip too deeply into principal.

While these two views have different policy implications, the difference between them is not something we can leave to technicians. They express two different approaches to life, and two different moralities. While most people would probably subscribe to the second, more generous view, we leave many of our decisions to specialists whose esoteric knowledge cloaks a value system akin to that of the hit-and-run driver.

Subtlety would depend on immense technological sophistication, but that would probably be the easy part. The tough, but crucial task would be to take the vast machinery of modern society off automatic pilot. We have to deal with the big questions, the ones that our specializations do not help us to answer. We must examine our pleasures to see how much they please us, and scrutinize our comforts to see if they truly comfort us. We must face our threats, perhaps to discover they are delusions, and perhaps to find that they come from those with valid grievances. We have to see if we can imagine lives that bring each of us more meaning, though possibly fewer things. And we have to turn our formidable powers toward creating a future in which we would like to live—even though we know we will not live to do so.

Afterword

"How does it all come out?"

That's a question I've been asked many times during the last couple of years while working on this book, and it has not been easy to find a polite way of saying that this is the wrong question. We're hooked on narrative. Aristotle told us there ought to be an ending. The Preacher in Ecclesiastes lamented that there seems to be none. And though literary theory tells us that we are only kidding ourselves, most readers feel cheated if a novel fails to come to some sort of resolution of the crisis it poses.

For my part, I've decided that it is possible to be cautiously optimistic about our fate. It does seem that there are ideas and means at our disposal that could make life better for ourselves and those who come after us, but it will require some changed patterns of thinking for such improvements to come to pass.

In order to draw such a conclusion, it is important not to fear being thought naïve. It certainly requires entertaining some thoughts with which I am not habitually comfortable. I set out with a protechnology bias and ended with a somewhat spiritual one. The effort surely requires a few leaps of faith. It entails encounters with great black holes of doubt. And as the writing ends, I am able to muster only one and a half cheers for tomorrow.

I started the book with an awareness of the millennium looming, though I failed to anticipate how rapidly and extensively millennial thinking would spread. The End of Things is in the air. Since I started on this project, I have read of the end of history, the end of art, the end of Communism, the end of nature, the end of the Cold War, the end of labor unions, the end of network television, the end of the middle class, the end of objective truth, the end of the American century, the end of industry. Some of these are undergoing profound changes, while it can be argued that some others never existed. But even as history is said to end, the affairs of people continue to change in profound and interesting ways, and most of the rest of the items on this endangered list give every evidence of going on indefinitely. Such a desire to find meaning and completion at the end of the millennium is, in part, a harmless exercise in numerological magic, and as I said earlier, this extremely round-numbered year provides a convenient benchmark for asking how we're doing.

Yet there is something about this hunger for the end of things that is troubling. It is a symptom of the extreme emotional isolation and selfishness at the root of many of our problems. I am reminded of a very old man I once knew, a longtime American resident who nevertheless treated his inherited title of European nobility with utmost respect. He spent his childhood in a world of dynasties and empires, and when he spoke of St. Petersburg, he was not talking about Florida. I knew him when he was in comfortable retirement among his aristocratic trappings, in a handsome and comfortable house, recently married to a woman much younger than himself. Few of us can expect to pass our ninth decade so pleasantly. Yet when he read his *New York Times* each morning, something about him became downright scary. He paid particular attention to East-West relations, and it was quite apparent that the closer the world came to an all-out nuclear confrontation, the happier he was. Gradually, it dawned on me that he thought he had a good shot at living to see the end of the world, and moreover, that he felt he was somehow entitled to it. He had had an exciting life, and had come in contact with many of the major forces that shaped the nineteenth and twentieth centuries. Hooked on narrative, like the rest of us, he wanted his own demise to coincide with that of human civilization, apparently so that he would not miss anything.

As we sat together at the breakfast table, he was scarcely aware that I, more than half a century younger than he, might not be quite so ready for the world to end. I know he viewed me as the product of a debased society and time, one in which he had prospered, but debased nevertheless. Nothing about life was getting better, so my loss would be small. While admitting that he just might be right, I was not willing to give up on life quite so easily. The patterns of history are one thing, but each of us knows that life has value in itself. Most people are extremely reluctant to give up on their lives sooner than is absolutely necessary. His solipsism was so great that he could scarcely see that across the table sat someone who wanted the opportunity to live the same rich and eventful life that he had. He did not really know he was being selfish. He just felt he had a right to an ending.

Likewise, those who are searching for endings are engaging in a similar sort of self-indulgence. They are viewing life as a work of art that must come to some sort of a satisfactory conclusion. They are viewing history as spectators, nature as aesthetes, while failing to become passionately involved in what comes next.

"How does it all come out?" is a compelling question, one with the same pop culture gravity as "Who shot J.R.?" or "Who killed Laura Palmer?" It's a stupid question, especially when it is asked by people who could have a great impact on its answer. I've decided that "What are you going to do about it?" is the proper response, though it seems a bit too hostile to incorporate in everyday conversation. If you view the future passively, it is probably not going to live up to your standards.

When I visited "The World in Motion" at Disney World's Epcot Center, the ride broke down. For more than twenty minutes, I was trapped in a little car somewhere in a dark passageway. Next to me, a cute caveman reinvented the wheel every few seconds, and a jingle blared, "It's fun to be free!" What had been a pleasant, if slightly mind-numbing paean to progress in transportation became, when the machine broke down, a working model of hell. In society at large, the machine seems to be breaking a good deal more often now, the apparent motion less convincing, but we remain, trapped in our little cars, awaiting what will come next. Many things have happened before us, and many will happen after us, and we cannot expect our own lives to be either aesthetically complete or uniformly entertaining. We are not consumers of history, but rather its makers.

I often reflect on my old friend. He didn't live to see the end of the story, or even to see the plot rewritten during the last five years.

And I also think of my grandmother, who lived through many of the same years as the old aristocrat, though not in such a cosmopolitan manner. When I was a little boy, she held me in her lap and told me about her girlhood in a little village in Ireland, and how, barely into her teens, she said goodbye to her parents for the last time and came to America. The story was long and it involved many hardships and blessings, not to mention an enormous amount of extraneous detail. (To this day, I can't figure out what made her like William Jennings Bryan so much.) Though she never said it directly, I knew that the story had no end because I was an important part of it. I cried when she talked about leaving her mother, but I also understood that it made my life and the opportunities I took for granted possible. It was up to me to know the story and make it a part of my life, add to it and pass it on. She did not look for completeness in her life, but it was obvious that she had found meaning.

Our lives are inevitably the wrong shape. They are too short to allow us to do what we want to do. They are too long, and as values change and verities disappear, we become embittered living in a world in which we cannot believe. Life's rewards are not distributed fairly. There is always less luck than we deserve. A span of a thousand years is beyond the scale of individual human life, but well within the range of history, so it is monumental yet meaningful. The end of such a period can be a good excuse to clear outworn notions out of the ideological attic, but we should not be preoccupied with endings.

To live each day as if the world were coming to an end gets us off the hook. It absolves us from responsibility for future generations, but it also drains our actions of weight and meaning. In 2001, another millennium gets under way, and if we and our descendants do things right, there will be more millennia after that one. A moral life has no sense of an ending. It is part of a longer story that will go on and on and on.

Readings
and Sources

Below is a list of some of the books that I have used in the making of this one. It is intended for further reading rather than as documentation. In fact, I consider some of these books to be questionable or even crazy, but in thinking about the future, it is as important to be as clear about what you don't want as about what you do. The list does not reflect the bales of newspaper and magazine clippings I used or the conversations and experiences I had, which also helped me shape this book. The list tends to be heavy on titles from the last two decades, while understating the importance of basic philosophical and historical works. Science fiction is also underrepresented, even though it provides an arena for the exploration of ideas unavailable elsewhere.

I also made use of *Future Survey*, edited by Michael Marien and published by the World Future Society, Bethesda, Md., an extremely valuable tool for anyone trying to get a sense of what people are thinking about the future, month to month. It is a compendium of abstracts of books and major articles on technology, politics, economics, ideas and values, often accompanied by terse commentaries and short essays that try to relate the ideas to one another. It is humbling, in writing something like this, to know how much you are not going to be able to read or deal with seriously. *Future Survey* at least gave me some concrete sense of what I did not know.

Another tool that helped shape these pages was *Global Data Manager*, a piece of computer software published by the World Game Institute of Philadelphia. It is a collection of economic and social data from all the countries of the world, presented in spreadsheet form and manipulable to point out geographical patterns, per capita statistics and such unlikely information as global energy consumption measured in Twinkies.

Abrams, Malcolm, and Harriet Bernstein. *Future Stuff*. New York: Penguin, 1989.
Adams, Henry. *The Education of Henry Adams*. 1918. Reprint. Boston: Houghton Mifflin, 1961.
Alexander, Christopher. "A City Is Not a Tree," in *Zone 1/2*. New York: Urzone, 1987.
Alexander, Christopher, et al. *A New Theory of Urban Design*. New York: Oxford University Press, 1987.
America in Perspective. Oxford Analytica, edited by Daniel Heath. Boston: Houghton Mifflin, 1986.
Anderson, Annelise, and Dennis L. Bark. *Thinking About America*. Palo Alto, Calif.: Hoover Institution Press, 1988.
Asimov, Isaac. *The Complete Robot*. Garden City, N.Y.: Doubleday, 1982.
Augustine. *The City of God*. Translated by Henry Bettenson. London: Penguin, 1972.
Bacon, Francis. *Essays, The Advancement of Learning, The New Atlantis and Other Pieces*. Published under the title *The New Atlantis*, 1627. Reprint. New York: Odyssey Press, 1937.
Baudrillard, Jean. *Simulations*. New York: Semiotext(e), 1983.
Bellamy, Edward. *Looking Backward*. 1888. Reprint. New York: Modern Library, 1951.
Bellini, James. *High Tech Holocaust*. San Francisco: Sierra Club Books, 1986.
Benford, Gregory. *Timescape*. New York: Simon & Schuster, 1980.
Beniger, James R. *The Control Revolution*. Cambridge, Mass.: Harvard University Press, 1986.
Berman, Marshall. *All That Is Solid Melts into Air*. New York: Simon & Schuster, 1982.
Bird, Caroline. *The Good Years*. New York: Dutton, 1983.
Birnbaum, Norman. *The Radical Renewal*. New York: Pantheon, 1988.
Brand, Stewart. *The Media Lab: Inventing the Future at MIT*. New York: Penguin, 1988.

Brown, Harrison. *The Challenge of Man's Future*. New York: Viking, 1954.

Brown, Lester. *Building a Sustainable Society*. New York: Norton, 1981.

Brown, Lester R., et al. *The State of the World 1988, 1989,* and *1990*. New York: Norton, 1988, 1989, and 1990, respectively.

Bureau of the Census, *Historical Statistics of the United States*.

———. *Statistical Abstract of the United States*.

Butler, Samuel. *Erewhon*. 1872. Reprint. London: Penguin, 1970.

Calder, Nigel. *Technopolis: Social Control of the Uses of Science*. New York: Simon & Schuster, 1970.

———. *The Green Machines*. New York: Putnam, 1986.

Calthorpe, Peter, and Sim Van der Ryn. *Sustainable Communities*. San Francisco: Sierra Club Books, 1986.

Calthorpe, Peter, et al. *The Pedestrian Pocket Book*. New York: Princeton Architectural Press, 1989.

Čapek, Karel. *R.U.R.* (1921), in *Toward the Radical Center: A Karel Čapek Reader*. Translated by Claudia Novack-Jones. Highland Park, N.J.: Catbird Press, 1989.

Cetron, Marvin, and Owen Davies. *American Renaissance*. New York: St. Martin's Press, 1989.

Clarke, Arthur C. *July 20, 2019*. New York: Macmillan, 1986.

Cohen, John. *Human Robots in Myth and Science*. South Brunswick, N.J.: A. S. Barnes, 1967.

Corn, Joseph J., ed. *Imagining Tomorrow*. Cambridge, Mass.: MIT Press, 1986.

Corn, Joseph J., and Brian Horrigan. *Yesterday's Tomorrows*. New York: Summit, 1984.

Csikszentmihalyi, Mihaly. "Memes vs. Genes," in *The Reality Club*. Edited by John Brockman. New York: Lynx Books, 1988.

Daly, Herman E., and John B. Cobb. *For the Common Good*, Boston: Beacon Press, 1989.

Deibold, John. *Making the Future Work*. New York: Simon & Schuster, 1984.

Dickson, David. *The Politics of Alternative Technology*. New York: Universe Books, 1974.

Drexler, K. Eric. *Engines of Creation*. New York: Doubleday, 1987.

Dreyfus, Hubert L. *What Computers Can't Do*. Rev. ed. New York: Harper & Row, 1979.

Dyson, Freeman. *Disturbing the Universe*. New York: Harper & Row, 1979.

———. *Infinite in All Directions*. New York: Harper & Row, 1988.

Eco, Umberto. *Travels in Hyper-Reality*. San Diego: Harcourt Brace Jovanovich, 1986.

Ehrlich, Paul. *The End of Affluence*. New York: Ballantine, 1974.

Ehrlich, Paul, and John Holdren, eds. *The Cassandra Conference*. College Station, Tex.: Texas A&M University Press, 1988.

Elul, Jacques. *The Technological Society*. New York: Knopf, 1964.

Etzioni, Amitai. *The Moral Dimension.* New York: Free Press, 1988.

Feather, Frank. *G-Forces Reinventing the World.* New York: Norton, 1990.

Feinbert, Gerald. *Consequences of Growth.* New York: Seabury Press, 1977.

Ferkiss, Victor C. *Technological Man.* New York: Braziller, 1969.

Feuer, Lewis, ed. *Marx & Engels: Basic Writings on Politics and Philosophy.* Garden City, N.Y.: Doubleday, 1959.

Fjermedal, Grant. *The Tomorrow Makers.* New York: Macmillan, 1986.

Florman, Samuel C. *The Existential Pleasures of Engineering.* New York: St. Martin's Press, 1976.

Forester, Tom, ed. *The Materials Revolution.* Cambridge, Mass.: MIT Press, 1988.

Garson, Barbara. *The Electronic Sweatshop.* New York: Simon & Schuster, 1988.

Geoghegan, Vincent. *Utopianism & Marxism.* London: Methuen, 1987.

Gilder, George. *Microcosm.* New York: Simon & Schuster, 1989.

Gitlin, Todd. *The Sixties.* New York: Bantam, 1987.

Glass, Bentley. *Progress or Catastrophe.* New York: Praeger, 1985.

Gleick, James. *Chaos.* New York: Viking, 1987.

Glenn, Jerome Clayton. *Future Mind.* Washington, D.C.: Acropolis Books, 1989.

Goldstein, Joshua S. *Long Cycles.* New Haven: Yale University Press, 1987.

Gribbin, John. *Future Worlds.* New York: Plenum, 1981.

Harris, Nigel. *The End of the Third World.* London: Penguin, 1987.

Hayden, Dolores. *Redesigning the American Dream.* New York: Norton, 1984.

Heilbroner, Robert L. *The Future As History.* New York: Harper & Brothers, 1960.

Heinlein, Robert A. *Stranger in a Strange Land.* New York: Putnam, 1961.

Henderson, Hazel. *The Politics of the Solar Age.* Indianapolis: Knowledge Systems, 1988.

Herodotus. *The Persian Wars.* New York: Modern Library, 1942.

Hughes, Thomas P. *American Genesis.* New York: Viking, 1989.

Huxley, Aldous. *Brave New World.* New York: Harper & Brothers, 1932.

I Ching. Princeton: Princeton University Press, Bollingen Series, 1967.

Jackson, J. B. *Discovering the Vernacular Landscape.* New Haven: Yale University Press, 1984.

The Jerusalem Bible. Garden City, N.Y.: Doubleday, 1966.

Johnson, George. *Machinery of the Mind.* New York: Times Books, 1986.

Johnson, Warren. *Muddling Toward Frugality.* Boulder, Colo.: Shambhala, 1979.

Kahn, Herman, and B. Bruce-Briggs. *Things to Come.* New York: Macmillan, 1972.

Katsiaficas, George. *The Imagination of the New Left.* Boston: South End Press, 1987.

Lasch, Christopher. *The Culture of Narcissism*. New York: Norton, 1979.

Lem, Stanislaw. *The Cyberiad*. New York: Seabury Press, 1974.

———. *Imaginary Magnitude*. San Diego: Harcourt Brace Jovanovich, 1984.

———. *Fiasco*. San Diego: Harcourt Brace Jovanovich, 1987.

Lovelock, J. E. *Gaia*. Oxford: Oxford University Press, 1979.

Macrae, Norman. *The 2025 Report*. New York: Macmillan, 1984.

Macvey, John W. *Space Weapons Space War*. New York: Stein & Day, 1979.

Marek, Kurt W. *Yestermorrow*. New York: Knopf, 1961.

Masuda, Yoneji. *The Information Society*. Bethesda, Md.: World Future Society, 1981.

McCord, William. *Voyages to Utopia*. New York: Norton, 1990.

McHale, John. *The Future of the Future*. New York: Braziller, 1969.

McHarg, Ian. *Design with Nature*. Garden City, N.Y.: Doubleday/Natural History Press, 1969.

McKibben, Bill. *The End of Nature*. New York: Random House, 1989.

Meadows, Donella, et al. *The Limits to Growth*. New York: New American Library, 1972.

Meikle, Jeffrey. *Twentieth Century Limited*. Philadelphia: Temple University Press, 1979.

Melman, Seymour. *The Permanent War Economy*. Rev. ed. New York: Simon & Schuster, 1985.

Mesarovic, M., and E. Pestel. *Mankind at the Turning Point*. New York: Dutton, 1974.

Miller, Donald I., ed. *The Lewis Mumford Reader*. New York: Pantheon, 1986.

Minsky, Marvin. *The Society of Mind*. New York: Simon & Schuster, 1986.

Moravec, Hans. *Mind Children*. Cambridge, Mass.: Harvard University Press, 1988.

More, Thomas. *Utopia*. Translated by Paul Turner. 1516. Reprint. London: Penguin, 1961.

Mumford, Lewis. *The Condition of Man*. 1944. Reprint. New York: Harcourt Brace Jovanovich, 1973.

———. *The Story of Utopias*. 1922. Reprint. New York: Viking, 1962.

———. *Technics and Civilization*. 1934. Reprint. New York: Harcourt, Brace & World, 1964.

Naisbitt, John. *Megatrends*. New York: Warner Books, 1984.

Naisbitt, John, and Patricia Aburdene. *Megatrends 2000*. New York: Morrow, 1990.

Nisbet, Robert. *History of the Idea of Progress*. New York: Basic Books, 1980.

Nora, Simon, and Alain Minc. *The Computerization of Society*. Cambridge, Mass.: MIT Press, 1981.

Oberg, James Edward. *New Earths*. New York: Meridian, 1983.

Office of Technology Assessment. *Technology and the American Economic Future*. Washington, D.C.: Congress of the United States, 1988.

O'Neill, Gerard K. *The High Frontier*. New York: Morrow, 1977.

————. *The Technology Edge*. New York: Simon & Schuster, 1983.

Pagels, Heinz R. *The Dreams of Reason*. New York: Simon & Schuster, 1988.

Parfrey, Adam, ed. *Apocalypse Culture*. New York: Amok Press, 1987.

Pawley, Martin. *The Private Future*. London: Thames and Hudson, 1974.

Peitgen, H. O., and P. H. Richter. *The Beauty of Fractals*. Berlin: Springer-Verlag, 1986.

Pirsig, Robert M. *Zen and the Art of Motorcycle Maintenance*. New York: Morrow, 1974.

Pynchon, Thomas. *The Crying of Lot 49*. Philadelphia: Lippincott, 1966.

Reich, Charles A. *The Greening of America*. New York: Random House, 1970.

Reich, Robert B. *The Next American Frontier*. New York: Times Books, 1983.

Rifkin, Jeremy. *Time Wars*. New York: Holt, 1987.

Roszak, Theodore. *The Cult of Information*. New York: Pantheon, 1986.

Schneider, Claudine. "The Global Challenge: Changing Habits or Changing Climates" in *The Future: Opportunity Not Destiny*. Edited by Howard F. Didsbury, Jr. Bethesda, Md.: World Future Society, 1989.

Schumacher, E. F. *Small Is Beautiful*. New York: Harper & Row, 1973.

Schwartz, Hillel. *Century's End*. New York: Doubleday, 1990.

Scientific American, September 1989 special issue. "Managing Planet Earth," especially articles on energy use, manufacturing, agriculture and sustainable economic development.

Shaker, Steven M., and Alan R. Wise. *War Without Men*. McLean, Va.: Pergamon-Brassey's International Defense Publishers, 1988.

Shelley, Mary. *Frankenstein*. 1918. Reprint. London: Penguin, 1985.

Snow, Chet B. *Mass Dreams of the Future*. New York: McGraw-Hill, 1989.

Stableford, Brian, and David Langford. *The Third Millennium*. New York: Knopf, 1985.

Stewart, Hugh B. *Recollecting the Future*. New York: Dow Jones–Irwin, 1989.

Stilgoe, John R. *The Common Landscape of America, 1580 to 1845*. New Haven: Yale University Press, 1982.

Theobold, Robert. *The Rapids of Change*. Indianapolis: Knowledge Systems, 1987.

Thompson, Alan E. *Understanding Futurology*. Newton Abbot, Eng.: David & Charles, 1979.

Toffler, Alvin. *Future Shock*. New York: Random House, 1970.

————. *The Third Wave*. New York: Morrow, 1980.

————. *PowerShift*. New York: Bantam, 1990.

Turkle, Sherry. *The Second Self*. New York: Simon & Schuster, 1984.

Villodo, A., and K. Dychtwald, eds. *Millennium—Glances into the 21st Century*. Los Angeles: Tarcher, 1981.

Virilio, Paul. *Speed and Politics*. 1977. Reprint. New York: Semiotext(e), 1986.

Virilio, Paul, and Sylvère Lotringer. *Pure War*. New York: Semiotext(e), 1983.

Voltaire. *Candide, or Optimism.* 1759. Reprint. New York: Signet, 1961.

Wagar, W. Warren. *A Short History of the Future.* Chicago: University of Chicago Press, 1989.

Warnock, John. *The Politics of Hunger.* New York: Methuen, 1987.

Wells, H. G. *The Time Machine.* 1895. Reprint. New York: Ballantine, 1983.

———. *The Island of Dr. Moreau.* 1896. Reprint. New York: Signet, 1988.

White, E. B. *One Man's Meat.* New York: Harper & Brothers, 1950.

Wiener, Norbert. *The Human Use of Human Beings.* Boston: Houghton Mifflin, 1950.

Woods, Lebbeus. *OneFiveFour.* New York: Princeton Architectural Press, 1989.

World Commission on Environment and Development. *Our Common Future.* Oxford: Oxford University Press, 1987.

World Resources Institute. *World Resources Yearbook, 1988–89.* New York: Basic Books, 1988.

Zohar, Dana. *The Quantum Self.* London: Bloomsbury, 1990.

Zuboff, Shoshana. *In the Age of the Smart Machine.* New York: Basic Books, 1988.

Index

Truman Doctrine, 55
Twinkie standard, 87–9
2001: A Space Odyssey (film), 66

ultimate sciences, 144
unemployment dilemma, 139–40,
    165
uniformitarianism, 42
United States
    agricultural resources, 83–5
    children, attitudes toward, 100
    Cold War, 117–18
    community, perspective on, 188–
        91
    consumer society, 129–31
    economic warfare, 118
    forward-looking society, decline
        of, 5–6
    homelessness, 13, 73–6
    the land, Americans' relationship
        to, 182–8
    military technology, approach to,
        117
    post-World War II period, 55–6,
        119–21
    private life, vision of, 186–7
    progress, attitude toward, 11–12,
        112
    robotics in, 152–3
    self-image, needed change in, 99–
        104
    unemployment, 140, 165
    universal landscape, 185–6
    utopian tradition, 49–51, 52–70
Utopia (More), 39–40, 41, 44, 239
utopianism, 30, 39–41
    American tradition, 49–51, 52–70
    change and, 48–9
    consumerism and, 52–3
    critiques of, 51–2
    experts, rule by, 50–1, 59–60
    materialism and, 54

people-institutions relationship,
    58–9
personal exploration, 66–7
space exploration and, 64–6
systems thinking and, 60–2
technology and, 47–8, 58, 124–6
usefulness of, 46
utopia of the country house, 19

Vancouver Expo '86, 9
Venus, 199, 205
video games, 124
Vietnam War, 56, 57, 63–4, 68
Virilio, Paul, 115
virtual realities, 165–6

Waiting for Godot (Beckett), 34
war
    age of population and, 80
    economic warfare, 118
    environmental impact, 162–3
    game theory and, 214–15
Warhol, Andy, 62
War Without Men (Shaker and Wise),
    162, 163
waste disposal, 225–7
wastefulness, sufficiency of re-
    sources and, 85–90
Watergate scandal, 68–70
Wells, H. G., 51–2, 231
Wiener, Norbert, 149, 214, 215
Wilson, Woodrow, 53
Wise, Alan R., 162, 163
women, labor of, 86
work-related issues, 135–8
    computerization, 141, 142–4, 149
    control aspects of technology,
        142–4
    deskilling of craftsmanship, 141–2

A Note on the Type

The text of this book was set in a digitized version of Janson, a typeface thought to have been made by the Dutchman Anton Janson, who was practicing type founder in Leipzig during the years 1668–1687. However, it has been conclusively demonstrated that these types are actually the work of Nicholas Kis (1650–1702), a Hungarian, who most probably learned his trade from the master Dutch type founder Dirk Voskens. The type is an example of the influential and sturdy Dutch types that prevailed in England up to the time William Caslon developed his own designs from them.

Composed by Graphic Composition, Athens, Georgia

Printed and bound by Fairfield Graphics, Fairfield, Pennsylvania

Designed by Iris Weinstein